For my wife, Jean, whose help and encouragement have been invaluable

Contents

Part three: Organisation for marketing

backcloth; The position of the UK; The UK, the
European Monetary System and Maastricht; Methods of
exporting; Marketing services and government support

Preface

The sixth edition updates and re-orientates, as necessary, a book which has been accepted for a considerable period of time, in many countries, as a concise, theoretically sound, yet practically oriented handbook for a wide variety of marketing students, teachers and managers.

What then are some of the really major changes that have taken place over recent years in supply/demand situations having a major impact on marketing planning and execution, and thus on education and training? They can be summarised as follows:

1. Marketing planning and execution

(a) International and national political and economic changes and their impact on marketing organisations, strategies and tactics.

(b) The very significant development of the marketing of services.

(c) The development of non-profit marketing, e.g. education, health, charities, political institutions.

(d) Privatisation and deregulation.

(e) Social and behavioural changes, e.g. the role of women, social mobility and life styles.

(f) The development of information and technology.

(g) Marketing developments, e.g. direct marketing, niche marketing, franchising, telemarketing, network marketing, media organisation, joint venture operations, credit trading and services.

2. Marketing education and training

(a) A broadening of the range of younger students taking up marketing studies arising from, for example, more vocational type studies in universities, colleges and schools.

(b) More postgraduates and significantly more work-based students/managers attending part-time day, evening and block release programmes leading to a range of vocational certificates and diplomas.

(c) More internal organisation training programmes with short- and medium-term career development and team approach objectives.

(d) More emphasis on individual and group projects based on actual organisations and situations.

This sixth edition accordingly takes into account these many changes with which students, teachers and instructors have now to cope.

Above all, the aim, as always, has been to set the subject of marketing in terms of a learning process involving knowledge skills and an analytical approach geared to a diversity of practical applications in changing circumstances.

GBG 1994

Part one
What is marketing about?

1

Marketing defined

The increasing importance of marketing

1. Historical development

At the beginning of the Industrial Revolution, Adam Smith in his *Wealth of Nations* said:

> Consumption is the sole end purpose of all production; and the interest of the producer ought to be attended to, only so far as it may be necessary for promoting that of the consumer. The maxim is so perfectly self-evident that it would be absurd to attempt to prove it. But in the mercantile system, the interest of the consumer is almost constantly sacrificed to that of the producer; and it seems to consider production, and not consumption, as the ultimate end and object of all industry and commerce.

It was not, however, until the early years of the present century that any serious thought was given by scholars to examining the activities and institutions involved in marketing processes. The practical implications of *consumption being the purpose of production* have only in the last decade or so been recognised by business organisations. As long as the sources and supply of goods were limited and customer demands were comparatively unsophisticated, it was possible for a manufacturing company to make profits – and to grow – by concentrating on production efficiency. The customer came at the end of a long chain of events. He or she was essentially a problem solely for the sales force, whose task was to sell what had been produced. In many cases, particularly with industrial products and services, it was even believed that goods were bought and not sold, and a reputation built for technical and for professional excellence would ultimately lead the customer to seek out the appropriate source of supply.

As production capacity increased, professional regulations were eased and competition became more intense, additional attention had to be paid to the selling process. Many companies still pay insufficient attention to selling and advertising; others have been forced to devote more and more attention and money to these activities, but often the customer still comes into the reckoning only in the final stages and advertising is ill-conceived and directed. The disappearance of economic, social, political and technological conditions which make possible an easy sellers' market has brought about in many other companies a complete reorientation of business philosophy. These companies have adopted or are in the process of adopting *the marketing concept which starts with the customer* in the belief that the most profitable business can come only, as Clive Barwell put it, 'by identifying, anticipating and satisfying customer needs and desires – in that order' (A. Wilson (ed.), *The Marketing of Industrial Products*, Ch. 1, Hutchinson, 1965.

2. Marketing and change

It may be thought surprising that a concept which was recognised from the very early days of civilisation – as soon as man ceased to be individually self-sufficient and began to make and exchange things with others – and which was enunciated by Adam Smith two hundred years ago, should have been lost sight of, and only recently emerge as new and even revolutionary. The reason lies in the process of industrialisation itself. At an ever-accelerating rate, Adam Smith's notions of the advantages of specialisation and division of labour spread into all forms of business. The emphasis was, not unnaturally perhaps, placed almost entirely on improving the *productive efficiency* of individually specialised units. Manufacturing specialists dealt with merchant specialists.

New worlds were opened up, populations grew and communications were developed. Soon large-scale operations were needed to satisfy the expanding demand and to capitalise on scientific discoveries and technological progress, as well as to provide economies of scale. Increased output levels required increased levels of consumption. Both combined to produce social changes at an unprecedented rate. The British Chartered Institute of Marketing aptly describes marketing as 'the management process which identifies, anticipates and supplies customer requirements efficiently and profitably'.

3. Major social changes
Among the social changes which have been and still are spreading from the earliest Western industrialised societies to all parts of the world, these are the most significant:

(a) The move from agriculture to industry – the growth of trade unions and worker co-operation; the increase in white-collar workers and salaried staff.

(b) The provision of greater educational opportunities – schools, colleges and universities for more and more people, whether rich or poor.

(c) The raising of living standards – greater and greater national wealth spread more and more evenly across all levels of national communities; a breakdown of traditional class barriers.

(d) The removal of barriers of distance – more extensive use of faster and more efficient means of communication.

(e) The extension of the average life span.

(f) The population explosion.

Sociological changes will take place over the next few decades at an even faster rate, speeded on by technological developments – new materials, the development of new energy sources, mechanisation and automation, and improved information and communication systems. The interactive nature of what may be considered environmental systems, e.g. the economic, technological, legal, political and cultural, must not be overlooked. There would, indeed, be grave dangers in forgetting that all markets consist essentially of people. The distinguished American academic Philip Kotler reminds us that

> Marketing is human activity directed at satisfying needs and
> wants through exchange processes. (Kotler and Armstrong,
> *Marketing: An Introduction* 1987)

It would be pertinent to examine currently the use of advertising and promotion by some service organisations. Sheer weight of advertising spending and the use of complex media technology may often be exceedingly wasteful if the first principles of the marketing philosophy are ignored.

4. Marketing: a vital business philosophy
It is the greater complexity of the interaction of the various factors of

change, the greater speed at which they are taking place, and the greater risks of business investment involved, which make it imperative that the factors of production be organised with as full a prior understanding as possible of the factors of consumption. Marketing thus demands the acceptance of *consumer orientation* by the boards of directors, chief executives, management and employees in every activity. The marketing philosophy then becomes the major driving and co-ordinating force of the whole enterprise.

It is important to distinguish between marketing as a concept of business management and marketing as a group of business activities undertaken by specialists within an organisation. Michael Baker, in one of his early marketing texts, when considering the broad view of the marketing concept, starts with the following proposition:

> If economies are comprised of people, and we are endeavouring to allocate scarce resources in order to maximise satisfaction, then it is satisfaction of people at which we are aiming. This being so it is essential we determine first what people want and then allocate resources accordingly. In other words, we must determine the nature and strength of demand and create supplies of goods and services to satisfy these demands. (Michael J. Baker, *Marketing: An Introductory Text*, 1979)

Macroeconomic planning may be viewed in this way. The macro approach is to view business organisations *as a whole* as integrated marketing organisations.

The concept constantly reiterated in each edition of this book thus involves three fundamental propositions:

(a) Customer orientation.
(b) Organisational integration.
(c) Mutually profitable exchange between customer and organisation.

Integration, profit and social responsibility

There are those who claim that the marketing concept has failed to live up to the high expectations of its early protagonists. The concept remains valid. What is often the problem is that the practical interpretation and application are too often woefully deficient – particularly with regard to the three propositions set out in 4 above. Special economic factors affecting the state of demand in the 1990s are referred to in 13.

5. Integration

Too frequently, marketing departments have been set up or marketing specialists introduced to an organisation with no essential change of attitude on the part of top management, of established functional specialists, or of new experts in computing systems, information technology, etc. The task of integration is particularly significant in organisations in which management personnel have powerful, vested professional interests of long-standing in production expertise, technical research and finance.

The concept of marketing applies as much to organisations producing industrial materials, components and capital equipment, and to those providing services such as banking and insurance, as it does to companies dealing in consumer goods. Initially, some technical and professional organisations wrongly identified the concept with special offers – 'three pence off' and the like – but in recent years, many have made significant steps towards the acceptance of marketing in relation to their own businesses. Nevertheless, these are often the very organisations in which traditional attitudes are firmly held by managers in various specialist functions and in which the total organisational reorientation is difficult to achieve. The importation of marketing specialists may improve very limited parts of the operation, but there is also a danger that marketing itself may be judged to have failed unless marketing orientation truly permeates the organisation structure horizontally and vertically.

6. Profit and social responsibility

Marketing involves an exchange – and a mutually beneficial exchange. Organisations exist to achieve objectives, and a prime objective of the private sector of business must be profit. It is, however, essential that the profit be judged by customers, governments, organised labour and the public at large as a fair return achieved by fair means. Customer orientation should not be allowed to degenerate into what appears to outside interests to be customer manipulation and exploitation. Consumerism is spreading fast.

Discussions on the responsibilities of organisations to society are currently claiming more media time and space. The issues include the adverse effects on society and the environment of products, manufacturing processes, factory sites, organisational rationalisation and redundancy. The British Chartered Institute of Marketing's definition of the concept, it will be noted, refers to the involvement of 'the labour force itself'. Profits will continue to be fundamental to business survival, but effecting a balance between the profit requirement and that of satisfying social demands in a changing environment will call for ever more attention to the acceptance in practice of fully integrated marketing.

Among the increasing number of issues which now come under public investigation are such matters as service availability and standards; pollution by product, by process and by packaging; and truth in advertising and pricing (e.g. the true cost of borrowing and unit pricing). Considerably wider issues than this are now posing problems affecting marketing decisions. Examples are the debate on the order and reordering of national priorities, urban development, social costs of services, race relations, quality control responsibility and liability, the impact of organisational size and market share in regional economic groups, the operations and behaviour of international firms, sponsorship and social and physical welfare.

These issues have sometimes led to economic bloc regulations and national legislation, such as the following:

(a) Race Relation Acts.
(b) Restrictive Practices Acts.
(c) Consumer Protection Acts.
(d) Watchdog/investigative bodies, e.g. Environmental Health Departments (UK) and the Consumer Consultative Committee (EU).

Inevitably, as such writers as Crozier, Cannon, Kotler and West stress, consumerism, environmentalism and company social behaviour will become increasingly serious issues in terms not only of responsibility, but also of liability.

In the UK, the Citizens' Charter has been launched with considerable publicity and has led to a multitude of individual organisational printed 'charters'. The actual effect internally and externally has still to be seen and measured.

7. Social services: marketing and cost–benefit exchange
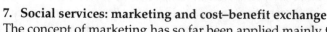
The concept of marketing has so far been applied mainly to business organisations providing material goods and services. The marketing of social and professional services has been one of the most significant developments in the more economically developed parts of the world in recent years. The growth of tourism and leisure markets can be seen in both developed and less economically developed parts of the world.

The service sector, like the material goods sector, has been privately owned in the main, and the profit motive has similarly exerted a strong influence on objectives and strategy. The question of public and private ownership is largely a political issue, and recent events in, for example, the UK and Russia indicate that even long-held political stances are changing to a greater or lesser extent. Whatever and wherever the specific changes, there will remain organisations which are seen not as primarily profit producing, but as seeking other objectives at a subsidised cost. Even in these organisations, however, cost effectiveness is likely to become increasingly important, and such organisations should also consider and adapt to it. Kotler and Zaltman stated, in an *American Journal of Marketing* paper in 1971, that 'marketing management occurs when people become conscious of an opportunity to gain from a more careful planning of their exchange relations'. In his book *Basic Marketing: a Managerial approach*, McCarthy refers to four key variables in marketing:

(a) Product.
(b) Place.
(c) Price.
(d) Promotion.

The provision of hospital services exemplifies the applicability of the concept. What facilities and services does the public require hospitals to provide (the product)? Where and how should particular services be offered (the place)? What is an acceptable level of cost input in return for services offered (the price)? In what way should the service communicate its services, its locations, and its use (and need) of resources (the promotion)?

Referring to the three propositions in 4, it is valid to ask:

(a) To what extent is a hospital service, for example, really customer oriented?
(b) To what extent is there organisational integration, e.g. among doctors, nurses and lay administrators, in terms of customer needs?
(c) Could the cost effectiveness of the service–customer exchange be improved, and what would be the additional mutual exchange effect of increasing or developing the level and/or nature of the resources?

The setting up of hospital trusts in the UK may lead to improved health care together with increased cost/output effectiveness. Cost effectiveness may in practice, of course, lead to an emphasis on cost reduction and decisions on patient care may be influenced mainly by cost criteria rather than the needs of the patient.

The coexistence of publicly and privately financed service organisations may present problems that require a range of strategic, operational and organisational solutions. The problem of acceptance of the marketing concept as set out in this chapter should not be one of the real difficulties, but often is in practice.

The role of marketing managers

8. Marketing management and general management

Edmund P. Learned, an American management expert, has stated that the minimum role reserved for the top general management in the largest firm involves the following responsibilities:

(a) Formulation or approval of objectives and strategy.
(b) Approval of major general policies in support of the strategy adopted.
(c) Review and approval of major capital commitments.
(d) Review of master plans, programmes and budgets.
(e) Selection and development of key executives.
(f) Provision for long-range planning.
(g) Review and appraisal of the results of operations.

The ability of one person to encompass fully all these tasks is restricted to only the very smallest organisations. As organisations grow, responsibility for specific tasks is delegated. Activities are grouped and appropriate relationships are established so as to bring about the most effective use of human and material resources in the achievement of objectives.

9. The activities of marketing groups

Activities appropriately delegated to marketing groups are as follows:

(a) Identification and anticipation of demand, its level, timing and character.
(b) Liaising and communicating with other activity groups in respect of resource allocation to provide products and/or services in line with (a) and company policy and objectives.
(c) Organising and implementing the strategy and tactics which are necessary to bring about a mutually profitable exchange between the organisation and its target markets through products and/or services, place (channels and distribution system), price and promotion (selling, advertising and other non-personal methods).

The role of the most senior marketing executive is thus quite different from that of the chief organisational executive. It is important that this distinction should be recognised and understood, since it is not un-usual to hear opponents of marketing claiming that its protagonists describe their role in such a way as to usurp the function of the chief executive.

10. Organisation of marketing activities

Marketing managers hold delegated responsibility both for staff ac-tivities, e.g. the provision of information and services, and for line activities, e.g. the implementation of a co-ordinated product/market plan. Organisation is itself a means to an end, and its efficiency – necessary for the achievement of that end – depends largely on the clear understanding by those concerned of the elements in the formal organisation structure: that is authority, responsibility, accountability and lines of communication.

Organisation of marketing involves both the co-ordination of indi-vidual marketing activities *and* the integration of the marketing function with the other functions in the business structure. Thus a marketing manager may have:

(a) prime delegated responsibility for:
   (*i*) sales forces
   (*ii*) advertising and promotion
   (*iii*) customer advisory services
   (*iv*) channel strategy
   (*v*) marketing research; and
(b) major shared involvement with other specialist groups in such critical decision areas as:
   (*i*) corporate planning
   (*ii*) product and/or service planning
   (*iii*) pricing
   (*iv*) physical distribution
   (*v*) education and training

11. Qualities needed in a marketing manager

It cannot be stressed too much that success depends on the harmon-ious integration of the whole, as well as on the individual parts. To achieve a profitable balance of products, price, promotion, service and other elements to meet objectives which are in line with the policy and multiple objectives of the board, marketing executives need more than a drive to achieve current sales volume targets, which is the usual objective of sales managers. They must be capable of objective con-ceptual forward thinking, with the ability to diagnose and analyse problems, to make plans and to see that they are implemented and evaluated. Experience must be combined with an understanding of economics, behavioural sciences, finance, statistics, mathematics and operational research.

Marketing theory

12. The essence of marketing theory

There are three basic approaches to the study of marketing:

(a) *Institutional analysis.* Marketing institutions are business organisations which are principally concerned with the distribution of goods and services, such as retailers, wholesalers, advertising and marketing research agencies, and commodity exchanges. These institutions have developed because of the separation between producers and consumers. This separation may be one of:

(*i*) distance

(*ii*) time (difference between time of production and time of consumption need) or

(*iii*) knowledge.

In addition, organisations such as banks, hire-purchase and insurance companies, telecommunications, water and power suppliers function as marketing institutions in that they constitute an exchange system between producers and consumers.

It is increasingly recognised that non-profit organisations such as charities are also involved in a form of marketing exchange system.

(b) *Functional analysis.* Marketing functions may be described as major marketing operational activities, such as pricing, selling and advertising.

(c) *Commodity or channel of distribution analysis.* A study of channels of distribution would involve tracing the passage of individual products or commodities through various marketing institutions from producer to consumer, investigating the functions performed at each stage.

It is important for students to understand the three basic approaches that are combined in this book.

13. The relevance of economics

In order to understand each of the three basic approaches and their interrelationships, it is necessary to draw on relevant concepts of economics. A study of economic aggregates (e.g. total consumption, total income and total employment) is described as *macroeconomics*, and this branch of study has relevance to marketing. For example, demand for goods and services may be subject to external constraints imposed by such organisations as the European Union, the G7 group, GATT and individual government economic policies. A study of the economy in detail, e.g. how prices of goods are determined, and what factors determine the quantity and type of goods produced, is described as *microeconomics* and has very special significance for the marketing student. The application of micro- and macroeconomics may be seen in the case of the demand for television sets, which may be affected by such considerations as the price, the hire-purchase facilities available, the number of producers and distributors, taxation policies and technological developments.

Until the late 1970s, governments of the more industrialised nations tended to follow Keynesian thinking with regard to total demand. Trade cycles were offset by stimulating money circulation in a recession and by money supply restriction in a boom. The process may be described in simple form as follows:

Depression	*Boom*
Lower taxes (to create budget deficit)	Raise taxes (to create budget surplus)
Lower interest rates	Raise interest rates
Increase public, especially capital, expenditure	Reduce public expenditure
Encourage spending and investment	Discourage spending and investment

In the UK, policies of this kind succeeded from the mid-1930s until the late 1970s in keeping employment high, keeping inflation within reasonable bounds, expanding demand overall, and improving material living standards – even if the percentage improvement in the UK was often not as good as that of other industrialised countries. Several major considerations have in recent years upset the economic scene: increased oil demand and more co-operative action by oil producers; the formation and extension of the powers of regional groupings such as the European Union; the emergence of greater Third World competition; the extension of multinational company activities; and the economic growth and activities of Japan and the USA.

In many industrialised countries, recession and inflation have actually coexisted. GATT negotiations on reducing trade barriers have been unduly lengthy, but some remedies appear to be emerging. In individual countries there have been many suggested prescriptions, such as incomes and prices control (neo-Keynesian) and control of the money supply (monetarism). The latter attacks inflation by means of high interest rates and exchange rates, and reduced public expenditure. Similar situations and sometimes similar measures taken by other major world powers, such as the USA, have led to internationally interactive effects which leave the marketer in unfamiliar low-growth situations. In times such as these, it should be realised that there are still some growth areas, and whether the need is for coping with demand reduction or for innovation, marketing has a very vital role to play.

14. The relevance of behavioural sciences
Production, marketing and consumption are carried on by human beings whose attitudes and decisions are the result of psychological or sociological influences which may be in conflict with rational economic motives. Marketing students must, therefore, make use of relevant concepts in the behavioural sciences.

15. The relevance of statistics, mathematics and finance
Marketing is concerned with the allocation of scarce resources to achieve output results compatible with resource availability and utilisation as well as corporate objectives. The marketing student should therefore learn to assess and control input and output wherever possible in quantitative terms. He or she must consequently become familiar with the relevant branches of statistics, mathematics, operational research and finance. It is highly significant that in the 1990s information technology has become the centre of a hi-tech revolution in British commerce – and certainly in marketing. However, many problems remain, such as nervous middle management, young systems specialists unable or unwilling to communicate, shortage of suitable software, too much choice available to ill-informed potential buyers, and changes in people and systems.

16. The approach of this book
Because of the complexity of real marketing situations, an interdisciplinary approach has been taken in this text. Institutions, functions and channels will be studied against a background of interacting and changing political, technical, economic and cultural conditions. In the remainder of Part One we shall first look at the key figure in this complex – the customer – and examine ways of understanding him

or her better by means of marketing research. Part Two is concerned with planning, distributing and communicating in such a way that customer and company goals are satisfied. Part Three is devoted to the operational strategy, organisation and control which are essential for growth, and even survival, in dynamic marketing conditions.

Progress test 1

1. What major social changes have contributed to the need for companies to be marketing oriented?

2. What are the three propositions contained in the concept of marketing, and what significance do they have in the practical application of the concept?

3. What tasks are appropriately delegated to marketing managers?

4. Give examples of high, moderate and low-growth markets in the 1990s. What explanations can you offer?

Assignment

Select two high-street businesses with branches in the same town/city. The businesses should differ in some significant way, e.g. essentially service or product; supermarket or estate agency; national, multinational, local or regional organisation.

Arrange and prepare interviews with a senior executive at each in order to assess the use of information technology in current marketing control and future planning. Discuss the timing and sequence of introduction of particular systems. Assess problems with the introductions, if any. Comment on similarities and differences and suggest possible reasons.

This assignment may be undertaken at the planning stage by small groups. Individual written reports should be followed by class/syndicate discussions.

2

Buyer behaviour

Stages in the decision process

1. Domestic consumer and corporate buying behaviour: categories of buying

Domestic consumers are those who buy goods and/or services for themselves, their families and friends, etc. Corporate buyers are those who are concerned with purchasing goods and/or services for their organisations – government departments, commercial businesses (e.g. banks, insurance companies, manufacturing, fishing, agricultural enterprises, etc.) and intermediaries (e.g. retailers, wholesalers and agents of various kinds).

Economic motives enter to a greater or lesser extent into all kinds of buying situations, but they are certainly not the only considerations. We will therefore examine the buying decision process first, since in all kinds of buying, and whether the decision to buy is made immediately or after a lengthy period of consideration, there are a member of common features:

(a) A general or a specific need is felt (*see* **2–5**).
(b) A period of pre-buying activity follows, i.e. an investigation of sources of supply which might satisfy the need (*see* **6**).
(c) A decision is taken (what to purchase, or even to make no purchase) based on the results of the pre-buying activity and the strength of the need (*see* **7**).

2. The basic need

This may be either *general* (e.g. I need a change of environment) or more *specific* (e.g. I need a holiday in Spain). The more specific need may arise spontaneously or it may be stimulated by creative marketing. The basic need is for a collection of utilities providing a psychological or social satisfaction, and not for a product or a specific form of service. Consequently, it is important that marketing programmes should be designed to identify products or services giving satisfaction of a need. An early classification of basic needs relevant to marketing is set out in **3–5** below; **6–11** present behavioural concepts.

3. Psychological needs
These cover the following:

(a) *The physiological* – the need to satisfy the bodily requirements, e.g. of hunger, thirst.
(b) *Pleasure satisfaction* – physical and aesthetic, appeals to the senses. Certain foods have a pleasurable flavour; certain furnishings bring aesthetic satisfaction.
(c) *Security* – the need to protect oneself from danger or worry.
(d) *Ownership* – the innate drive to possess things.
(e) *Self-esteem* – the desire to satisfy the 'ego'.

4. Sociological needs
These include the following:

(a) *Love of others* – particularly those in close family relationship.
(b) *Social acceptance* – the need to be recognised by the many formal and informal groups to which a person belongs. This need may be to conform or to be distinctive.

5. Maslow's hierarchy of needs
Some of these needs are stronger than others at particular times, in particular people and in particular societies. It will also be apparent that some of these needs are closely linked with others. Maslow has set out a five-stage priority of human needs, the first two of which are primary needs fundamental to existence, the last three secondary:

(a) Basic physiological needs (conditions affecting the human body – hunger, sleep, temperature).
(b) Safety needs (self-protection against present and future dangers).
(c) The need for recognition, love and belonging.
(d) Ego-satisfying needs (desire for self-esteem, self-respect).
(e) Self-fulfilment needs (realisation of complete self-creativity). This need is felt and satisfied by relatively few.

See A.H. Maslow, *Motivation and Personality* (Harper and Row, New York, 1954).

6. Purchasing activity
No two people 'perceive' things in exactly the same way. Past experiences, the way in which one's senses have been stimulated, condition

one's attitude towards objects, words and ideas. Accumulated experience builds up a perceptual framework over a period of time, so that one has a predisposition to see or believe what one expects or would like to see or believe. Once a buying need is felt, the perceptual framework is more vigorously activated and motivated at a conscious and subconscious level. The potential buyer's ultimate decision is now more likely to be influenced by advertising, displays or personal sales talks, or by other people's attitudes and opinions. This purchasing activity can be broken down into six stages as follows:

(a) Awareness.
(b) Knowledge.
(c) Liking.
(d) Preference.
(e) Conviction.
(f) Purchase.

7. The decision complex

The decision itself is really a result of a collection of decisions: for example, what class of product, what type or brand, what design, what quantity, in what place, from whom, at what price, and by what method of payment. One of the tasks of marketing is to communicate with the potential buyer in such a way that he or she not only becomes aware of the existence of the product or service offered, but develops a sufficiently strong and favourable attitude to go through the buying decision processes with a greater degree of confidence. Uncertainty and delay in making buying decisions are often the result of a conflict between rational economic motives and non-rational external and internal stimuli. So-called impulse buying is more frequently found where there is no economic anxiety – with comparatively inexpensive, frequently purchased products, where non-rational external stimuli (packaging, promotions, display) have a major influence.

The influences of 'augmented product' personality and environment

8. The augmented product/service concept

An early tutor of mine, Ed Bursk, maintained that in every buying situation the buyer needs some inner rationalisation to justify a decision which appears outwardly obvious. Kotler names this idea the 'augmented product/service' concept. He refers to the core product, the formal product and the augmented product. The 'core benefit' is step one; this is followed by the 'formal product', a reinforcing characteristic such as packaging, brand name and styling. The 'augmented product/service' adds yet more conviction of decision to buy, and includes such items as after-sales service, guarantee, free delivery.

9. Behavioural influences

Personality conditions a buyer's behaviour in an individual way according to his or her personal aspirations, temperament, cognitive and perceptual attributes, learning experience and state of motivation. Cultural and organisational influences also have a profound effect. Cultural differences are brought about by the sets of values to which individuals have been exposed from birth – as a child at home, as a pupil in a particular school environment, etc. Other social influences are later brought to bear. The organisation in which people work is a social institution where irrational values develop. This complex of influences is brought to bear on both consumer and industrial buying (**22**).

It would be impossible to devise a marketing programme to meet every individual circumstance and it is important, therefore, to identify significant group behavioural patterns. Consistent spending patterns may, for example, be related to the following variables:

(a) Urban and rural communities.
(b) Family income levels.
(c) Occupations.
(d) Education.
(e) Age.
(f) Sex.
(g) Informal social group membership.
(h) Race or nationality.
(i) Religion.

Conventional market profiles are dangerous. The problem, then, is to examine the behavioural patterns which emerge from combinations of those variables listed above, to uncover the underlying and not merely the superficial rationalisations of attitudes, and to determine which patterns are really significant.

10. Social grading

The most widely used scheme of grouping people for marketing purposes in the UK in terms of society divisions is based on occupation and income, and is carried out on behalf of the Joint Industry

• Committee representing newspaper and periodical publishers, advertising agencies and advertisers. There are six categories based on the occupations of the head of the household (*see* 7: **8**(d)). In fact, the six categories are normally grouped into four classes – most commonly AB, C1, C2, and DE.

Users are increasingly sceptical of these categories. The very high sales of Target Group Index data based on computerised results of many types of data are highly significant, as is the fact that 'occupation' is only one of several variables used by American researchers.

Changes in purchasing behaviour may be significantly affected by such variables as household size, previous buying experience, life-cycle stage, total family income and its use within the family unit. The researcher must also beware of the erosion of differentials in wages and salaries between some of the traditionally high- and low-income occupations.

The development of buyer classification by the ACORN technique is yet another sign of the unease felt in many quarters by conventional occupationally based data. The neighbourhood scanning technique has been used in the USA for a number of years, but has only recently been researched in depth and validated in the UK mainly as a result of the work of Richard Webster at the Centre for Environmental Studies. The initials ACORN are derived from the term A Classification Of Residential Neighbourhoods and the concept derives from the notion that life styles and behavioural patterns of particular neighbourhood groups have a great deal in common. Eleven family groups are most commonly used, although these can be further subdivided and related to postcodes and census districts. As an indication of this approach, which is gaining increasing favour, 17 per cent of households in Great Britain (classified under ACORN as groups) are living in modern, privately owned dwellings, and these are mainly populated by young families living on the outskirts of large towns or in small estates in commuter areas. There is an expectation of career development and residential movement. Incomes, education and car ownership are well above average.

11. Life styles and attitudes
Two specific fields of study in relation to buying behaviour which are currently attracting the attention of both academics and practising marketers relate to life-style patterns and attitudes.

The concept of life-style patterns and their potential application to marketing decisions was brought forward by William Lazer in 1963. Since then, continuous efforts have been made to identify groups of people according to their activities, interests and opinions. If significant correlations exist between life style and product use, television programme preferences, store choice, etc., the possibilities of devising appropriate products and/or communications directed towards similar life-style groups are opened up. Life-style data can, of course, be associated with more conventional demographic information, such as age, education, income, family size and occupation. The life-style approach has been applied in recent years not only to the marketing of consumer goods, but also to marketing service facilities such as bank credit cards and insurance.

Attitudes can be defined as predispositions to act in particular ways towards particular people, ideas or situations. They are not innate and can be changed, although it is difficult to effect changes since many attitudes have become deeply ingrained over time. Some attitudes are held with great intensity, and in general the evidence indicates a positive correlation between attitudes of high intensity, intentions to buy or not to buy, and ultimate buying action.

Until comparatively recently, attitudes have been difficult to identify and even more difficult to measure with the precision necessary for marketing application. Reference to new research techniques in this field is made in Chapter 3.

Corporate buying behaviour – the systems approach

12. Buying motives

Many products are bought as part of a total system: for example, even a domestic detergent is part of a system involving the whole organisation of the housekeeper's tasks and, in particular, is related to problems of time, equipment and availability, quite apart from its fitness for a particular purpose.

In the buying of industrial and commercial goods and services, the systems concept has become very important. Materials, components and machines are examined in terms of benefits and/or disadvantages within the total interactive system of operations. Thus in marketing services or products it is necessary to consider not only the mechanistic system, but also the subjective behaviour and values of personnel likely to be affected by any change. Construction materials, for example, must be acceptable to architects, engineers and contractors, objectively and subjectively. To meet this situation there is a growing movement towards systems marketing and within that concept to systems selling approaches. In certain large-scale contract situations, it is not infrequently an advantage for companies to combine in order to present a total system, as in the construction of electricity power stations.

13. The organisational buying complex
Successful organisational marketing requires that very special attention be paid to discovering the following:

(a) Who the buyers are.
(b) Where they are.
(c) How they may be reached.
(d) What they really want.
(e) What motives will induce them to buy.

It should not be assumed that company goods and services cannot be differentiated easily, and that success or failure depends only on a single combination of the right specifications, price and delivery. In the most non-differentiated commodity situations a whole range of differentials is possible, including better technical advice and more frequent or regular delivery. The way in which buyers 'perceive' a problem (*see* 6) can change. Technology changes, company policy changes, and company organisation changes.

Until comparatively recently, purchasing as a specialist activity had not received the attention it really merited. Of the gross output of goods in the UK, materials purchased represent some 60 per cent of the total.

14. New pressures in company purchasing
Classically, purchasing objectives are based on five key criteria:

(a) Quantity – ensuring availability.
(b) Quality – satisfying required purposes yet avoiding overspecification.
(c) Time – ensuring delivery.
(d) Source – evaluating possible suppliers.
(e) Price – negotiating appropriate terms.

More recently, increasingly sophisticated techniques have been applied, in terms of total organisational economics, to these criteria. Quantities are related more closely to the interrelated factors of alternative use of capital and space and the requirements of particular levels of output, stock turn, etc.

Buyers' stock and quality control procedures are becoming much more sophisticated. For example, sampling inspection alone may lead not only to faulty finished products, but also to wasted costs incurred by the processing of initially unsatisfactory materials. Companies such as Ford and Marks & Spencer use intensive quality control or assurance schemes which involve inspection and approval of suppliers' quality control systems.

The increasing flow of new goods and services is leading to a re-evaluation of existing supply sources and an exploration of new ones. In some cases, contact in the early stages of a project leads to joint development work and the establishment of relationships with a wider range of users, specifiers, financial approvers and professional buyers, each motivated in different ways.

The initial price of capital equipment is set against life-cycle cost calculations, involving taxation considerations, maintenance requirements, breakdown incidence, past availability, etc.

Value analysis and brainstorming techniques are being applied more regularly and systematically. Value analysis involves the careful analysis of components and materials by cost and function, so that existing use of particular designs, materials, processes, etc. can be questioned and alternative solutions advanced. These may save the company costs while taking nothing away from, and sometimes adding to, the customer's value perception.

Value analysis is sometimes associated with brainstorming – a technique by which a group of people, often from a diversity of specialisms within the organisation, are stimulated to make suggestions about specific problem situations. The suggestions can be completely wild, criticism is barred. When carefully handled, brainstorming often produces a number of completely different, useful approaches which merit further investigation.

Increasing attention is now being paid to the process of negotiation; this is particularly important in effecting large-scale national and international deals.

15. Specific behavioural questions
Key questions to be answered when marketing industrial products and service deals are the following:

(a) When repeated purchases are made, is each regarded as a major new decision or as a rebuying situation?

(b) How is a 'rebuy' or a 'new-buy' situation handled in terms of the decision process?

(c) Who are the major buying influences in various situations? Who plays a key role and when?

(d) What are the major motivations of these decision-makers and executives of key influence likely to be in particular situations? These motivations will not be entirely rational. There will be different formal and informal relationships, and different environmental backgrounds, training and interests.

(e) What is the effect of the formal and informal organisational structure on buying behaviour? The reward system, the status system, the authority system, the communications system and the extent of centralisation all have an important bearing (*see* 10:**2,15**). Good salespeople know intuitively that buyers are subject to normal human anxieties, frustrations and inertia. A more scientific study of behaviour would improve not only the effectiveness of the salesperson, but also the effectiveness of the whole customer-oriented marketing operation.

Major marketing stimuli

16. Product/service

A product or service may represent economic utility to a purchaser. He or she may, for example, believe that an electric drill will save the expense of hiring outside labour to make improvements to the house. The purchase of an electric drill, however, may not arise from purely economic motives. The prime urge may be to gain the admiration of others. Even if there are economic motives, these will be modified by the system of values of the individual, and the social environment which influences his or her attitudes and behaviour. The more affluent the society, the greater the spread of disposable income (money available after essential purchases have been made), and the greater the problem of choice. The choice is not simply between various types and makes of drill, but between drills and a whole collection of completely different items, such as holidays, refrigerators and furniture, and between buying now or saving. Similarly, choice between drills of different designs, performance and price depends on interacting economic, psychological and sociological motivations.

In commercial markets, there has been a rapid expansion of contract hire and subcontracting, the leasing or hire of transport, buildings and equipment, and debt and credit factoring. Many of these developments add to the growing strength of service activities and the need for more skilful purchasing and marketing activities. Industries such as transportation, communications, banking and insurance have long been recognised as a key service element in the economy of the more highly developed countries. To the growing proportion of economic output of the service sectors should be added health and welfare, education, technical services, building societies, consultancy and maintenance activities, transport and tourism.

17. The package
Packaging materials, design, colour, size, illustrations, brand names and associated symbols (logotypes), typefaces, copy and layout may affect to a very considerable extent a potential buyer's perception of a product. Packaging plays a vital role in stimulating memory, helping recognition, gaining shelf space, and providing use, storage and transportation benefits, but it has wider behavioural implications in terms of establishing customer preference, including recycling, environmental considerations, ease of opening, etc.

18. Price
The level at which a firm sets its prices will affect both sales and profitability. The demand for a car at £18,000 will be smaller than that for a car at £10,000. Under certain circumstances, it may be more profitable for a particular company to concentrate on the more limited market. From the basic economic law of supply and demand (i.e. the lower the price, the greater the quantity of demand), it is possible to construct graphs of theoretical demand quantities in relation to price. Some products will be seen to have much greater price elasticity than others: for example, the demand for a breakfast cereal might be reduced by one-tenth if prices were doubled, while the demand for a toilet soap might be cut by 70 per cent by a similar price change. It is important to study price elasticity considered in conventional economic terms, with regard to the availability of substitutes, durability, the ability to postpone purchase, income, population and the prices of competing products. It is also important to realise that, in developed economies, psychological aspects of pricing take on greater and greater significance. Lower price, for example, may be irrationally associated with poor quality (*see* Chapter 5).

19. The promotion
Many advertising campaigns are mainly planned in quantitative terms. How many people will be exposed to what weight of advertising during what period of time? To this quantitative thinking is added a target audience defined in broad socioeconomic categories. The most common measurements of effectiveness are based on recall (i.e. recollection of advertisements), but recall may be utterly unrelated to purchasing activity (*see* 7: **9–10**).

Advertising and communications must be directed towards stimulating favourable trade opinions and feelings about a company, as well as favourable customer attitudes towards product quality, price, delivery, sales and technical services. Concepts derived from clinical research and the findings of sociologists, psychologists and anthropologists may be used to determine why people buy particular products or services, and may lead to advertising which appeals to needs, wants and desires, so that potential buyers may rationalise the desire to buy. A ten-year guarantee originally given with mopeds in Germany inhibited sales, since many potential customers had guilt feelings about buying a product that they would expect to exchange for a car in two or three years. Advertising copy and visual elements are therefore designed in the light of anticipated connotations, i.e. the mental images aroused in the reader or viewer, beyond the superficial or explicit meaning.

In marketing a product, it is certainly important that the product itself, the packaging, the price and the promotion should have a consistent appeal in terms of the attitudes and motivations of potential buyers. This calls for deliberate research and planning. The recent growth in promotional expenditure in banking, insurance and financial services appears to call for very careful analysis of targeting and return on investment.

20. Distributive structure

Some products and services are bought direct from the producer; others are made available through various intermediary channels, such as retail and wholesale outlets, brokers, agents and mail-order houses. The producers and the 'channels' are all involved in marketing operations and it is important, in considering strategy and tactics, to understand the flow of the consumption system, the motivations of buyers and sellers along the chain, the relative importance of these channels and changing customer perceptions of them.

An organisation can either effect change in an established distributive system or react to change. A number of important movements are currently taking place for both these reasons in distribution patterns, among which the following changes are highly significant:

(a) The growth of vertically integrated systems, whereby an organisation moves into ownership or special contractual arrangements with the owners of organisations which come earlier or later in the consumption system. Thus, Marley has moved strongly forward into retail outlet ownership. Marks & Spencer has developed contractual relationships with suppliers on strictly controlled 'St Michael' speci-fications. New forms of franchising are developing. Franchising involves any contract under which independent retailers or whole-salers are organised to act together or with manufacturers to distribute given products or services.

(b) The growth of non-store retailing, such as home selling, e.g. Avon and Tupperware; the use of vending machines in offices and factories; and the spread of mail order, direct catalogue selling and network marketing.

(c) The growth of horizontally diversified trading. Supermarkets which previously restricted their retailing activities to grocery items are now offering clothing, furniture, electrical goods and self-service petrol stations. Producing organisations are also involved in acqui-sitions, mergers and development programmes leading in the direction of 'free-form' operation – a willingness to supply forward any products or services at a level which can be profitable.

(d) The growth of discount and cash-and-carry trading based on minimum services and décor, high volume and low unit margins.

(e) The growth of shopping centres with parking facilities away from the high street. Banks, insurance offices, solicitors, estate agents and other services are associated with these logistic shifts.

Growth has been particularly marked in new and diverse develop-ments in the financial services sector. The growth in credit trading has been made possible in the UK by a combination of government policy and aggressive marketing by the banks. Other service sectors showing very marked growth include tourism, international currency dealing, investment consultancy and brokerage, the leisure industry, building societies, and professional and technical services.

These changes give rise to the need to consider buyer behaviour in terms of buyers' perceptions of and attitudes towards organisations, products, brands, stores and suppliers.

21. The corporate image

A potential buyer's attitude to a product may be modified by his or her attitude to the organisation which manufactures or sells the product. A retailer may be more ready to handle a new product from a manufacturer whose products have yielded good profits in the past. A potential user may choose a plane of a particular brand because he or she has had good service from a saw made by the same manufacturer. In view of the fact that most companies now manufacture and/or market a wide range of products or services, increasing attention is being paid to the development of corporate images which are aimed at creating a widespread favourable company identification or image, by means of advertising, public relations, factory/store design, product design, stationery, transport and so on. Corporate image building is aimed not solely at potential customers, but also at other individuals and institutions on which future prosperity may depend, such as:

(a) shareholders and potential investors;
(b) the government;
(c) employees;
(d) suppliers;
(e) the public in the immediate vicinity of company premises; and
(f) schools and universities from which staff may be recruited.

> NOTE: In terms of specific product/service markets, this could, of course, have harmful as well as favourable knock-on effects.

The behavioural complex

The student of buyer behaviour would be well advised to examine in greater detail the following aspects of psychology and sociology.

22. Psychology
While psychology involves the broader study of living organisms, the student of marketing will derive most direct advantage from investigation of a limited number of aspects of human behaviour:

(a) *Motivation* – strivings or inner states which move people towards goals whether primary and physiological (e.g. hunger) or secondary (e.g. attracting attention); the degree of individual consciousness of particular motivations; their relative strengths; their interrelationships, etc.
(b) *Perception* – the way in which people interpret the information coming through the senses (e.g. words and pictures in different media).
(c) *Learning* – the changes in behaviour which lead to new habits or reinforcement of existing behaviour (e.g. brand switching and brand loyalty).
(d) *Personality* – the classification of a person's characteristic ways of reacting to situations.
(e) *Attitudes* – predispositions to behave in certain ways towards particular objects, ideas and situations.

23. Sociology

Sociology, the study of groups in society, tends to overlap with other sciences. For example, the interaction between individuals and groups is the subject matter of social psychology. Individuals when faced with a buying decision are likely to be reflecting to some extent values and behaviour patterns derived from identification with one or more social systems, including:

(a) the political system
(b) the economic system
(c) the family and kinship system
(d) the educational system
(e) the religious system.

Within these groups there will be primary groups (those who interact on a face-to-face basis); peer groups (those who have the same status in relation to a particular situation – evening class students, or managers of equal level in an organisation); and reference groups (groups which provide a model for an individual's behaviour, e.g. a junior clerk might aim to imitate the behaviour of the company's accountants).

The following simplified diagram is intended to illustrate the behavioural complex:

The individual	*Psychological processes*	*The environment*	
		Social	*Physical*
Attitudes		Primary	Geography
	–PERCEPTION→	groups	
Beliefs		Reference	Climate
		groups	
Values	←LEARNING –	Peer groups	Urban/
Motives			rural

Progress test 2

1. What is meant by 'the hierarchy of needs'?

2. What are some of the socioeconomic group factors to be considered in examining buying patterns?

3. What is systems selling? Give examples.

4. What are the five key criteria in company and organisational purchasing, and how has the application of these criteria been improved by new methods?

5. By what four major stimuli might a marketing organisation stimulate customer demand?

6. Comment on the development of vertically and horizontally integrated systems of distribution.

7. Why is it necessary to develop a corporate image? In what circumstances are there disadvantages? Give examples and discuss.

8. Explain the following behavioural terms: perception; attitudes; peer groups; reference groups.

9. Distinguish between product services and service industries. Give examples of differences in the development of the two sectors.

Assignment

Different systems of social classification are used for different purposes by different organisations. One member of a teaching/learning group should make appropriate contacts to obtain information on survey classifications used by the following:

– The Joint Industry Committee for National Readership Surveys.
– The British Registrar General.
– The International Labour Office in Geneva.
– The EU Socioeconomic Classifications.

Syndicates should be set up to discuss the findings (one system per syndicate). One member should then be prepared to talk to the whole class (group) and to answer questions on the system of classification previously examined.

3

Marketing research

Marketing research and decision making

1. Decisions and risk

Marketing decisions are inevitably made under conditions of uncertainty. Uncertainty involves both risk and opportunity. The use of marketing research does not and cannot eliminate either risk or opportunity, but its intelligent use can reduce risk and indicate the degree of probability of the various possible outcomes of opportunity. Markets are increasingly dynamic and competitive; their successful exploitation calls for greater investment and more frequent innovation. Decision making, therefore, must be faster and less susceptible to many of the needless errors of intuitive judgement.

2. Marketing research: definition and application

Marketing research may be defined as the objective and systematic collection, recording, analysis, interpretation and reporting of information about: existing or potential markets (i.e. market research, see 5), marketing strategies and tactics, and the interaction between markets, marketing methods and current or potential products or services (see 4–7). It can therefore play a major role in enabling the modern executive to apply a truly analytical approach to decision making. It can also assist in the evaluation of the effect of decisions which have been taken.

3. Origin and development

Marketing research has a comparatively recent origin, the first formal marketing research organisation having been established in the United States in 1911. From slow beginnings, in recent years there has been a growing sophistication in methods and methodology (see 17), and in the application of statistical techniques and behavioural science concepts (see 34), and the early scepticism of managements and the sometimes exaggerated claims of pseudo-researchers are rapidly disappearing. The use of marketing research in consumer markets is now reasonably widespread. The need for the objective evidence which marketing research as a decision-making tool can provide for management in producer goods or industrial markets is probably even greater than in consumer goods markets, but its value in these areas has been too little realised and research activity has consequently been more limited (*see* 11: **6**).

The scope of marketing research

4. Marketing research and management problems
In the following paragraphs (**5–7**) are some examples of the enormous range of problems on which management may require information, whether on the markets for their products (or services), on marketing strategy, or on the products themselves seen in this context of markets and marketing methods.

5. Markets
An up-to-date knowledge of the market is essential for successful marketing. Management must ask themselves the following questions:

(a) What is the *size* of a market for a product or service (in terms of volume and/or value)?

(b) What is the past *pattern of demand*; what factors (economic, social, political, technological) might affect future demand, and when? Is demand subject to seasonal or cyclical variations?

(c) What is the *market structure* (e.g. is it based on industry, on size or numbers of companies, on income groups, on sex, on age, on geographical distribution)?

(d) What are the *buying habits*, motivations and procedures of domestic customers, retailers, wholesalers and professional service and industrial buyers?

(e) What is the company's *market share* and how does this compare with competitive shares over various time periods?

(f) What are past and future *trends* – rate of change in population, national income, retail sales, industry output?

(g) Which *overseas markets* present the best immediate or long-term opportunities?

6. Marketing policy and strategy
Armed with a knowledge of the market, management can consider their overall marketing policy and tactics. They will require further

information about competition, costs, and the probable results of different courses of action. For example,

(a) Where, how and at what cost do competitors advertise? What are competitive pricing structures and practices?
(b) How do marketing and distribution costs compare, in total and by individual elements, with competitive cost?
(c) What are the most effective channels of distribution?
(d) How do sales differ by territory, industry and type of outlet, and why?
(e) What effect on demand will there be if a new product is introduced under an established corporate image or a separate brand name?
(f) What would be the effect of a change in pricing structure on the number and frequency of orders, or on factory and store inventory levels?
(g) What amount of service, at what cost, is it necessary to provide to maintain or improve profitability?
(h) What is the effect of sales promotional activity?

7. Products and services
The third factor to be considered is the product/service range, in terms of suitability for the market, design and manufacture, competitive advantages and profitability. Examples in terms of products are as follows:

(a) What is the company reputation or image for products, presentation, technical service and delivery? What are the major weaknesses of products – own and competitive?
(b) How are products used and what characteristics are considered most important? What should be the range offered, e.g. prices, sizes, colours, designs?
(c) What changes will be necessary in materials used, advantages offered and functions performed, and when? Should certain products be dropped, and when?
(d) What is the best pricing structure for a new product? What might be the effect on the profitability of a product or volume sales of a price increase of, say, 4 per cent?
(e) What patents, licensing agreements or other legal restrictions might affect manufacture or sale of a product?
(f) What do reactions to products in test markets indicate in terms of national or international operations?

The basic concepts of product/market and marketing information needs can be applied to service organisations. D.F. Channon, in his excellent book *Bank Strategy and Marketing* points out, for example, that a clear distinction between commercial and merchant bank activities no longer exists. Lending and credit services, however, differ considerably in range, variety and emphasis. In addition, banking service products may now include consultancy services to individuals and corporate bodies, factoring, international transfers and a variety of special fee-paid activities. The student may ask what information and research was undertaken prior to the acquisition of estate agencies by some banking organisations.

8. Marketing research and company organisation

The range of studies which the marketing researcher may be asked to undertake extends across departmental or functional barriers. Examples of studies in which executives other than those in marketing divisions would be concerned are as follows:

(a) Plant location studies.
(b) Economic forecasting in connection with budgets.
(c) Studies of companies under consideration for acquisition.
(d) Analysis of transport utilisation.

In any company organisation, marketing research must therefore be placed under the control of an executive who is sympathetic to its importance, its need for adequate finance and its essential objectivity (it must be protected from personal pressures to find support for the subjective judgements of management). The data and recommendations produced should be regularly and easily available to appropriate decision- and policy-makers, whether they be individuals or committees. In small companies, ideally a marketing research manager should report to the chief executive. In large companies, with a marketing director at policy-making level, marketing research might report to that executive. Many companies have no marketing research staff of their own, but too frequently when specialist staff are employed their effect is negligible because they are too remote from major decision centres. (Where company marketing research departments do exist, they are usually small and a number of projects are assigned to outside independent agencies.)

9. Dangers in use of terminology

Specialists in marketing research departments must combine skills from economics, psychology, sociology, mathematics and statistics. One of the major dangers is that these specialists may forget that their prime aim is to assist in the solution of marketing problems and may become too involved in research methodology (*see* **17** (a), **44**) for its own sake. Personal communications with other executives and final research reports can be hampered by an overemphasis on technical terminology. Findings and methods should be explained in language non-specialists can understand.

Sources of information

10. Data types
Data are generally classified as either primary or secondary.

(a) *Primary data* – information which has originated directly as a result of the particular problem under investigation.
(b) *Secondary data* – data which already exist and may be used for an investigation, but which have not been collected for that specific purpose. It is usually cheaper to use this kind of data than to set up special investigations, but care must be taken to ensure that the data are relevant, can be adjusted to the problem, and are reliable.

11. Sources of secondary data
These can be divided into internal and external sources.

(a) *Internal.* There is invariably a mass of marketing information in a company's own records – particularly sales records. This information may not have been collected systematically or in the most appropriate form, but it is clear that marketing researchers should turn first to the sources which, properly organised, can provide continuously relevant current data as well as information for occasional and special investigations. Data-processing equipment, computers and the systems approach are making the extrapolation of appropriate information easier and faster.
(b) *External.* In addition there is a wealth of published information available from external sources, such as agencies, consultants, government departments, trade associations, banks, professional bodies, research organisations and the press. Some of these are outlined in paragraphs **12–16** below. A fuller list of various bodies and publications which provide useful information is given in Appendix 1.

12. Specialist marketing research agencies
Large numbers of these agencies, varying enormously in size and

specialisation, exist in the UK and in many parts of the world. The larger agencies usually offer a wide range of services but some concentrate on projects requiring more specialised skills, such as field interviewing in connection with industrial and/or service markets, motivation research and research connected with specific industries.

Special services offered by agencies include the following:

(a) The *A. C. Nielsen food and drug indices*, which provide extensive data at frequent intervals obtained from a large sample (*see* 21 below) of product sales by brand, retail purchases, inventory levels and movement, retail and wholesale prices, percentage distribution, etc. Data are broken down in various ways: for example, by geographical area and type of store.

(b) The advertising research services of the *Gallup* and *Starch* organisations. Gallup tests advertising research in mass circulation printed media, while Starch attempts to evaluate whether particular current advertisements are or will be read more than past advertisements or competitive advertisements.

(c) The *Audit Bureau of Circulation*, with a membership of 2,000 publishers, advertisers and agencies, which provides certified information on the circulation of printed media. It should be noted that many specialist magazines do not subscribe to the Audit and there is no objective measurement of the circulation figures claimed.

(d) *Measurement of television audiences*. Commercial television audience ratings are published weekly from JICTAR (Joint Industry Committee for Television Audience Research) figures. These figures are derived from statistics provided by Audits of Great Britain Ltd (AGB), who use both paper tape recordings from set meters fitted to receivers and family diaries. The Broadcasters Audience Research Board (BARB) was set up in August 1981 to be responsible for commissioning television audience research and to rationalise the differing research methods previously used by the BBC and IBA. Problems of more refined measurements, such as the number of persons watching particular programmes or advertisements, their actions and subsequent buying behaviour, are as yet unsolved.

13. Advertising agencies

The demands of clients for more comprehensive marketing information as part of a total marketing plan, together with the growing need for agencies to be competitive, has led to a considerable extension of marketing research departments in advertising agencies. The cost of sustaining these services is leading more often to an additional charge

above the 15 per cent commission on which agencies have traditionally operated (*see* 6: **23**).

14. Advertising media proprietors and contractors
Much of this research is basically intended to show the effectiveness
of the particular media being sold, and great care is needed in interpreting the studies. Nevertheless, the practice of producing such
research data is gaining ground rapidly and much of the information
may be free from promotional bias.

15. Trade associations
Studies are usually very limited in scope and statistics may be difficult
to interpret if important companies or groups of companies are
omitted. However, studies which are available are particularly useful
in service and industrial marketing research, where there is a comparative lack of sources of secondary data (*see* Appendix 1).

16. Government departments and international organisations
These are invaluable research sources. British government departments provide both annual and monthly statistics on many topics,
and foreign governments provide information through their embassies or issue bibliographical lists from the appropriate trade
ministries. Other statistics are published by various international
bodies, such as UNO, OECD, IMF and EU Statistical Office.
   Some of the great number of reports available are listed in Appendix 1.

Executing marketing research studies

17. Steps in the market research process
Research projects are not susceptible to any one complete and inflex-
ible sequence of steps, and the types of problem to be studied will
determine the particular steps to be taken and their order. The following steps provide, however, a useful procedural guide:

(a) Definition of the problem is the step of the greatest importance.
Frequently, management initially pose an ill-defined problem or one
which is a superficial aspect of a more fundamental problem. Care
must be taken to verify the objectivity and validity of the background
facts and to agree upon the problem in writing with the executive or
executives concerned with its circumstances.

(b) Specification of the information required.
(c) Design of the research project, involving consideration of:
  (*i*) the means of obtaining the information;
  (*ii*) the availability and skills of company marketing research staff and/or agencies;
  (*iii*) methodology, i.e. a detailed explanation of the way in which selected means of obtaining information (e.g. library/desk research, observation studies, individual and group interviews, questionnaires etc.) will be organised, sequenced or combined, and the reasoning leading to the decisions;
  (*iv*) the time and cost of the research.
(d) Sample design.
(e) Construction of questionnaires and/or preparation of briefs for field interviews.
(f) Execution of the project, with arrangement for checks on the reliability of data being collected.
(g) Analysis of data.
(h) Preparation of report and recommendations.

18. Sampling

When field studies are undertaken, considerations of time and cost almost invariably lead to contact being made with a selection of respondents. The respondents selected should be as representative as possible of the total population to be investigated in order to produce a miniature cross-section. The selection process is called *sampling*. The word 'universe' is often used to describe the whole population from which the selection is made. Samples are of two basic types:

(a) *Probability or random samples* – samples which are so constructed that every element from the total population has a known probability of selection and the limits of probable error in relating results to the whole population are thus known mathematically in advance.
(b) *Non-probability or purposive samples* – samples based on the choice of the selector.

19. Comparison of probability and non-probability samples

Probability samples enable experimental error to be measured, but they do not necessarily provide more accurate marketing research results than non-probability samples. A small probability sample may yield a high experimental error; even with a large sample, errors may arise because of variability in the characteristics of the population being examined, such as attitudes and habits. Non-probability samples are subject to error in sample selection, but the risk of selection bias has to be weighed against the risk of experimental errors arising from smaller probability samples. In industrial marketing research, executive judgement is likely to be more accurate than in consumer marketing research because of a more exact knowledge of a comparatively small universe. Concepts of probability are frequently used in non-probability samples and judgement is applied to give 'weighting' to factors according to their likely importance in the majority of marketing research surveys.

20. Modified probability samples
Statisticians have developed a number of specialised probability procedures which are of particular value in marketing research. The most significant are considered in **21–25** below.

21. Systematic sampling
Only the first unit of the sample is selected at random. The following units are selected at fixed intervals. If, for example, questions were to be asked of householders in a road and the third house were selected randomly as the starting point, there would be systematic sampling if subsequent interview were carried out at fixed regular intervals: for example, at the eighth, thirteenth, eighteenth and twenty-third houses, and so on. The cost can be controlled by the intervals selected. The basic assumption is that all elements of the population are ordered in a manner representative of the total population. A systematic sample of a list of customers arranged according to their annual purchases would meet this assumption, whereas there is a possibility that every fifth customer entering a store on a given day may be unrepresentative of the weekly clientele.

22. Stratified sampling
If there is evidence that certain elements of the population are more significant for the purpose of a survey than others, it may be desirable to weight these elements in proportion to their significance. If, for example, tea consumption of a household were significantly related to family size and particular age groups, a stratified sample would give due weighting to respondents who conformed to the significant criteria. Stratified samples may be especially useful in industrial marketing research if, for example, volumes of output or number of employees are known significant factors. Interviewers are sometimes instructed to survey fixed proportions of a given population, such as 50 per cent of large firms in a given geographical area. This is

described as *quota sampling*. This technique is not based on probability, but in situations in which a relatively small percentage of the universe accounts for a very large percentage of usage or sales, weighted, stratified sampling would be more likely to produce results in keeping with the real situation than a scrupulously random sample.

23. Cluster and area sampling
Geographical dispersal of interviews creates cost problems. Cluster sampling reduces cost by concentrating surveys in selected clusters: for example, in particular sales areas, counties, local authority areas, or towns. The principle of statistical random selection could be applied in the selection of clusters and units within the clusters. Clusters may be selected on the basis of predetermined strata – if home ownership is an important factor, it may be necessary to identify clusters according to known data on home ownership.

24. Multi-stage sampling
This is a development of the principle of cluster sampling. The first stage may be to select large primary sampling units, such as counties, then towns and finally districts within towns.

25. Sequential sampling
This is a complex technique. The ultimate size of the sample is not fixed in advance, but is determined according to mathematical decision rules on the basis of information yielded as surveys progress. This technique is frequently used in industrial market surveys where it is particularly difficult initially to define the universe in terms of critical criteria (e.g. turnover of companies, machine utilisation), or in order to build up to a specified quota of strata in the stratified sampling (*see* **22**).

   The objective of sequential sampling is to determine the smallest sample that can be used to produce confidence intervals within given margins of error. In marketing research a confidence of 95 per cent is commonly accepted, i.e. there is a 5 per cent chance that the true population statistic may fall outside the margins of error indicated. The basic problem here is to determine how much extra cost should be incurred to reduce risk. In this connection it should be noted that, while a high degree of precision is associated with larger samples (the size of the sample being more important than the size of the sample universe), sample size has to be multiplied by four to double the precision. For further information on sampling, readers are advised to consult Elliot and Christopher's *Methods in Marketing Research*, but it would be well for them to remember that more real practical problems are associated with stages (e) to (g) of the market research process set out in **17** than with sample design and sampling error.

Bias is a particularly acute problem and is more likely in interactive methods such as interviewing than in non-reactive methods like observation. A combination of both types of approach is often recommended as a means of drawing attention to particular biases which may otherwise remain undetected.

26. Methods of collecting data
Data can be collected either through observation or through direct communication with respondents, whether by mail, telephone or personal interview. The advantages and disadvantages of these methods are outlined below (**27–30**).

27. Observation
The observation method is commonly used in studies of consumer movement in stores, in poster-passing traffic counts, etc.

(a) *Advantages*
(*i*) If the observer records accurately, subjective bias is eliminated (direct communication methods are susceptible to bias which may arise from either questioner or respondent).
(*ii*) Information relates to what is currently happening; it is not complicated by consideration of past behaviour, future intentions or attitudes.
(b) *Disadvantages*
(*i*) It is usually an expensive method.
(*ii*) Information provided is very limited.

28. Mailing and questionnaires
This is the method most extensively employed (*see also* **33** below).
(a) *Advantages*
(*i*) Low cost even when spread widely geographically.
(*ii*) Lack of interviewer bias.
(*iii*) Some respondents are difficult to interview – particularly in industrial markets.
(*iv*) Respondents have more time to give considered answers.
(*v*) Respondents may prefer anonymity.

NOTE: Questionnaires may be used in various ways: for example, they may be mailed, or they may be used in a verbal interview in strictly structured form (questions asked in order and word sequence as set down). They may be used for telephone interviews, or in a two-part verbal interview – partly structural, partly open-ended (the respondent is free to make any responses). (*See also* **29, 30**.)

(b) *Disadvantages*

(*i*) Limitation of information. To be successful, mailed questionnaires should be comparatively short and simple. Questions may be dichotomous (yes or no answers), multiple choice (alternative answers listed) or open-ended. The latter are often difficult to analyse. A specialised form of multiple-choice questions involves *scaling*. For example, respondents may be asked to rank products in order of preference, or to indicate an attitude according to its strength, say from 'like very much' to 'dislike intensely'. One of the problems arising from scaling questionnaires is the difficulty of establishing the exact intervals: for example, are products 1 and 2 seen to be more equal than 4 and 5?

(*ii*) Problems of having constantly to up-date mailing lists.

(*iii*) Low rate of return and the difficulty of knowing whether willing respondents are truly representative. Sometimes a number of personal field interviews or telephone enquiries are carried out to check on the validity of the sample of questionnaires actually returned. It should be noted that the rate of return will depend on such factors as the skill of questionnaire construction and time of mailing.

(*iv*) Possible ambiguity of replies or omission of replies to particular questions.

(*v*) Inflexibility – the difficulty of amending the approach once questionnaires have been despatched. Pilot testing is, in any case, very desirable to avoid question construction faults which may lead to answers which defy analysis.

NOTE: Questionnaires should contain 'control' questions which indicate the reliability of the respondent. For example, a question designed to determine consumption of particular materials may be asked first in terms of financial expenditure and later in terms of weight. Again, one or two questions not directly related to the purpose of the survey may produce answers which cast doubt on the reliability of the respondent.

29. Telephone interviews

Although this method has many advantages, particularly in trial surveys, it is only now beginning to be used more widely in the UK.

(a) *Advantages*
    (*i*) More flexible than mailing.
    (*ii*) Interviewer can explain requirements more easily.
    (*iii*) Faster than other methods.
    (*iv*) Cheaper than personal interviewing.
    (*v*) Ease of recall.
    (*vi*) Access can sometimes be gained to respondents who would neither be interviewed personally nor answer questionnaires.
    (*vii*) Replies can be recorded without embarrassment to respondent.
    (*viii*) Higher response rate than from mailing.
    (*ix*) Useful for radio and television surveys when checking that programmes are actually being heard or viewed.

(b) *Disadvantages*
    (*i*) Possibility of interviewer bias.
    (*ii*) Little time given to respondent for considered answers.
    (*iii*) Surveys restricted to respondents who have telephones or, in industrial surveys, have easy access to telephones.
    (*iv*) Personal approach can inhibit replies.
    (*v*) Extensive geographical coverage may be restricted by cost considerations.
    (*vi*) The number of questions must usually be limited.

30. Personal interviews

These can be carried out in a highly structured way: the interviewer follows a rigidly laid-down procedure, asking questions in a prescribed form and order. The interviewer may, however, be allowed varying degrees of freedom in conducting the interview. The greater the freedom allowed, the higher is the skill required in the interviewer and the more complex are the problems of analysing the results.

(a) *Advantages*
    (*i*) Greater flexibility and more opportunity to restructure questions.
    (*ii*) More information can be obtained – and in greater depth.
    (*iii*) Resistance in the respondent can often be overcome by the skill of the interviewer.
    (*iv*) Products, advertisements, etc. can be shown or demonstrated.
    (*v*) Observation methods can be applied. In addition to recording verbal answers, interviewers can physically check stocks or note reactions to questions.

(*vi*) Personal data regarding respondents can be more easily obtained.

(*vii*) Sample can be controlled more effectively. Missing returns cause obvious difficulty in analysis. A skilled interviewer can arrange calls at appropriate times or make recalls if respondents are out, or rephrase questions to which there is initially no response.

(b) *Disadvantages*

(*i*) Relatively expensive if a large, widely scattered geographical sample is taken.

(*ii*) Possibility of respondent bias, to please the interviewer, to create a false personal prestige image, or to end the interview quickly.

(*iii*) Possibility of interview bias.

(*iv*) Certain types of individual, such as important executives and people in high income groups, may be difficult to interview.

(*v*) If the sample is large and if recalls are necessary, the time factor in completing a survey may be high.

31. The use of panels

Panels consist of *selected samples* of the universe (*see* **18** above) and are most frequently used in consumer marketing research. Members of these panels agree to regular interviews and/or the maintenance of diaries; sometimes panel members are given small financial incentives in return for their assistance. Panels are used by company marketing research units and by marketing research agencies. Examples are the A.C. Nielsen company and the AGB rating system (**12**(a) and (d) above).

(a) *Advantages*

(*i*) Trends in attitude, usage, etc. can be observed in easily controlled situations.

(*ii*) Panel members are obviously co-operative and usually supply very complete information.

(*iii*) Panels may be divided in order to compare reactions of different groups, for example, to products or advertisements – again under readily controlled conditions.

(*iv*) Appointments can be made, thus avoiding the expense of recalls.

(*v*) Individual behaviour can be studied over time periods. When different samples are taken, only group trends can be examined.

(*vi*) Panel members learn instruction procedures and time may thus be saved in the future.

(*vii*) Conversations can be recorded on tape and played back.
(b) *Disadvantages*
(*i*) Willingness to co-operate in a panel may indicate certain characteristics in members which are not truly representative of any particular universe.
(*ii*) If panel members drop out from time to time, it is difficult to ensure that their replacements have similar characteristics.
(*iii*) There is a tendency to develop a 'panel sophistication': that is, constant interviewing may lead to specially conditioned responses.
(*iv*) Individual responses may be conditioned by the fact that people in groups may adapt their behaviour to what is considered to be socially acceptable.

Problems of accuracy

32. Response accuracy
It is clear that, if marketing research is to provide information to guide decision making, information must be as accurate as possible, taking into account the limitations imposed by time and cost. As we have seen, sampling itself involves a calculated risk in relation to accuracy, and even in probability samples confidence limits are set. This problem is intensified by the fact that the statistical confidence limit presupposes that the questions posed are those to which accurate answers can and will be provided.

33. Factors in assessing accuracy of information
The following are some of the factors which must be considered in assessing the accuracy of information:

(a) Questions involving opinion are susceptible to greater inaccuracy than those involving fact, but even questions of fact may lead to inaccurate answers. If, for example, a physical check of stock in a store or pantry is taken, the only problems are whether the count itself is accurate and whether all stock has been seen. If, however, one asks what programme was seen on television three days earlier, the information may be inaccurate because of faulty memory or a conscious or subconscious desire on the part of the respondent to mislead. Although most respondents do not consciously try to deceive, memory can be very fallible.
(b) Respondents may not understand properly what they are being

asked. The difficulty may be in the phrasing of the questions, and it is wise to pre-test questions to avoid widespread misinterpretation.

(c) Respondents may not be willing to answer certain questions.

(d) The appearance or manner of the interviewer may influence the answers given. A respondent may give answers calculated to please or displease.

(e) Where questions relate to future actions, the reliability of answers depends on the extent to which people are likely to change their minds over given time periods.

(f) In posing questions on attitudes, there is the problem of assessing the intensity of a favourable or unfavourable response.

(g) If questions involve the respondent in supplying reasons for an action, the reasons may be inaccurate because previously they have never been consciously analysed or because they are based on false assumptions. A housewife may, for example, indicate that she buys a certain brand of tea because of its price, when in fact she always buys tea at a particular shop where many brands are not available.

(h) Answers on purchasing behaviour or attitudes may be supplied by persons who make only a contribution to the decision-making process. Other members of the household or company may influence the decision to a greater or lesser extent.

(i) Buying reasons or attitudes may be subconscious and not known to the respondent.

(j) Answers may be given in order to convey a false status image: for example, newspapers read, or cultural interests.

Behavioural and motivational research

34. Depth interview
The behavioural sciences, psychology, sociology and cultural anthropology, are concerned with investigating the reasons for human behaviour. The key word in this kind of research is *why*. An understanding of why people behave as they do in given situations, or why certain statistical relationships exist, leads to possibilities of planning how to effect change as well as planning to 'key in' to states of mind. (*See* 2:**22** and **23**.)

Specialists in these disciplines may undertake 'depth' interviews. The term 'depth' is used since the interviews are designed to discover underlying motives and desires. Depth interviews are usually undirected and require great skill and considerable time. There are difficulties not only in establishing the right degree of confidence and eliciting answers, but also in interpreting the qualitative information provided. This type of research is obviously expensive and, in practice, group rather than individual interviews are more commonplace.

35. Criticisms of depth interviewing
Among criticisms of the method, the following are those most usually advanced:

(a) Samples are too small for meaningful conclusions.
(b) The findings are not quantified.
(c) It is difficult to know whether these investigations into the reasons for behaviour really do indicate a purchasing need or a motive. Attitudes revealed under research conditions may change in actual buying situations.
(d) Individual reactions in group situations are conditioned artificially by the structure and behaviour of the group.

36. Techniques in motivation research
Among the special techniques employed in motivation research are the following:

(a) Sentence completion tests.
(b) Word association tests.
(c) Story completion tests.
(d) *Verbal projection tests.* In these, the respondent is asked to comment on or explain what other people do: for example, why do people smoke? Answers may reveal the respondent's own motivations.
(e) *Pictorial techniques.* An example is the 'thematic apperception' test, in which the respondent describes what is happening in an ambiguous picture. One of the most common of these tests is the Rorschach test, in which people are asked to describe what they perceive in two symmetrical ink blots. Another pictorial technique takes the form of a series of cartoons with words inserted in 'balloons' above. The respondent is asked to put his or her own words in an empty balloon space.
(f) *Sociometry.* This is a new technique through which an attempt is made to trace the flow of information among groups and then to examine the ways in which new ideas are diffused. Sociograms are constructed to identify leaders and followers. This approach has been applied to the diffusion of ideas on drugs among medical practitioners.
(g) *Attitude-scaling tests.* A number of scaling techniques have been developed, but perhaps the best known is the semantic differential

technique developed by C.E. Osgood. Basically, the idea is simple, the respondents being invited to rate particular words in relation to objects, services, products, companies, etc., along a bipolar scale, e.g. 'weak' to 'strong', 'cold' to 'hot', 'small' to 'large'.

(h) *Role-playing.* In these situations, the interviewer invites the respondent to act a simple role, such as a person advising a friend on how to set about buying a car.

37. Successful motivation research

Despite the criticisms, motivation research has been successfully applied to problems such as product design, package design, advertising, public relations, service facilities and pricing. It should also be added that some authorities maintain that valuable motivation research can be carried out by good marketing researchers who are not expert in behavioural science, provided that structured questions are used and that training and direction are given by experienced psychologists.

Data analysis

38. Preliminary care in collecting data

The care and speed of analysing data depend to a large extent on the care which has been taken in devising and executing a research project. Attention is therefore drawn to the considerations outlined in **39–42** below.

39. Constructing the questionnaire

(a) If the survey is to be conducted by means of structured questionnaires to which the possible answers are predetermined, data can be readily machine processed. Questions (and possible answers) should, therefore, be coded.

(b) The length of questionnaires should be kept to a minimum.

(c) Questions should proceed in logical sequence, moving from easy to more difficult questions, constantly maintaining the interest of the respondent. Personal and intimate questions should be left to the end.

(d) Technical terms, vague generalisations and expressions capable of different interpretations should be avoided.

40. The answers

(a) Replies to open-ended questions lead to difficulties in analysis, and manual methods of analysis will have to be employed. For this reason, and also because respondents and/or interviewers have to construct replies rather than simply provide an answer by means of underlining, crossing out or using a symbol such as a tick or a cross, the time allocated for the completion of the survey will need to be correspondingly greater.

(b) Adequate space for answers should be provided for ease of editing and tabulating.

(c) There should always be provision for indication of uncertainty, such as 'don't know' and 'no preference'.

41. Scaling and non-parametric data
There are, in fact, four types of scale:

(a) *Ratio scales*. Such scales have equal intervals. Each is identified with a number. The numbers can be added, subtracted, multiplied and divided, and the units are interchangeable. Speed and length, for example, are measured in ratio scales.

(b) *Interval scales*. These are similar to ratio scales, but lack a true zero. The intervals are equal but the zero is fixed arbitrarily – 70°F is not twice as hot as 35°F. A similar deficiency attaches to Osgood's semantic differential scale.

(c) *Ordinal scales*. These range ideas or objects in an order of priority or preference. This form of scaling is used in market research when respondents are invited, for example, to list products in order of preference. The intervals between ranks are unequal.

(d) *Nominal scales*. These are merely attempts to assign identities to words, such as 'yes', 'no' and 'dislike', so that it is possible for a researcher to categorise in numerical form the distribution of respondents' answers.

When data can be measured in units which are interchangeable – such as weights (by ratio scales) and temperatures (by interval scales) – those data are said to be *parametric* and can be subjected to most kinds of statistical and mathematical process. When data are measured in units which are not interchangeable – such as product preferences (by ordinal scales) – the data are said to be *non-parametric* and are susceptible only to a limited extent to mathematical and statistical treatment.

Unfortunately, most behavioural data come into the non-parametric category, but some of the most promising developments in behavioural research have been associated with the development of new measurement techniques which open up completely new horizons. These techniques fall under a general classification of *multidimensional scaling* and include several approaches to both parametric and non-parametric data. They promise a great advance from a series of unidimensional measurements (e.g. a distribution of intensities of feeling towards single attributes such as colour and taste, or a preference ranking with indeterminate intervals), to a perceptual mapping in multidimensional space of objects (company images, advertisements, brands, etc.). Such techniques, which require sophisticated computer programs and data generation by behavioural specialists, have already indicated surprising product gaps and promotional inadequacies.

For those who have difficulty in conceptualising the idea, imagine that you have an outline map of your own country. You then obtain data on the distances between each pair of the largest towns and/or cities (perhaps twelve or fourteen). You now convert these distances into ranks by assigning rank 1 to the shortest distance, and so on. By the application of a computer program, a configuration remarkably close to the actual town and city locations can be revealed.

Now transfer the idea to the mapping of opinions, life styles, attitudes, etc. The argument may now be advanced that opinions, life styles and attitudes derive from a constellation of components: for example, attitudes towards a product may derive from colour, design, country of origin and many other factors. If, of course, all these variables were discrete, the number of potential spatial maps would make their use impracticable in marketing. In fact, there are usually significant intercorrelations, so that a comparatively small number of factors appears to account for an attitude formation. This can then be mapped in a manner more akin to an actual buying situation, rather than by examining on conventional lines single factors in isolation or in simple cross-classifications.

42. Conducting the survey

(a) Interviewers should be carefully selected, trained and briefed.
(b) Occasional field checks should be made to ensure that interviewers are neither cheating nor deviating from instructions. Control questions should be inserted in mailed questionnaires (*see* **28** above).
(c) Advance provision should be made so that appropriate action may be taken if selected respondents refuse to co-operate or are not available when an interviewer calls.

43. Editing, tabulating and analysis
When the data have been edited and tabulated, analysis can begin.

The type of information required for analysis should, of course, determine to a considerable extent the manner in which the survey is planned and executed, as was indicated above (**38–42**). A careful watch should, however, be kept for *unanticipated factors* of significance.

In the process of analysis, relationships or differences supporting or conflicting with original or new hypotheses should be subjected to statistical tests of significance to determine with what validity data can be said to indicate any conclusions. For example, is it more probable that differences in the buying pattern of two groups of people, as shown in survey results, arise from chance selection in the sample or indicate an actual difference? (*See* Chapter 19 of W.M. Harper's *Statistics* in the M & E Handbook series.)

Marketing research reports

44. The content and layout of reports
The importance of the final report cannot be over-emphasised. This is the document which is seen by the busy executive, often unfamiliar with specialist terminology, and to which he or she looks for clearly expressed findings. The following guides to report presentation are therefore offered:

(a) *Layout*
  (*i*) All reports should carry a title and date.
  (*ii*) There should be a table of contents, so that information that the decision-maker wishes to examine closely can be located without difficulty.
  (*iii*) The report should contain a clear statement of the objective of the research, and an explanation of the methods.
  (*iv*) A statement of findings and recommendations in non-technical language should appear at the beginning. If findings are extensive, they should be summarised.
  (*v*) The main body of the report should be presented in logical sequence and broken down into readily absorbed and identifiable sections.
  (*vi*) Technical data, such as questionnaires, sample information and statistical tables, should be put in an appendix.
(b) *General rules*
  (*i*) Reports should be written in a concise and objective style, avoiding vague expressions such as 'it seems' and 'there may be'.

(*ii*) The inclusion of charts and illustrations in the main body of the report should be seriously considered if they present information more clearly or forcibly.

(*iii*) Any constraints or calculated confidence limits should be stated.

Marketing experiments

45. Simple models for difficult marketing conditions

In scientific experiments carried out under laboratory conditions, research takes place under controlled circumstances. A variable is studied and observed, and any change is measured in situations where the surrounding environment is maintained under strict control. Statistical measurement can be carried out to discover whether the variable has caused any change and, if so, to what extent. Such ideal circumstances are virtually impossible in marketing. There are so many uncontrolled variables, including competitive activity, economic changes, and decisions made by human beings. Yet it is important to attempt to measure change in sales, profits and market share by making changes in products (e.g. design, colour, taste), in packaging (e.g. colour, visual images, shape), in service (e.g. level, kind, cost), in distribution methods, locations and dealer conditions, and in promotion (e.g. media selections, usage, level, frequency). A further complication is the time factor. In this context, advertising demonstrates the problem very readily, in that its effect(s) may be the result of a single advertisement, but more probably will be the cumulative result of a series of advertisements – what is often described as the 'carry over' effect.

46. The experimental method in marketing practice

Marketing researchers in practice have to accept the limitations of the dynamic nature of the real world of commerce in devising their experiments.

Peter Chisnall in his book *Marketing Research: Analysis and Measurement* sets out the simplified model of the experimental method in marketing shown in Figure 3.1. *Primary variation* refers to output changes caused by input changes: for example, increased sales caused by rerouting of the sales force. *Secondary variation* refers to variation in output caused by environmental changes: for examples, reduced sales caused by changes in indirect taxation. *Error* refers to faulty experimental conditions, such as measurement mistakes.

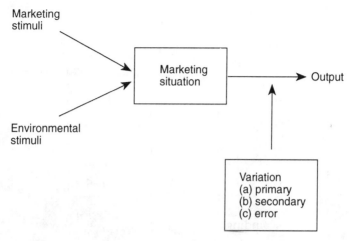

Figure 3.1 *Model of the experimental method in marketing*

Examples of simple experiments are as follows:

(a) Identical marketing campaigns run in similar environmental situations except for a single difference in marketing stimuli: for example, advertising (paid) used in some outlets, no advertising in others (control); rearrangement of display units in some stores, usual arrangement in others (control).

(b) Comparative tests: for example, 'split runs' in advertising. This involves using two different advertisements (e.g. in terms of space, place, copy and illustrations) in different editions or runs of a publication, and checking on the results. This is most likely to be useful where the 'carry-over' effect is minimal, as with a special coupon offer.

(c) Test marketing is one of the most common forms of experimental marketing. Further reference will be made in 4: **16–19**.

More sophisticated experimental designs are now being used with, for example, multiple variables to measure the effect of combinations of variables. Prices might be held constant, and changes made in the type of display merchandising, in the use of trade incentives, and in the expenditure on each in a variety of combinations. Factorial designs and analysis of variance techniques are now fairly frequently used where the potential variations in outcomes justify the cost.

James Rothman in his *Consumer Market Launch Handbook* gives the simple Latin square design in Figure 3.2 used for a store test on a product with very high sales in four stores during a period of one

Store

	1	2	3	4
Week	A	B	C	D
	B	D	A	C
	D	C	B	A
	C	A	D	B

Figure 3.2 *Simple Latin square design*

week. A, B, C and D represent marketing stimuli and in the illustration are designed so that each of the stimuli is used once in every week and once in each store.

Marketing information systems

47. Data sources

Over recent years, the need for more integrated marketing information systems has been realised. Traditionally, information comes from many different sources within an organisation – and from external sources – and is often used for different purposes. Examples of internal sources are salespersons' call reports, accounting data relating to costs and revenues by product and market, etc., regular and special marketing research reports, test market results, marketing experiments and models. External data may come from such sources as government, banks, media, and international and regional bodies.

48. Integrated information systems

All this miscellaneous information needs to be collected, processed and presented in meaningful terms to appropriate marketing decision-makers. Some of the information will be directed at current operations: for example, results over an operating year may be compared with targets. Other information will be required to assist longer-term decision making in such areas as new product/market/service development and in measurement of potential risks and rewards.

An ideal information system will also contain appropriate statistical methods, models, etc. so that data may be processed quickly in various ways and, ideally, will respond on visual display units to 'what if' questions and so on.

Progress test 3

1. What kind of questions on products or services might be answered by the use of marketing research?

2. What are the main sources of secondary data?

3. What are the main types of modified probability sample?

4. What are the advantages and disadvantages of using mailed questionnaires?

5. What are the advantages and disadvantages of personal interviews?

6. What factors affect the accuracy of replies?

7. What techniques are used in motivation research?

8. What is meant by 'non-parametric data'? What is the significance of the use of these data in marketing applications?

9. How should marketing research reports be presented?

10. Illustrate the use of the experimental method in three kinds of marketing decision.

Assignment

Arrange for small groups each to visit a local business. The following list will serve as an example of the wide range of choice:

- a supermarket
- a main dealer/distributor for a major car manufacturer
- a clearing bank
- a building society branch
- a small shopkeeper (one outlet only)
- a cinema or theatre
- a private hospital

– a manufacturing company
– a brewery.

The class/group leader should endeavour to persuade the manager, or one of the manager's nominees, to give a short talk on the business (what goods and/or services it provides and how it keeps in touch with its customers and markets). The group should ask what marketing research, if any, is carried out locally or is available from other sources. The nature and frequency of information exchange between local branch management and HQ marketing departments should be explained if appropriate.

After the visits, short talks should be prepared in order that information may be exchanged, differences noted and constructive suggestions made on important particular marketing information needs and practicable ways of improving specific marketing information systems.

Part two
Product/service policy and the marketing mix

4

Product/service policy and planning

1. Nature and scope of product policy

Product policy is concerned with defining the type, volume and timing of the products and/or services that a company offers for sale. It therefore involves both existing and new products and services, such as bank housing loans.

Such decisions should be consistent with corporate strategy which may be influenced by:

(*i*) what has been described as product/market scope (customer targets, functions served and technology employed);
(*ii*) 'thrust' – competence or critical advantages; and/or
(*iii*) investment and risk objectives.
In line with these considerations, product/service policy must take into account the following criteria:
(a) The company's total use of financial and staff resources. These resources have to be planned to meet short-term and long-term objectives.
(b) The kinds of customer or market area at which products or services are aimed.
(c) The promotional methods to be used.
(d) The reputation of the company.
(e) The company's position as a leader or follower.

The product mix

2. Product lines and ranges

Few companies manufacture or offer a single item (*one line*) at a single price (*one range*). In the case of most companies, there are several lines and ranges. The total assortment of products that a company offers may be described as the *product mix*. In its range of assorted items, a company may offer a wide variety of different items and/or a large number of quality or style variations. The product mix may be extended in various ways:

(a) By variations in models, styles and service packages.

(b) By variations in quality offered at different price levels.

(c) By the development of associated items: for example, cameras and photographic accessories.

(d) By the development, acquisition or licensing of completely different products or services in terms of customer needs, manufacturing processes, etc. ICI, for example, produces industrial chemicals, household paints and plastics among its range of products.

Product policy requires continuing attention, since decisions on adding or dropping products will constantly arise. The more volatile the market, the more frequently will decisions have to be made, but the speed of change even in less volatile market areas (e.g. capital goods) is such that policy decisions are equally or more important, since more time and more financial and labour resources are usually required to effect change.

The model of analysis described above can be adapted to situations where a business or non-profit-making organisation is clearly in the service sector: for instance banking, tourism, legal services, accounting, health care and employment agencies. Differences in practical applications should, however, be recognised. Service industries have, for example, special problems with quality control, lack of inventories and matching supply and demand, as well as differences in customer/supply company personal relations.

Attention at this stage should be drawn to the expansion of the activities of many manufacturers and retailers into profit-oriented service activities: for example, the provision of financial credit, leasing and maintenance contracting. 'Product' in this chapter covers goods often further distinguished into durables and consumables. 'Services' include primary services, such as medical services, and goods-related services, such as extended service contracts and car financing schemes.

3. Advantages and disadvantages of multiproduct operations

The greater the variety of products offered, the greater, theoretically, is the market opportunity and the less the threat of complete loss of business. On the other hand, the costs of development, manufacturing and marketing may be too high to effect economies of scale, and effort may be so thinly spread that the strategic advantages of concentration are lost. Short production runs, for example, lead to high unit manufacturing costs, while advertising and selling effort scattered across a wide range of miscellaneous products and markets may be both costly and ineffective.

Unless, however, there is a British, European or International Standard specification laid down and conformity is forced on competitive organisations, there are advantages in expanding associated lines. Such advantages include the following:

(a) Increased production of minor variations may lead to lower unit costs resulting from a greater absorption of overhead, provided that there is sufficient increase in sales revenue.
(b) Sales force costs may be reduced if similar outlets are involved.
(c) Advertising of a broad range or line may be more effective.
(d) Distribution may be more readily achieved along the channels of distribution if there is a satisfactory range in terms of consumer choice and in terms of buying economies.
(e) The opportunity of short-circuiting inefficient intermediaries and controlling sales effort directly or closer to the end user may result.
(f) Development plans may involve the gradual build-up of customer-related items in a 'systems' strategy. Customer functions may be related in a manner not initially recognised by producers: for example, office systems covering a wide range of technology, expertise, etc.

4. The product life cycle

The sales of many products appear to follow a typical pattern, showing a gradually increasing growth to maturity, a levelling-out as saturation point is reached and then a decline. This is illustrated in Figure 4.1.

(a) Prior to the introduction of a product to the market, there is a *development stage* during which there tends to be greater and greater investment. This investment cost must be either charged against future earnings or written off, and it is not unnatural to find that a company which has invested large sums in a particular development project will be reluctant to abandon the research. The product life-

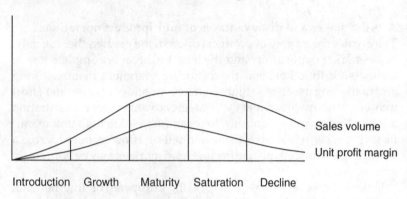

Figure 4.1 *The product life cycle*

cycle concept is useful in determining the time and cost of development projects in relation to the ultimate pay-off. Frequently, large-scale development projects take much longer than originally expected, and it is important at regular periods to review progress made against life-cycle expectations.

(b) In the *introductory stage*, costs of production and marketing will be high, but if there is a genuine product differential (an advantage not enjoyed or easily copied by other companies), a company may benefit in various ways, such as high initial pricing or rapid market penetration.

(c) During the *growth stage*, the initial marketing efforts should lead to the greatest rate of sales expansion, but according to the rate of technical change, the rate of market acceptance and the ease with which competitors can imitate and enter the market, buying resistance will build up. Management must therefore be ready to phase in new products and adjust marketing tactics in line with the anticipated cycle.

(d) The *maturity and saturation stages*, for example, may be the times for changes in pricing, in advertising and promotion, or in design or quality range.

(e) At the *stage of decline*, profit margins become very small and every effort has to be made to reduce costs and improve distribution efficiency. Price becomes the major issue and this may, for example, lead to a restriction of distribution to large outlets. A product which is at the decline stage in one country may, however, find a growth market in a country with a less highly developed economy. The cost of maintaining business at this last stage of the cycle must be weighed against the opportunity for investment elsewhere. The latest portfolio management techniques developed by the Boston Consulting Company involve sophisticated life-cycle analysis.

5. Eliminating products

Company profit contribution frequently comes mainly from a small number of items in the product mix. Dropping products which make little or no contribution can frequently make very significant improvements in overall profitability. Weak products are very costly in ways which are not readily seen in accounting returns. For example:

(a) They take up a disproportionate amount of management and selling time, shelf space, stock control and administration.

(b) They involve short runs and high production setting-up costs.

(c) They often require special warehousing and transportation consideration – stock turn is vital in retailing and wholesaling.

(d) They are incurring expense which could be directed to more profitable developments.

(e) They may cause customers to think of the company as being unimaginative and technically unprogressive.

6. Resistance to dropping products

Frequently resistance to dropping weak products arises, for various reasons. For example:

(a) Management is more concerned with new product development than with balancing the current product mix.

(b) There is a sentimental attachment to products which were successful in the past – particularly if they were part of the original mix.

(c) Sales forces tend to fear loss of individual orders without having access to the facts of the complete marketing situation.

(d) Hopes of revival tend to linger for an inordinately long time.

(e) Falling sales or profits are attributed to weak advertising or selling operations rather than to the product.

(f) Dropping products may lead to the assignment of personnel to new tasks and vested interests operate to resist changes of this kind.

Products must be considered truly objectively and not continued for reasons such as these.

7. The product mix and sales growth

Companies seek to achieve profitable sales growth in the following ways:

(a) By increasing sales of existing products in existing markets through more efficient or more aggressive selling and promotion, or application to new uses.

(b) By developing improved products for existing markets.

(c) By developing new products for existing markets (but *see* 8).

(d) By offering existing products to new markets.

(e) By offering modifications of existing products to new markets.

(f) By developing new products for new markets.

8. Market segmentation and product specialisation

It should be stressed that many companies seek to develop completely new products when it might be more profitable to exploit new market segments. The economies of scale possible in capital-intensive industries, such as chemicals, draw attention to the need to exploit markets on an international scale just as much as the need to develop new product ideas. For instance, the growth in demand for paper tissue has been stimulated not only by introducing new use concepts (e.g. paper towels) and by extending the range in size and colour, but also by exploiting new market segments (e.g. industrial markets). The development of a segmentation strategy may:

(a) Secure new user market segments.

(b) Enable concentration on most profitable buyers by means of product design or promotion.

(c) Stimulate distribution channels.

(d) Build up a reputation for progressive leadership.

(e) Provide sales forces with renewed drive.

(f) Force competition into defensive strategies.

(g) Stretch product life cycles at comparatively low cost.

There is a difference between product differentiation, based on such general notions as the need to offer variety and customer choice so that a wide range of needs are catered for fairly well, and *planned* market segmentation. The latter implies that a distinctly homogeneous group of needs has been identified clearly with a particular group of potential customers, and that there is a distinct demand/profit curve associated with satisfying the needs of that group. The traditional means of segmenting markets (e.g. by organisation size, geography, business classification, socioeconomic grouping, age, sex, etc.) are now beginning to be supplemented by behavioural research into such areas as life style, attitudes and priority spending patterns. These new approaches are often combined with more conventional data, and have been used not only in product development and promotional programmes in repeatable consumer goods markets, but also in connection with the marketing of such diverse services as bank credit cards and residential property. One other important application has been in determining the positioning of products in international markets.

New product planning

9. Requirements for new product planning
New product planning involves targets and timetables for:

(a) research, engineering, architects, designers, etc.;
(b) plant and equipment development;
(c) commercial development;
(d) staff development; and
(e) provision of financial resources.

10. Risks in new product planning
All new products involve risk, which is at its highest when the investment is high. The period of return on investment is long, and the product involves new areas of research, new manufacturing techniques and 'know-how', and entry into new markets requiring new marketing skills and resources.

In order to reduce risk, the greatest possible care should be taken during the stages of *exploration, screening* and *specification*. Design testing and marketing are the really costly stages, involving many more people and greater plant and equipment resources than exploration, screening and specification.

It has been estimated that the rate of new product failure in the USA is as high as 80 per cent. The cost of failure would probably be only one-tenth if probable failure could be detected before the design stage, by more thorough and accurate exploration and screening.

11. Risks in major new service planning and decisions
In many new service market situations, major decisions have been and are taken on the subjective opinions of experienced senior managers and board members with input–output and time-related accounting support. Consider decisions by some UK banking organisations to acquire estate agency businesses in recent years – and the consequences!

The American Institute of Management Sciences published an illuminating paper in 1989 on a truly marketing approach to questions relating to the design, size, location and facilities required by the

Marriott Corporation for a new chain of hotels which would meet the requirements of business and non-business travellers. One aspect of initial marketing research was to examine key facets or attributes of such hotels, namely external factors, rooms, food-related services, lounge facilities, leisure-time activities, general service availabilities and security. These facets were subdivided into 50 specific attributes. Analytical techniques such as those covered in Chapter 3 and many more advanced analytical methods of extracting key information probability data were used (a much fuller account is given in *Managing Services* by C.H. Lovelock). The Marriott Corporation had set up three test hotels in 1987, and by 1993 the newly named Courtyard by Marriott 'product' – very different from the usual Marriott hotel and appealing to a distinct market segment – had expanded to some 300 hotels with results within 4 per cent of predictions.

12. Sources of new product ideas
Ideas for new products can come from many sources: for example,

(a) research and development personnel;
(b) marketing personnel;
(c) associated companies in other countries;
(d) customers;
(e) outside technological or scientific discoveries;
(f) employee suggestions;
(g) brainstorming sessions of executives;
(h) competitors;
(i) knowledge of government needs;
(j) individual executives;
(k) a study of unused patents.

13. The screening process
Screening is the process of eliminating ideas which are out of line with company objectives or resources, or which carry high-risk cost and little profit opportunity (*see* **14**).

Screening and later stages of the product development process require contributions from a range of specialists, such as market researchers, engineers, development specialists and accountants. If there is no separate product-planning group – and these are becoming more common – there must be detailed arrangements for *co-ordination* (*see* **29**). In technologically based industries, there is frequently too much reliance placed in the early stages on the opinions of technical specialists working in comparative isolation.

14. Screening considerations
Screening involves considerations such as the following:

(a) *Demand considerations*
(i) What is the potential demand and in what markets?
(ii) What is the likely life cycle of the product? What is the pattern of demand? Information data systems should yield valuable clues.
(iii) What is the possibility of substitution or product obsolescence? Loss of foreign markets by import substitution should not be ignored.
(iv) What are the possibilities of modifying the product to enter new market segments or lengthen its profitable existence?
(v) Will the product produce a stable or seasonal sales or production pattern?
(vi) What is the maximum development time for profit exploitation?
(vii) What are the growth prospects of the product in terms of the total market?

(b) *Considerations of resources*
(i) Is the new idea in line with company policy and objectives (e.g. profit, image, market growth, product lines)?
(ii) Is the new idea in line with company resources (e.g. capital, physical resources, 'know-how')?
(iii) What time, equipment and money will be required to carry out the project, and what other opportunities will have to be delayed or missed as a result?
(iv) Are sufficient numbers of qualified personnel available, or can they be made available by recruitment or training?
(v) What is the availability of materials and bought-in components? What are the likely price variations and how will these affect final price and demand?
(vi) What manufacturing problems will arise?
(vii) To what extent will the product assist in reducing production or marketing costs of other products?
(viii) What will be the effect on inventory levels?
(ix) Can existing distribution systems be used?

(c) *Competitive considerations*
(i) What patent considerations are involved – either the company's own or competitive patents?
(ii) What is the competition – number, size and resources of companies, and their strengths and weaknesses? Do not forget international competitors.

(*iii*) How do the company's likely costs compare with those of potential competitors?

15. Commercial evaluation

The screening process will throw up the more obvious pitfalls and opportunities which a new product offers, but desk and field market surveys will assist in defining the market or markets by size, location, structure and buying habits. Information can also be obtained on competition and other possible external factors, and thus calculations can be made to indicate the share of market likely to be obtained at various time periods at various costs, and by the use of various methods of distribution, pricing and sales. Companies such as Unilever are using decision theory and discounted cash flow techniques at this stage.

16. Product testing and test markets

Once the product has passed through the development and design stage, full-scale production risks are avoided by building models or prototypes, or by using a pilot plant. It may also be feasible to carry out limited tests of the product in the marketplace. In the marketing of consumer goods, a geographical area – possibly one of the smaller television areas – may be selected to test consumer and channel reaction to both product and marketing methods. A gradual extension of the test market can follow, which allows for a gradual build-up of manufacturing capacity, inventory and selling effort.

17. Arguments for and against test marketing

The main argument against test marketing is that competitors immediately become aware of what is happening, and can take steps to counter the development before national distribution or the growth stage of the product life cycle is reached.

Against this, it could be argued that test markets assist in providing a realistic picture of the way in which competitors will react. The problem is to weigh the risk of failure against the advantage of a time lead – a particularly acute problem in narrowly differentiated consumer markets.

18. Operating test markets

Test markets need to be operated against controls, and companies frequently use the areas on which they have previously accumulated considerable data in connection with other product launches. Competitors may, of course, react by introducing unusual variables which make interpretation of results difficult: for example, running special promotions on a scale which would be uneconomical on a national basis.

Other problems arise in operating test markets. For example:

(a) *What should be the size and structure of the sample* – which towns, cities, rural areas, etc.?

(b) *Over what period should a test market run in order to obtain reliable information?* What time should be allowed for initial purchase and repeat purchases, without providing invaluable cost and revenue data to competitors, or incurring disproportionately heavy expenses in analysis, and production at uneconomic levels?

19. Selecting test markets

Criteria employed in the selection of test market areas have been ranked by the American journal *Sales Management* as follows:

(a) Typicality of distributive outlets.

(b) Relative isolation from other cities.

(c) Availability of advertising media that will co-operate.

(d) Diversified cross-section as to ages, religion, etc.

(e) Representative as to population size.

(f) Typicality as to per capita income.

(g) Previous good record as a test city.

(h) Stability of year-round sales.

20. Consumer panels

In addition to, or as alterations to, test marketing, use is frequently made of consumer panels. Consumer panels are often used at an early stage of development to determine consumer attitudes or strength of preference. In industrial markets, prototypes or limited batches may be tested in the working environment on company customers or potential customers of various sizes and types. It is currently often argued that 'concept testing' is a low-cost guide in early go/no-go situations.

21. Forecasting accuracy

Product testing on the other hand almost always brings about changes in production methods, in design, in packaging, in pricing or in marketing procedures. A Nielsen investigation of 141 consumer products reveals that forecasting accuracy increases the longer products are on test, up to a period of 9 months. The chances of a correct projection of sales based on limited tests were as follows:

After 2 months – 1 in 9
After 4 months – 1 in 7
After 6 months – 1 in 2
After 8 months – 2 in 3
After 9 months – 5 in 6

The break-even concept

22. Break-even point

It is important to calculate in advance the likely relationships between cost, volume and profit over various time periods. Break-even charts are often used for this purpose. Figure 4.2 is based on certain assumptions:

(a) That fixed and variable costs can be separated clearly and meaningfully.
(b) That variable costs change in direct proportion to output.
(c) That price does not change at different levels of output.
(d) That the relationships are real only at a particular point of time.

The level of output at which break-even occurs can be calculated from:

$$1 - \frac{\text{Total fixed costs} \qquad (\text{£s})}{\text{Margin of contribution (£s per unit)}}$$

The margin of contribution is derived from subtracting the unit variable cost from the unit selling price.

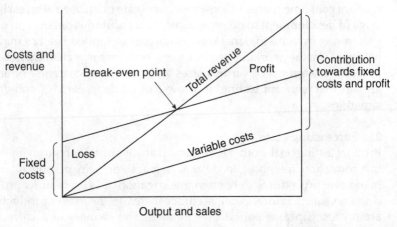

Figure 4.2 *A break-even chart*

It is often important to know the amount of net sales revenue at which break-even is reached on a variety of units at different selling prices. In this case, fixed costs should be divided by the margin of contribution expressed as a percentage of net sales. The margin of contribution as a percentage of net sales may be calculated from:

$$1 - \frac{\text{Total variable costs}}{\text{Net sales}}$$

This formula derives from the fact that it is the complement of the percentage of total variable costs of net sales, i.e. the percentage contribution margin to net sales.

23. The effect of variable factors on break-even points and profit contributions

A decision to increase volume, other than for strategic reasons, can only be justified if additional revenue is at least equal to additional variable costs, and will provide funds for contributing to fixed costs and thus add to profit.

Break-even calculations can show the likely effect of an increase in price, or increased costs arising from the purchase of additional equipment, increased wage rates, changes in material prices, and so on. It will be clear that the higher the fixed costs, the more important is the volume consideration. Capital-intensive industries are particularly susceptible to volume changes and normally demand high plant utilisation. A high investment in plant, as in certain sectors of the chemical industry, may lead to a situation where home markets are insufficiently large to reach really profitable volume levels, but high plant investment and utilisation achieve the enormous economies of scale which are necessary for competitive prices in internationally competitive markets.

24. Break-even and cost concepts

Calculations of profitability depend to some extent on accounting conventions and company accounting practices. Methods of assessing costs differ considerably, as will be seen from a study of the following paragraphs (25–7).

25. Fixed and variable costs

Fixed costs theoretically remain constant over all levels of output. *Variable costs*, such as direct labour or materials, vary with changes in output level.

Fixed costs per unit of output therefore decline as production increases; variable costs per unit of output may increase if there are changes in wage rates or material prices, or decrease if, for example, materials are bought at more advantageous quantity terms. Some costs, such as power, may be partly fixed and partly variable: power for lighting may be classified as fixed, while power for operating machines may be classified as variable.

Classification into categories of fixed and variable costs depends on accounting practice and the time over which the costs are calculated.

26. Opportunity costs

In economic terms, a cost incurred for any item or project means that there is a consequent loss of the opportunity to spend that money in another way.

(a) *Return on investment (ROI)*. The cost of development of a new product involves the loss of opportunity to use resources elsewhere, and consideration should therefore be given to rates of return on alternative investment opportunities. In assessing new development possibilities, the following equations are useful:

$$ROI = \frac{\text{Percentage of profit}}{\text{per unit of sales revenue}} \times \frac{\text{Annual sales revenue}}{\text{Capital invested}}$$

$$ROI = \text{Percentage profit} \times \text{Capital turnover}$$

(b) *Discounted cash flow*. Conventional accounting procedures frequently place a penalty on new developments by ignoring the fact that marketing research, technical development, tooling up, initial advertising and similar expenses are investment costs and should be treated quite differently from normal operating costs. Cost must, of course, be recovered. The problem is to establish a relevant time base and a realistic means of allocating costs directly involved in development projects.

Projects occupy differing periods of time and bring in varying flows of profit over their life cycle. One of the techniques which is being increasingly used to cope with the problem of alternative investment decisions over varying time periods is *discounted cash flow*. This technique seeks to translate future cash flows to present values by a process of *discounting* – taking into consideration the many implications of cost of capital and the return over various time periods. Alternative investment proposals are therefore ranked qualitatively, and not purely quantitatively as in the accounting-rate-of-return method or the pay-back-period method. The notion of *opportunity cost* is involved in using discounted cash flow to decide on problems such as:

(*i*) whether to build a new factory or expand other facilities;
(*ii*) whether to replace existing plant by plant with a higher productive capacity or rate of production;
(*iii*) what alternative methods of financing should be adopted;
(*iv*) whether to lease or buy. This is an increasingly important issue and has led to major developments in the hiring of vehicles, warehouses, office premises and many items of capital equipment.

27. Incremental cost
Incremental cost is the additional total cost charge which arises from the making of a new decision. Clearly, it is important to ensure that the additional cost incurred by a particular decision is more than covered by the additional revenue resulting from that decision. The concept would be particularly relevant in decisions on changes in levels of production output or in deciding whether to accept a special order at a special price. In the latter event, it would be necessary to compare the outcome of order acceptance against the outcome of order refusal. Consideration would also need to be given to the possible effect on other prices in the future as well as the possible loss of alternative investment (opportunity cost).

Organisation for product planning

28. Principles of product-planning organisation
It is dangerous to generalise about ideal organisational arrangements for product planning, since companies differ in so many ways. There are, however, certain important principles which should be observed:

(a) Product policy depends greatly on the attitude of top management, and it is vital that top management should be constantly alive to change in the market.
(b) If product planning is to be consumer oriented, marketing personnel should be closely involved, from the earliest stages of development and throughout the life cycle of the product.
(c) Product planning involves the co-operation and co-ordination of specialists with different attitudes – engineers, scientists, accountants, marketing personnel, and production, distribution and communications specialists. It is necessary, therefore, to set up clear definitions of responsibility and authority in relation to product decisions, and to ensure that there are easy and known systems of communication (*see* 8:1).

29. Co-ordination through groups

One of the problems of organisation for product planning is to ensure that vested interests do not dominate or produce conflicts. There will, in fact, often be a strong case for establishing a *new product planning group*, as well as *product managers* responsible for the co-ordination of activities and the profitability of existing products or product groups. The product-planning group may consist of a committee of executives which meets at regular intervals, or a permanent 'staff' group freed from the problems of day-to-day line operations. The completely separate staff group is most commonly found in large organisations and is normally concerned with new product development. Existing products are, in these cases, under the direction of product or product-group managers, reporting in turn to the senior marketing executive. When new product planning is carried out by an independent group, it is important that a mechanism exists for decision making, so that new products can be moved over to line product managers at the appropriate time.

30. Use of networks in product planning

One of the ways in which the many necessary activities of different people at different times can be effectively co-ordinated is by the use of network analysis. A network is a graphical representation of a project, showing all activities linked sequentially in such a way that interdependencies are clearly seen: that is, when the beginning of one activity depends on the completion of other activities. Timings are shown so that it is possible to see the earliest and latest times at which an activity can begin. The shortest possible time for completion of the project can also be traced along the network. This is the *critical path*, any delay along which will cause a hold-up in the completion of the total project. Cost elements can also be built in, if desirable, as well as a range of alternative time estimates.

31. Decision tree

Another technique which may be used in product planning is the *decision tree*. It has been made clear that product planning involves a sequential decision-making process, and that at various stages a decision to stop the project or to follow an alternative course of action could be taken. The decision tree is based on the notion of probability. At each decision point an estimate is made of the probability of success or failure and the consequent effect on loss or gain. In Figure 4.3 (taken from a paper by J.F. Magee in the *Harvard Business Review*)

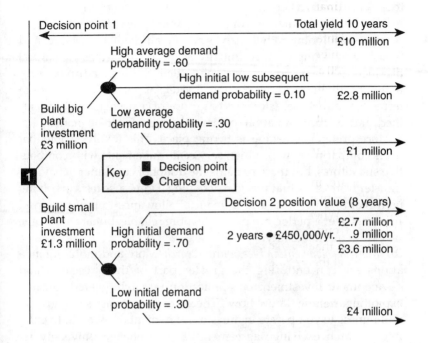

Figure 4.3 *Decision tree*

a decision tree is used to show the likely outcome of alternative investment decisions.

32. Cost, revenue and price

Determination of product policy and planning the most profitable product mix are highly important and complex areas of management. Cost and revenue considerations have to be calculated and estimated as precisely as possible. The effect of price on costs and revenue will be examined in the next chapter.

33. Product-market planning – recent developments

The very high fixed levels of cost associated with single-purpose plant and equipment, and the increased risk of substantial operating losses in the product-market pioneering stage (particularly in large organisations), have led to a number of significant developments in connection with product-market planning:

(a) *Concept testing.* New product concepts are tested before any money is invested in product research and development. The idea is to seek out product benefits and buyer attitudes before and after trial, mainly by depth interviewing. The gains appear to be mainly in product positioning rather than as an overall predictor. Marvel and Smash, for example, were initially seen as substitutes of natural products for lazy housewives, and their findings affirmed promotional strategy and positioning. Pockets of potential resistance in terms of product characteristics or groups of customers can be identified, and an approximation of demand structure can be made.

More preference testing is taking place. This involves potential users comparing new product/service arrangements with competitive substitutes, but there remains the doubt of consumer behaviour transfer from test situations to real buying. Home-use tests involving both real product tests and a financial allowance to buy preferred products over a period are probably more reliable, but are still some way from market reality.

(b) *More development and less pure research.* More and more organisations are concentrating the greater part of their research and development investment on application research, geared towards exploiting existing 'know-how'. There are already signs of a greater willingness to co-operate in areas of fundamental research, to enter into research exchange agreements and to engage university researchers on a retainer basis.

(c) *More formal systematic review of progress and expenditure on research projects.* This is set against market timescales, by multidisciplinary groups representing all vital functions.

(d) *The setting up of venture groups.* These are small groups of personnel specially selected to liaise with operating functions – research, production, purchasing, industrial engineering, marketing, finance – in order to speed up the process of product development to the point of commercialisation. A prime requirement for such groups is an effective leader – one who can achieve results, by working informally with a multidisciplinary team through existing operational units, which have their individual priorities and vested interests. The most successful venture groups have been appointed essentially on a temporary basis for one major project.

(e) *Systems approaches and corporate auditing procedures.* Many organisations have seen the need to achieve real economies of scale through the development of 'families' or 'systems' of products. This approach allows all assets (e.g. finance, technical skills, productive capacity, marketing expertise) to be audited, harnessed and developed towards the fulfilment of a succession of product-market objectives over time.

Products and packaging

34. Growth and importance of packaging

The growth of self-service stores and the importance of gaining distribution, shelf space and display have made packaging decisions in the field of consumer goods a highly important area of decision in regard to product policy and planning. Even in the marketing of industrial goods, packaging is taking on increasing significance and extending beyond the obvious necessity of providing for protection, transportation and storage.

The demand for packaging has led to an enormous increase in the range of packaging equipment and materials available. There have been spectacular increases in the use of flexible packaging involving special papers, plastics and aluminium foil. New printing methods have been developed, such as flexography, by which process it is possible relatively inexpensively to reproduce photographs or art-work in a wide range of colours on a wide range of materials. Computer graphics now enable changes in colour, size and position-ing of design elements to be viewed on screens in a matter of seconds, opening up tremendous new possibilities in package design.

Packaging design is influenced by the cultural, social and political environment. In the USA, for example, the housewife buys approxi-mately 90 per cent of her weekly purchases from supermarkets and self-service shops in one day. In the UK, the percentage of food purchases from self-service outlets is lower and there is still a great deal of daily shopping. In Latin countries, pre-packed foods are rather slow in sales growth. Attitudes to colour differ: white is symbolic of mourning in many Far Eastern countries as opposed to purple in Latin countries.

35. Factors to consider in package design

A package should be designed to perform many functions:

(a) *Provide protection.* This may be necessary at any stage in the distribution process and ultimately in the home or factory of the user or consumer (e.g. against product damage, contamination, evapora-tion, chemical change, pilferage): *see* **36** below. For example, surface treatment of packaging avoids deterioration of appearance after tran-sit and/or storage.

(b) *Offer convenience.* This covers handling, storage and opening of packages at all stages of distribution, and frequently in eventual use, reuse and disposal.

(*i*) *Convenience of storage in warehouse, shop and home.* In designing the package, there must be a consideration of the economies of stocking large quantities of bulky, slow-moving, low-profit-margin products, and the difficulties of stacking certain carton shapes.

(*ii*) *Convenience in use.* There must be a consideration of the development of new materials and functional designs – aerosol containers, vacuum cans for vegetables, flip-top cigarette packets, etc. New packaging ideas may lead to new products or product formulation, as with hair sprays or cheese spreads. Safety features should also be considered: for instance, designing easy-opening cans to eliminate the possibility of cuts and fingernail damage. The wider 'green movement' is spreading fast, and legal and environmental considerations are at the forefront of the switch to CFC-free aerosols and organic foods with special packaging requirements.

(c) *Reduce transport costs.* This is achieved by the use of lightweight yet adequately strong materials, especially important when goods have to be transported by air.

(d) *Provide opportunity for reuse.* The package may be deliberately designed so that it can be used for the storage of other items once the original product is consumed: for example, plastic and aluminium containers. On the other hand, some packages are designed so that refills may be bought. The design may be so differentiated that only a refill of the same product can be used in the original container.

(e) *Create a favourable product image.* The package has frequently to represent the product symbolically – to convey its buying advantages. The packaging 'image' will be reinforced if there is a close tie-in with advertising and promotion (*see* 7: **21**).

(f) *Establish product differences.* The package is often the major way in which narrowly differentiated products are distinguished. The difference may be in the art design, the shape or the materials used. A package can be used to convey an impression of quality differences. Gift packages are a good example of extending the range through packaging.

(g) *Establish corporate identity.* Some companies aim at promoting individual products in their own right. Others deliberately aim at creating a company rather than product loyalty, such as ICI and Marks & Spencer.

(h) *Gain display at retail level.* The package must be easy to arrange on shelves or racks and at the same time should attract the potential customer. Developments in printing techniques, such as flexography (*see* **34** above), combined with newer packaging materials, such as polyethylene film, are significant in this connection. Stock turn is critical in retailing, so stock numbering is invaluable.

36. Packaging and promotion

In considering some of the more sophisticated uses of packaging, the protective aspects of packaging should not be disregarded. Attention is therefore drawn to the following hazards against which packaging should provide a defence:

(a) *Damage by mechanical handling.* Most damage occurs in the handling process, and the more frequently products are handled in the distribution process, the greater is the need for protection. One of the advantages of the liner train and other container transport developments is that they result in less damage through handling. Damaged goods have to be replaced and are likely to cause loss and inconvenience to seller and purchaser. Often slightly damaged products may not be returned, but may inhibit repeat purchase.

(b) *Product loss.* Liquids and powders are highly susceptible to loss (e.g. powder leakage, liquid evaporation).

(c) *Pilferage.* Loss through pilferage can be quite high – especially if there are many handling points.

(d) *Contamination by dust or dirt.* Clothing, food and fine machinery are obvious examples of products liable to damage in this way.

(e) *Moisture gain and loss.* Many products have an optimum moisture content (e.g. cement, ceramic paints, frozen foods).

(f) *Chemical change* (e.g. metal corrosion, coffee rancidity).

(g) *Flavour loss or change.*

(h) *Mould* (e.g. in canned foods, paints).

(i) *Insect attack* (e.g. moths in clothing).

37. Product development in service industries

The significance of marketing and product development in a fast – developing service organisation such as Royal Mail was highlighted in a 1993 recruitment campaign for market development managers, new product development managers and marketing analysts.

Progress test 4

1. What are the advantages and disadvantages of multiproduct operations?

2. What is meant by the 'product life cycle'?

3. Why is there resistance to dropping products?

4. What are the main considerations in screening ideas for new products?

5. What criteria might be used in selecting test markets?

6. Construct a break-even chart.

7. What is meant by (a) 'opportunity costs'; (b) 'incremental costs'?

8. How might networks be used in product planning?

9. What is a decision tree?

10. Why is more attention now being paid to packaging?

Assignments

1. The Mars Company in the UK has had a very successful history in marketing chocolate confectionery, holding third position in this field in the early 1980s with an output of 140,000 tonnes and a turnover considerably exceeding £200 million.

The company was interested in entering the savoury snack market of potato crisps, nuts and snacks, a rapidly growing field. A crunchy wafer cheese sandwich bar, 'Sprint', was developed and put on test market in 1981.

Plant costs were comparatively low, since unused machinery was redesigned and modified for 'Sprint' production. The Harlech TV area was chosen as the test market, which ran for one year.

Outlets were supplied direct from six Mars depots and this was believed to be quick and economical. TV advertising was heaviest in the first three months, but continued throughout the year; 200 poster sites were used for one month; there was initially a postal coupon campaign with a free product offer; at stores there was a free product option on six wrappers in month 1; and mailed bulletins were also used.

A temporary 'commando' sales force handled the test market and sought access to over 15,000 outlets. Price was considered very reasonable (the product was zero rated for VAT). Consumer research had been carried out throughout the test using Mars employees.

One year after the test market launch, the decision was taken not to launch 'Sprint' nationally.

Examine the problems that a company such as Mars might have faced in arriving at a go/no-go decision in a development of this kind. Your analysis should cover the following:

– choice of test market

– duration of test market
– choice of product/market segment
– use of non-regular sales force
– advertising programme
– user information and market research
– information requirements for a major investment decision.

2. In 1992 Royal Mail had nine operating divisions in the UK. During the financial year 1992/93, each division set up a number of 'key initiatives', such as the establishment of business partnerships with major customers, the development of customer awareness and personnel training.

It is suggested that a small number of syndicates be set up to investigate the following:

(a) What were the names and geographical market areas of these divisions?
(b) Select one, two or three divisions and explore the marketing/customer aspects of key initiatives.
(c) How successful were the end-of-year results of these initiatives, and how were they measured?
(d) What steps, if any, have been taken to improve customer awareness throughout the organisation?

A key challenge of this assignment is to determine and locate relevant secondary and primary sources of information.

5

Pricing and demand

Problems of pricing

1. Perfect competition

A great deal has been written by economists on the interaction of price and demand. Much of this writing was based on a situation in which price was the dominant variable differentiating products or services. *Perfect competition* demands that goods from different producers are identical, that there are identical circumstances under which a sale takes place, that complete information on products and markets is equally available to all potential buyers, and that there are sufficient producers to prevent restriction of supply to one (monopoly) or a limited few (oligopoly) producers. Such conditions hardly ever exist and the growth of an affluent society has further complicated the quantitative assessment of elasticity: that is the sensitivity of demand in relation to price.

2. Imperfect competition

More recently, it has been realised that in a society where everyone is living above mere subsistence and exercising discretionary spending power, with ever wider ranges of goods available from competing producers, qualitative variables take on an increasing importance. *Imperfect markets* and *imperfect competition* are a feature of a sophisticated capitalist or mixed economy. This is not to deny the existence of varying degrees of demand elasticity. Economic pricing theory has relevance to practical marketing situations. The more a product or general product category is regarded as a necessity, the more inelastic is demand likely to be. If discretionary incomes fall, the demand for food will continue whereas the demand for washing machines will decline. Likewise the demand for exotic expensive foods will decline much more than the demand for bread. Again, with all products there is an upper and lower price level, outside which demand would fluctuate sharply; the problem is to determine those levels. Within a given price range, some products have a more elastic demand pattern than others, but too little is known of these more subtle elasticities since there is a tendency for competitors to follow each other's pricing systems fairly closely in order to avoid the risk of the unknown. Demand is a measure of the *utility* that a product has for a consumer or a market, and price is only one aspect of that utility.

3. Factors of demand
Factors which may affect demand can be subsumed under four broad headings:

(a) Market considerations (*see* 4).
(b) Company and product considerations (*see* 5).
(c) The demand for other products (*see* 6).
(d) The cost and availability of money.

4. Market considerations
Demand is affected by the size of the market and the needs and desires of the people constituting that market.

(a) *Population.* Total population in most parts of the world is growing, and the size of markets is increasing. On the other hand, populations are becoming more mobile and even industrial concentrations are shifting – sometimes as a result of government economic policy. Demand for both goods and services will, therefore, depend to some extent on the direction of marketing effort to particular market sectors.
(b) *Disposable income.* A highly developed industrial society has a large proportion of the population with considerable discretionary incomes. Countries in early stages of development have fewer people above subsistence level, but there may be a small layer of society with exceedingly high levels of disposable income. Government economic policy, especially taxation systems and regulation of credit and interest rates, may affect actual and anticipated disposable income levels very considerably. Expectation of earnings or profits has a marked effect on demand for deferrable items, such as luxury goods, plant and equipment, housing, repairs and replacements.
(c) *Customer satisfaction.* People are motivated to buy goods and services for a whole host of economic, social and psychological reasons. Current fashion, individual taste, prestige, imitation of others, and the relative importance of comfort, convenience or security, may all have a bearing on buying behaviour. Some products may even sell better in certain markets because they are higher in price.

5. Company and product considerations
Demand for a product is obviously influenced by the ideas people

have about that product and the company that manufactures it.

(a) *Company or product reputation*. The higher the price range of the product, the more is it likely to affect health or security; and the more influence it may have on the performance of other products, the more likely a purchaser is to avoid untried commodities from little-known firms.

(b) *Advertising and promotion*. A product must be known before it is bought. Selling skill or the creation of a favourable product image through advertising may have a very considerable effect on purchasing action. *Promotional elasticity* is a measure of the changes in demand relative to advertising expenditure.

(c) *Service*. The provision of pre- or post-sales advice and servicing facilities may more than compensate for an initially high price.

(d) *Credit and terms of trading*. This has been a major consideration in many countries in recent years.

6. The demand for other products
The following factors are important:

(a) *Cross-elasticity*. The demand for goods may be influenced by the demand for other goods, which may vary according to price.

(b) *Competition*. Demand will depend not only on the price of competitive products or substitutes, but on their reputation, availability, performance, aesthetic appeal, length of service, flexibility of use and so on.

(c) *Derived demand and choice*. The demand for almost all products is conditioned by the demand for others. Sometimes the buying problem is a question of deciding on the use of limited resources to buy one make of car as opposed to another – or to go on an overseas holiday instead of buying a car. Sometimes there is a close dependency in the demand for one product on the demand for another. The demand for nylon depends on the demand for nylon-finished products. The demand for machines depends on the demand for the goods that the machines produce. It is sometimes possible for the manufacture of derived demand goods to stimulate primary demand: for example, the promotional campaigns of manufacturers of fabrics in artificial fibres led to an increased demand for the fibres and for the raw materials and machinery.

7. The problem of changing variables
The problem of pricing is intensified not simply because of the increasing *number* of variables affecting demand, but also because those

variables are in a *constant state of change*. It is a basic task of marketing to determine which of the variable factors of demand have greatest significance in particular markets at particular points of time. Attempts to determine the factors at present range from sheer guesswork or intuition to the construction of complex mathematical models. Successful product differentiation depends on the determination of the relevant factors and the creation of some of the elements of monopoly benefits.

8. Specific problems facing the price-setter

Among the many problems often solved intuitively or by conventional cost-based formulae are the following:

(a) Establishing an initial price structure for new products.

(b) Reacting to changes in competitive prices.

(c) Forecasting the role of price in relation to the various stages of the product life cycle (*see* 4:4).

(d) Determining the sensitivity of resellers to prices and margins.

(e) Estimating the relative sensitivity to price of basically similar products or services supplied to different markets or market segments.

(f) Organising price schedules for products with interrelated production costs.

(g) Arranging prices for products differing in cost and profitability, but which are purchased only in combination.

(h) Determining the appropriate timing, frequency and amount of price changes.

(i) Channel of distribution, traditional margins, stock turn and return on investment benefits.

9. Top-level management objectives, policies and constraints

Too frequently, in practice, price-setters lack clear statements by top management of the objectives and policies which must be accepted as given constraints by executives at a lower level, who have to make pricing decisions in relation to specific markets, products and/or services – and indeed specific situations. Some of these top-level decision areas are as follows:

(a) Does the company intend to communicate a corporate image which is closely identified with price levels, such as a reputation for high quality only?

(b) Does the company have short-run and long-run objectives in terms of overall profitability, and to what extent are these objectives to be applied to individual products or product groups regardless of their stage in the life cycle? Are different criteria to be applied to different home markets, or to overseas as opposed to home markets?

(c) What is the company's commitment to market penetration or share maintenance, and to what extent is it prepared to sacrifice short-run profit to gain strategic ends?

(d) Does the company seek price leadership and subsequent competitive price stability? Is it prepared to take aggressive action against 'inconvenient' price-cutters?

(e) What is the company's attitude towards risk, in which parts and in what proportion of its business?

(f)   What is the company policy on transfer pricing (*see* **36**)?

Specific competitive/marketing pricing strategies and practices

Increasingly, firms are concerned with financial goals which may influence earnings, the timing of earnings, the pattern and timing of cash flows, etc., and these goals have a bearing on pricing policies. Subject to such considerations, organisations may adopt particular strategies to achieve specific market and/or competitive goals in price-setting circumstances such as those discussed in **10–16** below.

10. Market penetration
Low prices are set in order to penetrate markets and to gain a major market share – usually in a comparatively short time. This policy can only be valid if the market is very price sensitive, and/or if production costs fall significantly in line with volume increase, and/or if competitors will be discouraged. If penetration targets are achieved and competitive activity has been restricted, the problem of whether to raise prices or reduce margins to intermediaries such as wholesalers and retailers might arise.

A market penetration strategy designed to capture a major market share by attracting new buyers, increasing existing buyers' usage or deepening existing user loyalty and regularising users, depends not only on demand forecasting confidence, but on the ability to meet increased demand in an appropriate time. Otherwise, it is likely that sales will have been gained at a sacrifice of revenue and profit.

One argument advanced has been that, in conditions of great demand uncertainty, provided a 'satisfactory' profit is made in the short run, prices can be moved up if market demand exceeds expectation.

Such an argument has no practical validity in situations where governments impose statutory price constraints – an increasingly important consideration in inflationary situations which governments may attempt to control by some form of prices and/or incomes policy. Prices geared essentially to costs, lacking close analysis of short- and long-run supply/demand considerations, are particularly vulnerable in inflationary conditions.

11. Short-term profit maximisation
A policy of setting very high prices in order to make as much profit as possible in a short time is normally valid only if the producer has an innovation of such significance that there is a ready price-elastic market with virtually no immediate competition but likely competition in the near future. The producer must also normally be prepared to move out of the business when it has made its quick profits. The Reynolds International Pen Company introduced ballpoint pens at a retail price of $12.50 and in three months made a profit after taxes of $1,558,608 on an investment of $26,000. Competitive pressure forced prices down and the company closed, but the originator made a fortune. A primary objective of most companies, however, is to stay in business.

Short-term, profit-maximising (or 'skimming the cream') pricing objectives have sometimes been applied successfully to segment markets, to recover costs quickly in conditions of uncertainty, or to compensate for high development costs. Books are often produced first in a limited expensive edition and then, in the light of demand indications, cheaper paperback editions may follow. New drugs are often extremely expensive initially, but prices fall rapidly after the first one or two years of the product life.

12. Satisfactory rate of return
Some companies fix their prices on the basis of a traditional rate of return over a given time period, related to the extent of risk or investment involved. In its most sophisticated form this becomes *target pricing*. Target pricing is aimed at securing in a given period of time a predetermined rate of return on investment. The process involves the calculation of an average mark-up on average costs and at the same time projecting sales revenue at various stages of the product life cycle. Target pricing is thus directed towards the twin objectives of stabilising prices and yet achieving a given return on investment over the product life. At particular points of time the return will be high, at others low.

Target pricing demands accurate forecasting and accurate costing in terms of levels of output and marketing expenditure. Problems lie in the fact that, despite the importance of other factors, price remains a factor of demand, and this method ignores the influence of different price levels on volume.

13. Product-line pricing

Many companies selling a wide range of products gear pricing to a range of products rather than to individual products. It may be considered that certain products yielding a comparatively low profit-able return are necessary to support products which yield a high profit. At the extreme, some products may even be *loss leaders* – products which are basically non-profitable or just cover costs, but which stimulate buying of other profitable lines. Loss leaders are a feature of large retailing operations: for example, someone who buys low-priced aspirin tablets may be tempted to buy at the same time a perfume carrying a high profit.

14. Variable pricing

This is most commonly applied to products or services with known variable time demands. It may be used to take advantage of extra profit at peak periods, or to reduce production and overhead costs by stimulating demand in non-peak periods. Hotel rates may be high in peak holiday seasons and low in winter and autumn. Specially re-duced rates for the use of electricity at off-peak periods may be introduced to utilise output more effectively and even cut the produc-tion load.

Occasionally, differential pricing may be negotiated with individ-ual customers, although this is a risky practice, or disproportionately high profit margins may be demanded for unusual extras, such as a television set with a particular type of wooden cabinet or a car with special chrome fittings. Variable pricing is, in fact, a well-established practice in the automotive industry, often involving not only charges for special features, but charges for delivery, allowances for 'trade in', etc. It is perhaps significant that Japanese companies in this field offer 'all-in' prices, featuring it strongly in promotion and advertising.

15. Competition-based pricing

Most companies set prices after careful consideration of competitive price structure. Deliberate policies may be formulated to sell above, below or generally in line with competition. One of the problems here is that cost and profit structures and practice will differ. The more closely a company's price policy is geared to match or undercut competitive prices, the more important it is to bring cost into line, to accept a lower rate of return or to provide a product package which is really different.

Many companies attempt to keep price levels in line with an average rate for the industry (the 'going rate'). The going rate is a valid policy where market conditions are highly competitive and where products are narrowly differentiated. This is a major problem of commodity and raw material trading, upon which many underdeveloped countries depend so much.

Close competitive pricing is also found in markets where one company or a small group of companies is in a highly dominant position, and can either directly or indirectly regulate prices of materials or components used by small price-cutting organisations, or stand the strain of a price war much more readily. In some cases, one company clearly emerges as a price leader.

16. Bid pricing
When contracts are awarded as a result of tender (e.g. government contracts and large-scale plant construction), companies must clearly attempt to determine the level of competitive bids. If the object is to obtain the contract, cost will be the main consideration when determining the minimum price level. Calculations of anticipated profit against probability of tender price acceptance may be undertaken. Mathematical models have recently been developed with some success, especially to cater for situations in which a previous history of competitive-bid data exists: for example, in open-tender conditions. In some cases, models take account of both past data and subjective probability estimates, by knowledgeable executives, of success or failure at a range of price levels. The significant advantage of models which are in use is that the successful bid price is regularly above that which would have been the outcome of conventional methods.

Some special aspects of service pricing

Some services are charged at a fixed rate: for example, the rental of installations, equipment, etc. over a contractual time period. The cost of supply is charged according to quantities used and/or time of usage. Electricity supply and telephone charges are examples of this kind of pricing.

Consultation charges in private medical treatment often consist of a charge for initial consultation with lower rates for follow-up consultations and/or treatment and a separate charge for medicines, etc.

Some large hotel/restaurant groups offer special rates at stated times and on certain days to those over a certain age.

Reduced 'stand-by fares' are offered by some tourist aircraft and sea cruise operators to potential customers who can take advantage of these offers at short notice.

The examples given all show an awareness of the critical distinction between fixed, variable and semi-variable costs together with price/demand relationships. The application of these concepts calls for close study of the nature of the services: for example, individually prescribed services (e.g. professional advice) or more generally offered service (e.g. public transport); fluctuating demand patterns and capacity constraints (e.g. fire and police services, hotels and restaurants); means of delivering services (e.g. the customer visits the service provided, as in concert halls; or the customer is visited by the organisation representative, as in letter mail services. It will be seen from these and other examples how great is the significance of cost/price demand analysis and action plans appropriately tailored to given situations. This theme is continued in the following paragraphs.

The cost base

In practice, the build-up of price consists of an estimate of cost and a mark-up on that cost. In determining cost, three principal approaches are in common use:

(a) Full, total or absorption costing.
(b) Direct costing.
(c) Marginal costing.

17. Full, total or absorption costing
The essential feature of this approach is that an attempt is made to apportion all expenses, whether or not they can be traced directly to a product. Apportionment of overheads follows some 'reasonable' convention, but is of necessity arbitrary. It is claimed that this approach avoids the danger of incomplete recovery of overheads and appropriate profit. No account is taken of the fact that some products will inevitably be more price sensitive than others, and its acceptance for all pricing decisions will normally lead to both under- and over-pricing, since market forces are ignored.

Oil has presented very special pricing problems, since in power industries such as oil it is often impossible to avoid producing several products simultaneously. There are thus difficulties in allocating joint costs to particular products under reasonably stable world conditions. Between 1973 and 1975, however, the decline in demand for OPEC oil was around 20 per cent and an overall period of general economic recession was set in train in the majority of Western industrialised countries.

In spite, however, of some changes in world trade in recent years, such as the growth of less developed countries in the Far East – Hong Kong, Thailand, Malaysia, Taiwan, Singapore, South Korea – over three-quarters of the exports of the developed world are still exchanged with other developed countries. In the case of the less developed countries in the Far East, two major factors are the growth of tourism, and links with manufacturing companies from the developed world. Both developments call for new approaches to pricing policies – one of service industries and the other of inter-company transfer deals.

18. Direct costing

This approach represents an attempt to include in a product or process cost calculation only those costs which are directly incurred and which could be avoided in the medium or long term if the particular product or process were discontinued. Such costs may include factory costs, selling costs and other costs (e.g. research and physical distribution) which are specific to a product or product range.

Both fixed- and variable-cost elements are also included. Although organisations using direct costing methods have developed reasonably sophisticated systems for charging production cost at a given standard level of output, there is often a lack of data analysis in terms of direct marketing expenditure incurred in connection with specific product and customer market groups. As there is increasing evidence that a very high proportion of business potential is concentrated on relatively few customers, products and geographical areas, there is a need to develop more detailed information wherever possible on marketing costs directly attributable to specific product-market groupings.

Perhaps the most important disadvantage of direct costing methods is that, since these ignore the distinction between fixed and variable costs, it is not possible to assess the effect of volume changes.

19. Marginal costing

The essential feature of this costing method, which is known as *variable costing* in the USA, is the emphasis placed on the separation of costs into two main sections, namely fixed and variable. Fixed costs are those which tend to remain constant, regardless of changes in output. Variable costs are those which tend to vary with output. Marginal cost differs in accounting practice from the economist's use of the term. Marginal cost to the economist is the increment to total cost of the last unit produced. The accounting approach takes average variable costs within given ranges of output.

The method has great advantages in its ability to highlight the effect of changes in volume, price or costs. Once an appropriate price/volume relationship has been established to cover variable costs, additional revenue becomes a 'contribution' towards recovery of fixed cost, overhead and profit. Profit/volume sensitivity is of particularly great importance where the level of committed fixed costs is high. Clearly, the level of committed fixed costs also indicates the level of price above which an order is preferable to having plant idle. At the same time, marginal costing methods also allow for a consideration of opportunity cost in decision making: for example, what would be the likely outcome of raising price on product X, with a resultant loss of some volume and revenue, if this loss could be more than offset by using the released capacity to generate additional sales revenue on product Y?

The two principal arguments against marginal costing are as follows:

(a) There is often a practical difficulty in segregating fixed and variable expense – and such a segregation can only be valid for specified ranges of output and time.

(b) There is a danger that, if every price decision is taken on the basis of marginal cost, fixed expenses and profit will not be adequately recovered, and this situation can be intensified if short-term pressures on price become hardened in the longer term.

It is important for marketers to understand the principles, advantages and disadvantages of the main approaches to costing. Different cost conventions may be required for different decisions. Some cost bases will certainly represent the pricing floor. Total costing represents neither the true floor nor the true ceiling for good strategic decisions. Marginal and direct costing approaches, on the other hand, may both be regarded as valid – and sometimes complementary – approaches to the strategic managerial aspects of pricing decisions.

Discounts

Discounts involve the offer of reductions (differentials) from a base price and must also be considered when price policy is being determined. The following are the most usual forms.

20. Trade discounts

In areas where there is resale price maintenance (RPM), such as in some parts of the USA, the fixed retail price is usually the base. Elsewhere, as now in the UK, a suggested or expected retail selling price might be used. Prices to retailers might be at list price less a percentage discount to cover the retailer's margin. Prices to wholesalers might be at list price, less retail discount, less a discount to cover the wholesaler's margin. Although, except in RPM conditions, there is no control over resale prices, discounts have some stabilising influence on final prices.

> NOTE: Some companies argue that RPM is itself an important stabilising influence, and that marked price disparities at retail can lead to such a value uncertainty in customers' minds that demand is seriously inhibited.

21. Quantity discounts

Price advantages might be offered on the basis of order size or particular assortments.

Quantity discounts might be applied to retailers and wholesalers within their own prices structure, or there may be a general quantity rate-pricing structure which gives bulk-buying advantages to retailers and wholesalers equally – size of business or order being the only criterion.

Quantity discounts may attract large buyers or induce smaller buyers to order large quantities. Most quantity discount arrangements apply either to single orders or single deliveries, and these involve economies of scale in transportation and administration. Some discounts are paid retrospectively on the basis of orders received or goods delivered. In some countries, such as the USA, there are legal restrictions on discount procedures. Quantity discounting is found in both goods and services: for example, fleet owner discounts in the cases of company car purchases and discounted rates to contracted organisation employees offered in private health insurance schemes.

22. Cash discounts
Most business transactions from manufacturer to wholesaler and/or retailer are conducted on credit terms. The length of time allowed for payment varies considerably, and payment in practice is often de-layed beyond the duration of the officially stated credit terms. When this happens the supplier has the problem of deciding how rigidly to press for payment, and whether to refuse to supply further goods or services. Some suppliers offer a special discount for payment within a stipulated period from the date of invoice.

23. Seasonal discounts
These may be offered to stimulate sales at special times of the year or day: for example, 'off-peak' railway tickets.

24. Geographical differentials
These are differential rates offered in relation to distance from supply base, examples of which are petrol zone pricing and new car delivery.

> NOTE: Transportation costs may or may not be included in the price, and this is particularly important in the import/export business. For example, FOB (free on board) indicates that the vendor is selling at a price which includes all charges incurred in placing the goods on board the vessel. Once they are on board, the buyer bears the risk and any subsequent expenses. A CIF price covers the cost of goods, insurance and freight, the buyer taking no responsibility until he/she takes the goods from the ship at their destination.

Price change and customer attitudes

25. Problems of price changing
The risks involved in price change either upwards or downwards are so great that suppliers are usually slow to act. They are particularly slow to move prices upwards, knowing that such action will affect competitors, ultimate buyers and intermediaries, and will also be subject to government scrutiny. The fact that prices of particular types of product tend to move upwards or downwards at a particular time may be the result of any of the following:

(a) Unofficial inter-company communications.
(b) Changes in cost factors which affect all suppliers, such as variations in material costs and new wage agreements.

(c) A fear of loss of business if prices are not competitive.
(d) Action which should have been taken previously, but which has been delayed in order to avoid placing the company in an isolated pricing situation.

26. Estimating reaction to price changes
Some of the methods of pre-judging reaction are as follows:

(a) Attitude surveys – field interviews based on statistical samples.
(b) Mathematical models constructed from significant and controllable socioeconomic variable factors.
(c) Statistical estimates based on regression analysis and simple or multiple correlation (*see* **27** below).
(d) Experimental pricing in limited test markets.
(e) Operations research techniques, such as game theory, to anticipate likely competitive reaction (*see* **28** below).

27. Regression and correlation analysis
Regression analysis is a statistical method of examining the past trends of relationships between one variable (e.g. sales volume) and one or more than one other variable (e.g. advertising expenditure, cost of sales staff). Correlation analysis is a statistical method by which it is possible to measure the closeness of those relationships. Regression analysis will show that there is a relationship between disposable personal income and the sales of most consumer goods. Correlation analysis will show how close that relationship is in the case of specific consumer items.

When an increase in one variable coincides with an increase in another, the two variables have a positive correlation. When an increase in one coincides with a decrease in the other, the variables have a negative correlation. The highest possible correlation is expressed at ±1. Simple correlation is restricted to the relationship between two variables. Multiple correlation takes into account the simultaneous relationship of more than two variables.

28. The use of operations research techniques
Operations research is a comparatively new science derived from many disciplines, including mathematics, physics, engineering and economics. A basic concept is the building of a model, usually mathematical, consisting of sets of equations relating significant variables in a situation to the outcome. Professor Stone of Cambridge has constructed a model of the economy, for example, in an effort to study

and forecast the effect of changes in variables such as gross national product on the whole economy and on other variables. Other more sophisticated models have now been developed.

Operations research is essentially designed to assist in resolving complex problems. After being developed in the 1940s to tackle military problems, it is now being applied increasingly to business situations.

The most familiar type of pricing model is based on multiple regression, a linear functional relationship being sought between sales and marketing input variables such as personal selling efforts and costs, level of advertising, distribution and service support, etc. Regression analysis can also be used to produce models which aim to give decision-makers the chance of experimenting with various levels and combinations of strategic input to simulate probable outcomes. Some experiments have been carried out in the application of games theory technique, by which there is an attempt to examine systematically the possible reactions of a competitor or competitors to a company's change in pricing strategy – and the consequent company outcomes (pay-off) (*see also* **16**).

In practice, few pricing models are in regular use, and the employment of purely historical economic data is unlikely to lead to models of predictive usefulness. Behavioural factors must also be considered.

29. Behavioural factors
Psychological and sociological factors have a considerable influence on buying decisions in both consumer and industrial markets. There is, for example, a great deal of evidence to indicate that a buying choice is influenced by a high 'perceived' element of risk. Lack of confidence in assessing the relative quality of items leads to the acceptance of a higher price as a quality indicator and, in many cases, to buying at a high price to avoid risk. Risk may be perceived to be low in buying some products which have come to be regarded as non-differentiated commodities, such as salt. Value judgement is seen to be much more difficult in the purchasing of stereo equipment or carpets, and price becomes a quality indicator – particularly so if there is the reinforcing support of peer-group experience or opinion.

In industrial markets, research work has indicated that in cases where a product-buying situation has become a routine procedure, with an established buyer–seller relationship, it is rare for that relationship to be broken at all – and similar products and services are unlikely to be considered on a price basis unless the differential is in the order of 10 per cent or more. Even then the risk avoidance factor is strong if other processes or products are likely to be affected, and if the decision is to be taken by a single buyer isolated from the comforting support of other executives.

Among other considerations are the following:

(a) It may be thought that a product is *faulty* or comparatively unacceptable, and therefore has to be at a reduced price. However, established price values do persist and, provided there is *quality acceptance*, reduced prices may be seen as bargains.

(b) Experienced buyers may anticipate *further reductions* and wait until they judge prices have reached their lowest level.

(c) It could be imagined that there was a *danger of obsolescence*. Price reductions sometimes precede the entry of new models.

(d) Buyers – especially industrial buyers – may prefer *maximum price stability* as an indication of reliable trading practice. Frequent price changes may give an impression of financial instability.

(e) Many purchasers – particularly domestic consumers – are *unaware of the precise price* of a wide range of goods and only become aware if there is a change, when they tend to reassess the values of competing products.

(f) Customers may not have a precise knowledge of prices of existing products, but they usually have firm ideas of upper and lower limits, or a *price zone*. Prices outside the zone may have to overcome additional psychological barriers. The price zones for new products are much more vague and there is little or no opportunity to compare. This greater pricing latitude for new products is not always utilised by manufacturers.

(g) Some people like to be *innovators* or to be seen as innovators; others follow. Price attitudes of leaders and followers may be quite different.

(h) Price notions may be geared to the *coinage system*. Elementary use of this idea, such as £1.99 instead of £2, is still sometimes effective, but there maybe other price barriers associated with coinage which we know little about.

Pricing tactics and demand

30. Pricing and research and development costs

Frequently, companies set prices for new products with the objective of recovering research and development costs in a given time period. Research costs do not necessarily relate to individual product success, however and an attempt to recover disproportionately high research and development costs by high pricing may reduce profit by inhibiting demand.

There is much to be said for covering the costs of research and development by aiming at the highest revenue above marginal cost. Consumers will pay not for research as such, but for the *distinctive utility* – economic, psychological or social – which the product offers. In the last resort, products should be measured by the contribution they make to overhead and profit. Working in reverse and basing prices on arbitrary allocation of general overheads, whether they be management, research or clerical administration, can never be justified except perhaps for a 'one-off' guaranteed sale.

31. Indirect pricing differentials
Non-listed special allowances, service provision and other concessions are sometimes given (to major customers) in non-differentiated product markets. Other indirect concessions may take the form of margin guarantees, special credit terms and allowances to wholesaler, retailer or agency advertising or promotional campaigns.

Indirect price competition is openly seen in many consumer markets in offers of various kinds: for example, the use of coupons for free trials or for purchases at reduced prices. There are banded packs with two similar products at a special price, premium offers of gifts on purchase, and 'trade-in' concessions for durable items. These special offers to domestic consumers may be supported by special deals to channel intermediaries. Some offers are described as self-liquidating – goods are supplied at bargain prices in return for tokens indicating product purchase. Theoretically the 'bargains' are achieved by the promoter obtaining goods at bulk prices and passing on the advantages to individual customers.

32. Reasons for special promotions
In general, however, special promotions represent a temporary price cut and are used for various reasons:

(a) *Novelty appeal.* It is claimed that permanent price cuts are easily imitated and it is difficult to return to the original prices. Promotions on the other hand have a novelty appeal and can be a way of differentiating one product from another.
(b) *Psychological advantage.* Promotions, it is said, have a psychological advantage in creating a greater impression of extra value than a price cut.

(c) *New customers.* A special offer may be the means of persuading people to try a product for the first time and some of the business gained will be retained when prices are normal; loyal customers also gain the advantages of the temporary price cuts.

(d) *Opportunities for selling.* Promotions in highly competitive consumer markets provide salespersons with a series of new presentations and an opportunity for acquiring shelf space. These promotions are almost invariably supported by display materials.

(e) *Uneven demand.* Promotions may help to smooth out uneven demand.

In general, promotions are more frequent at the launching of a new product campaign.

Over recent years, as far as many consumer goods markets are concerned, the balance of power has tended to move away from the major manufacturers to the large retailing and wholesaling groups. This move is associated with two important developments which have led to greater in-store display and promotional activity. First, there is the growth of private label brands; second, there is the more intensive application – certainly at retail group HQ level – of the criterion of return on investment. To counter the first of these developments and to capitalise on the second, manufacturers are spending greater proportions of their advertising budgets on special promotions and deals, and the battle for shelf space is, in some cases, being waged in retail outlets not only by sales personnel but by special teams of merchandisers.

33. Pack size and price

It is sometimes difficult for a customer to compare prices of similar products, since there is often a wide range of pack size and differences in the weight of the contents. Although it may be necessary legally for the manufacturers to stipulate on a carton the weight of the contents, the purchaser may completely disregard weight–price comparison, or be unable to make the comparison, for example, between grams and cubic centimetres. The increase in pre-packed consumer goods has made direct price comparison much more difficult. Frequently virtual price increases are disguised by decreasing the size of the pack, as in confectionery.

34. Competitive pricing and company policy

Pricing policy, as has been seen, is related intuitively or by calculation to cost, demand and/or competition. Companies should, therefore, study not only their own costs but also the likely competitive cost structure. If competitors change prices, it will be necessary to decide on a line of action. The more products are seen to be similar, the more likely it is that prices will move in line. On the other hand, there have been examples of a company's maintaining prices when competitive prices move up and yet successfully improving market share or profits.

If products are differentiated, a company must consider what part price plays in the total marketing mix. After determining why a competitor has reduced price, for example, it will be necessary to estimate whether the price change is likely to be permanent and what the likely outcomes of various reactions might be. Competitive price cuts could be met by temporary indirect offers or a change in packaging, or an increase in advertising and sales effort. The timing of reaction will be important. It may be essential in some market situations to adjust prices immediately – in others there will be an opportunity to wait.

35. Information systems' needs for pricing decisions
It is evident that there is a pressing need for more sophisticated information systems to be established, so that specific pricing decisions in rapidly changing market situations can be made reasonably speedily, easily and effectively, yet be in line with a consistent overall company policy. The following list, adapted from the work of A.L. Oxenfeldt, covers data that might be used to design a price-monitoring system:

(a) Current sales in units and revenue for different product-market combinations set against previous annual sales.
(b) Current and previous years' sales at 'off-list' prices as a percentage of total company, product, product-group, customer or customer-group sales.
(c) Market shares – current and previous year.
(d) Current competitive prices by product and market category compared with previous year.
(e) Current and past marketing costs; actual production costs, and production costs at accepted level of maximum output.
(f) Stocks of company and, where appropriate, reseller finished goods – the incidence of significantly high and low levels, including 'out of stock' situations.
(g) Behavioural studies of customers' attitudes towards the company and its pricing practices.
(h) Salespersons' and customer reports of price dissatisfaction.
(i) Incidence of new customers, lost customers and enquiries, by product-market categories.

Behavioural aspects of price must be taken into account in developing practical models which will reveal to pricing decision-makers: (a) the key sensitive variables in defined product-market segments to which attention must be paid; and (b) the likely outcomes of alternative courses of action.

36. Transfer pricing

This relates to the policies and procedures to be followed when determining appropriate prices for inter- and intra-company transactions where there is common ownership. A process of vertical integration, with goods being transferred from one company to another at various stages of production, is a classic illustration of the need to determine, subject to statutory limitations, a clear pricing policy. The trend towards decentralisation, with, for example, divisions being treated as profit centres as a prime method of performance measurement and motivation, can conflict with a requirement to optimise corporate profitability. For example, managers who believe they are judged essentially by profitability measures may feel aggrieved if they are compelled to 'sell' a substantial proportion of their output to other divisions at a price artificially depressed below that which they could achieve in the open market.

The morale problem is often mainly attributable to faulty communications – a lack of explanation of the rationale of the system and assurance of due recognition of imposed constraints in performance assessment. It is impossible to generalise about the extent to which decentralised divisions should be compelled to supply their own company's captive markets at dictated prices. Sometimes, from the point of view of the purchasing division, there is a belief that more favourable terms should be obtained elsewhere. Therefore, many economically integrated companies have introduced a degree of 'arm's length' trading which has to be delicately balanced so that the main advantages of integration are achieved, but the inter-company parties to buying/selling transactions may indulge in price negotiation – and indeed, on occasion, buy or sell elsewhere. For aspects of transfer pricing in international markets, *see* Chapter 12.

Recent pricing developments

(a) There is much more extensive use of credit and deferred payment schemes. One reason for this is that, following bank deregulation, credit cards have been strongly promoted by banks and non-bank financing organisations. Some retailing organisations, such as Marks Spencer, have set up their own credit card operation. Another consequence of the extensive use of credit has been the willingness of some selling organisations to accept prices below those marked in return for immediate cash payment.

(b) Prolonged downturns or virtually no growth economic conditions have in many sectors – but especially in the retailing of deferrable items, such as cars, furniture/and household appliances – led to 'special' sales becoming almost continuous rather than seasonal. Such tactics are almost invariably defensive and are, not infrequently, linked with cuts in employment and other high-expense areas.

(c) Pricing competition has become much more severe in insurance and assurance markets. Some organisations, such as the UK Automobile Association, offer a comparative cost service derived from potential customer information and a database system covering charges and conditions pertaining to various providers of such services.

(d) Services provided by some organisations previously using full-time employees (e.g. electrical goods repairs, clothes alterations) have now been subcontracted to external independent operators. This has inevitably brought changes in pricing and convenience, and has, in many cases, opened up opportunities for new small and part-time business operators.

(e) There is greater evidence of initial period cost/price advantages in the marketing of durable goods, such as cars and financial services. Specific examples in the mid-1990s are:

(*i*) the offer by an investment group of a 2 per cent discount for specified investments of £1,000 or more received by a specified date;

(*ii*) the offer to purchasers by a Japanese car manufacturer of a three-year/60,000 mile manufacturer warranty plus two years' free servicing plus one year's free RAC membership. These special advantages occupied virtually the whole of a full-page advertisement. Other details such as buying prices notably exclusive of delivery charges and number plates were given in 'small print'.

37. Conclusion

Pricing is a key marketing decision area. Doing nothing, provided this is a deliberate decison, is a policy. Successful pricing decisions will always be the result of a combination of art and science, but it is increasingly possible to measure the probabilities of the effect of external forces in the environment in which a company operates. More certainly, it is possible to devise pricing policies which meet company objectives. No longer should a company be in the position of effecting a hasty compromise between conflicting objectives in complete ignorance of the likely market response.

Progress test 5

1. What are the major factors influencing demand?

2. What is meant by 'penetration' pricing and 'product line' pricing?

3. To what extent do companies set prices in line with those of competitors?

4. What are the main types of discount?

5. In what ways can the effects of price changes be estimated?

6. What behavioural factors influence the attitudes of buyers to price?

7. What are the reasons for special promotions?

8. What data might a company need to establish a comprehensive information system for pricing decisions?

Assignments

1. Prepare a five-minute talk on 'Price and other factors of demand'. Illustrate your talk by reference to enquiries you made among 10 males and 10 females of your age group in which they were asked to state:

– five items bought during the past month;
– in each case what factors affected the decision to purchase (e.g. brand name, attractive price, convenience of buying point, user experience, packaging); and
– which factors were the most important and which the least important.

2. Arrange for interviews to take place at local service establishments, such as a theatre or cinema; an hotel or restaurant; a radio, TV or video rental organisation; a travel agency; a bank.
    The objective of the visits/interviews is to examine the stated specific problems of regulating supply and demand, and the role of pricing in contributing to an appropriate answer.

Advertising and promotion: objectives and institutions

1. Definitions

Advertising is non-personal communication directed at target audiences through various media in order to present and promote products, services and ideas. The cost of media space, time and advertisement production is borne by the sponsor or sponsors, and this activity is sometimes described as 'above the line' advertising. It should be distinguished from *publicity*, by means of which an organisation derives benefit from favourable free showings, descriptions and discussions of its products and/or services in a variety of media (*see* 7:**41**).

Retailer/wholesaler merchandising, trade shows, exhibitions, product sampling, special offers, demonstrations, etc. are classified as *sales promotion* and are sometimes described as 'below the line' activity.

2. UK media and expenditure

Over £8,000 million is being spent annually on various forms of advertising in the 1990s. Of this a growing proportion goes on television advertising. It is too early to estimate the effect of the introduction of cable TV and 'the satellite revolution'. Big advertisers are certainly interested, but the reservations in the early stages are concerned mainly with the ability of the satellite and cable operators to 'deliver the audience'. A secondary problem will be one of convincing advertisers of target audiences to suit their product/service needs. The press – national and regional, magazines and periodicals, trade journals, directories, etc. – still accounts for considerably more than TV expenditure. In addition, spending on sales promotion is increasing and spreading from retailing to a wide variety of service industries.

Apart from the highly significant advent of cable and satellite TV, there are other areas of vastly increased activity that are worthy of note – advertising freesheets, sponsorship and commercial radio (e.g. Capital Radio, Classic FM and telemarketing). Advertising Association statistics show that there are some 500 free newspapers and newsheets. A Verified Free Distribution Audit is now well established, and this has, no doubt, assisted in attracting advertisers. The quantity of the editorial material has increased and the layout has improved over the years, attracting the attention of the 80 per cent of the adult population now receiving these publications.

Sponsorship is also very much on the increase, not only because of the very positive advantages of on-site posters, TV and other media exposure, but also because of public relations offspin and the buyer/executive hospitality opportunities presented. Glyndebourne Opera attracts corporate membership from such companies as the Midland Bank, IBM and Costain, and the building of a new Opera House in 1993-4 owed much to commercial financing. Tents and marquees at the Henley Regatta proclaim the names of such companies as the Reed Group, BOC and Norwich Union, while at Wimbledon, Beecham, Barclays, Norwich Union and other company backing is very evident. Individual company sponsorship of an ever widening range of sporting events, including soccer, cricket, rugby, tennis, golf, athletics and snooker, is increasingly evident. The costs are often very high – estimated at a total of over £250 million in the mid-1990s – and the business advantages are very difficult to identify and measure.

Direct mailing is also increasing rapidly. Some 2,500 million items were distributed in 1993 at a cost of over £1,000 million.

Advertising by companies marketing consumer services and industrial goods is increasing sharply. It is not surprising, of course, to see organisations such as Unilever, Procter & Gamble, Mars and Nestlé heading the top 20 companies in advertising expenditure, but by the mid-1990s service organisations such as British Telecom, the Electricity Association (Electricity Council), British Gas, the National Westminster Bank and the Halifax Building Society, as well as government ministries and departments, were among the top 20 users of TV, press and radio.

Leisure and tourism is now a vast complex growth industry, covering for example air, rail, road and sea travel, accommodation, travel agents and tour operators, and using a wide range of media and other forms of communication nationally and internationally. The British Tourist Authority has become a major spender in its promotion of tourism, and the opening of the Channel Tunnel is expected to lead to vast increases of tourist and commercial trade.

Political power and influence during the 1980s and early 1990s has had effects which are clearly to be seen directly and indirectly in UK advertising. Privatisation and deregulation have been two of the major areas of statutory and government policy change which have affected structural and operational developments within the advertising industry, as well as the external communications strategies and tactics of many commercial and professional institutions, including legal, financial and educational.

Commercial TV has flourished in the UK during the past decade. The government exercises some controls, specifically through the granting of TV franchises for a ten-year period. In 1993 a group of ten ·people representing the Independent Television Committee examined the tenders for sixteen of the franchises and the outcome was that four of the existing franchisees had to withdraw, and were replaced by Carlton TV, Sunrise, Meridian Broadcasting and West Country TV. These new franchise holders – unlike their predecessors – will contract out a substantial part of programming to independent companies. This devolution provides opportunities for smaller, specialised operators, but has inevitably caused redundancies and structural changes in the companies whose bids were unsuccessful. It is also widely predicted that TV agencies will be fighting for a fairly static £1.6 billion of sales for some time.

The 1990s will bring about, on the one hand, much greater consideration of the possibilities of supranational advertising and, on the other, much greater attention to very specific targeting of decentralised buying decision making by formal organisations and informal personal groupings. In this latter connection the lively activities of independent local radio together with two national networks, Classic FM and Virgin 1215, cannot be disregarded.

Media availability and use currently differ from country to country and from region to region. The differences depend on a number of factors, among which are the following:

(a) The technical development of communication systems.

(b) County size as well as geographical, topographical, cultural, religious and ethnic differences.

(c) Buying power – particularly the distribution of discretionary consumer income.

(d) Educational development – particularly standards of literacy.

(e) National legal restrictions on advertising.

(f) The structure of distributive systems.

(g) The relative costs of the media which are available.

(h) Technological developments, such as the development of telemarketing and digital broadcasting, and the current market increase in videos for promotional material.

(i) Stages of economic development and structure as well as government or economic group policies and regulations.

Advertising is a part of total marketing communications and must be considered in terms of markets and products/services at very different stages of development.

Total communications and the marketing mix

3. The marketing mix
The complex of marketing decisions which may stimulate sales is frequently called the *marketing mix* – a term first used by Professor Neil Borden of the Harvard Business School. The marketing mix may be seen to consist of elements concerned with the product (e.g. range, price, quality), with channels of distribution, and with communications. Communications involve the whole process of communication with markets, including advertising, personal selling and public relations. The sales-task approach to fixing and measuring the effectiveness of advertising expenditure depends on an understanding of the various possibilities for combining elements of the marketing mix. The basic elements of the marketing mix for machine tools may be products of rigid quality-control standards, high unit prices, low advertising expenditure, high personal selling cost, and direct distribution from manufacturer to user. In contrast, the basic marketing mix for flour may involve greater product-quality variation, low unit price, comparatively high advertising expenditure with low personal selling cost, and indirect distribution through wholesalers and retailers.

Just as marketing goals and strategies depend on the formulation of corporate goals, strategies and policies, so total communication goals and strategies depend on those of marketing.

4. The integration of marketing and communication objectives
In a handbook of this kind it is not practicable to explore the great diversity of marketing goals and strategies which might be applied to specific products or services in specific situations. Fundamentally, however, a business organisation may be following an aggressive strategy to expand a total market and/or its share of that market. It may seek to achieve this by increasing the business it transacts with existing customers and/or by gaining new customers. In some circumstances, it will be pursuing basically a defensive strategy, such as

seeking to maintain an existing market share. Advertising and promotional objectives and strategies should be integrated with
marketing goals and strategies. Objectives are a prerequisite for decisions on budgets, message strategy, media selection, timing and
frequency, and the measurement of effectiveness.

5. Objectives and measurement

As advertising is one of a number of variable elements of marketing
strategy, operating in a constantly shifting market environment, it is
virtually impossible, except in mail-order selling or certain direct mail
campaigns, to quantify exactly its contribution to profits. The more
precise the objectives are, however, the easier it is to estimate the value
of a campaign and to design an effective one.

The following are examples of objectives:

(a) To inform potential customers of a new product or service.
(b) To indicate new uses of an existing product.
(c) To remind customers of an existing product in order to maintain
loyalty against competing pressures.
(d) To give information about desirable qualities of a product.
(e) To stimulate enquiries.
(f) To give reasons why wholesalers and retailers should stock a
product.
(g) To provide technical information about a product.
(h) To build a corporate company image.
(i) To give information on price changes, special offers, etc.

Some of these objectives can be regarded as action objectives: for
example, stimulating enquiries and increasing wholesaler or retailer
stock levels. Others are designed to create a mental awareness and/or
favourable attitude towards an organisation, its products, services,
policies, etc. Although the exact contribution to profits of a particular
advertising campaign may be impossible to measure, since, for
example, a favourable attitude does not necessarily stimulate purchase, communication objectives should nevertheless be set and the
communication achievement measured.

6. The sales-task approach

When sales tasks can be closely defined – to increase product awareness among decision-makers in a given percentage of a market during
a predetermined number of months, or to expand dealer stock levels
by a certain percentage over a given time period – it is possible not
only to direct campaigns specifically towards the achievement of

stated tasks, but also to assess the contribution advertising is likely to make towards the accomplishment of those tasks.

7. Advertising and the sales process
It has been said that the sales process consists of six basic steps, namely:

(a) making contact;
(b) arousing interest;
(c) creating preference;
(d) making a specific proposal;
(e) closing the sale; and
(f) retaining business.

It is possible to assess the contribution which can most effectively be made by advertising towards the achievement of one or more stated objectives at each of the six stages. The justifiable cost of achieving the contribution by means of advertising can then be assessed in relation to total marketing expense. Consideration can also be given to the cost of alternative means of communication, such as employing extra salespersons. In this way a more realistic measurement of the economic level of advertising expenditure can frequently be made.

8. Factors influencing buying decisions
The sales-task approach to fixing and measuring the effectiveness of advertising expenditure is not always possible, and when it is used, it is clear that the probability assessments of the contribution that advertising can make towards the attainment of objectives must rely on judgement as well as on facts. Apart from the problems involved in estimating the external changing market forces affecting sales (e.g. competitive activity, economic climate, customer attitudes, trade attitudes, government controls), a marketing organisation has to take into account the wide range of forces it can bring to bear in order to influence buying decisions. A potential customer may be influenced to a greater or lesser extent by any combination of the following:

(a) Performance of the product.
(b) Aesthetic design features.
(c) Packaging.
(d) Service facilities available.
(e) Advertising.
(f) Promotions which give temporary special incentives to buy.
(g) Personal selling efforts.

(h) Channels of distribution – outlet images, location.
(i) Margins allowed to dealers along the distribution channels.
(j) Distinctiveness of the product (e.g. branding, quality).
(k) Price to the ultimate buyer.
(l) Credit facilities.
(m) Store display.
(n) Convenience of handling in transportation, warehousing or end use.
(o) The opinions of others.
(p) Ready availability of goods or services.

Advertising – expenditure and strategic considerations

9. Advertising expenditure

Advertising expenditures in relation to total marketing costs (costs of physical distribution and promotion as opposed to production costs) vary very widely. Sometimes they may be as high as 40 or 50 per cent; sometimes as low as ½ per cent. In general, the percentage of advertising expenditure is a greater proportion of marketing costs in the case of consumer than of industrial goods and services. Regularly repeatable consumer products with mass distribution objectives, such as soap and chocolates, are particularly heavily advertised. There has, however, in recent years been a noticeable increase in marketing activity in service industries, and banks, building societies, airlines, insurance companies, electricity, gas and transport undertakings have become substantial advertisers. In some cases, government advertising in the UK has been on a large scale: for example, in connection with privatisation and stock market issues as well as public information notices in connection with such matters as food risks and medical conditions such as AIDS.

With ever increasing expenditure, a purely subjective approach to budget decisions is unacceptable. Marketing research, costing studies and operations research can increasingly assist in determining the appropriate budget to be allocated to advertising and promotion elements of the marketing mix.

Some of the attacks made on high levels of advertising expenditure take no account of the cost frequently incurred by other elements of the marketing mix. In the 1966 Monopolies Commission investigations, evidence was provided to show, for example, that, while detergent advertising and promotions accounted for 16 per cent of marketing costs as opposed to 6 per cent in the case of ice-cream, trade margins for detergents were restricted to 19 per cent, while they were as high as 32 per cent for ice-cream. The strategies of individual companies marketing similar products may differ considerably. The optimal allocation of funds to the various elements of the marketing mix at various times and in various product-marketing contexts continues to present enormous problems. The most voluminous research activity is being devoted to the building of mathematical models. At the same time, there is a growing exploration of the use of pay-off matrices based on various expectations of risk, competitive response and marketing mix options. (*See Marketing Techniques for Analysis and Control* by P. Allen.)

10. Pull and push strategies
When greater reliance is placed on the personal selling efforts of a company's sales force or of distributor salespersons than on advertising, an organisation may be said to be pursuing a *push* strategy. A push strategy is typical of the marketing of industrial machinery, for example. Where it is not possible to bring strong direct selling pressure to bear on the end customer, a *pull* strategy may be used. Manufacturers selling grocery products, for example, usually feel that there is inadequate personal selling effort directed by wholesalers and retailers, and great attention is paid to advertising and promotion which 'pull' the product along the channels of the distribution and into the hands of the ultimate buyer. Push and pull strategies are therefore related to the types of product being marketed, and also to the external forces bearing on markets and company policies at particular time periods.

Advertising and the public interest

11. Criticism of advertising
The following criticisms of advertising are frequently made:

(a) Advertising is wasteful, particularly in times of scarce internal resources.
(b) In certain circumstances heavy advertising by a dominant supplier may restrict competition by preventing new entrants to its markets.

12. Economic justification of advertising
One answer to the first charge (**11 (a)**) is basically that successful

companies must be profit-minded and organise their expenditure in a way calculated to obtain the best return. From a company point of view, advertising may be justified when the increase in revenue is greater than the cost of advertising, provided that this is the most satisfactory – and profitable – of the various possible uses of scarce resources. It is interesting to note that, as far as Western European countries are concerned, advertising expenditure has generally increased in recent years, and notably in Germany, the UK and Spain. The main differences are in the availability and use of major media – newspapers, magazines and TV.

13. Advertising and the danger of monopoly

The second point of criticism (11 (b)) implies that by means of advertising a company can create such a consumer loyalty that it can build up the level of its sales to a scale where advertising becomes a very small proportion of individual unit costs; the resulting economies of scale will provide the opportunity for pricing flexibility along the distribution chain. This pricing flexibility, it is argued, could be used to prevent the entry of competition not having advantages of large-scale production and distribution. This goal achieved, prices could be raised to a level of unethical exploitation of the consumer. A monopoly, or oligopoly, operating contrary to the public interest could thus be created.

This second criticism is based on the premise that companies lack ethical standards, a premise which could be argued at length. The larger and more successful a company becomes, the more its policies are under public scrutiny and business ethics are no longer a matter of academic discussion; they are the vital concern of boardrooms.

Accepting a lack of ethical considerations, however, the criticism rests upon *the mistaken notion that products and markets do not change.* Examples of companies which have been able to enter fields dominated by more powerful organisations, by providing products having demonstrable technological or economic advantages, are not difficult to find. Wilkinson's inroads into the razor-blade market against the powerful Gillette; Lloyd's Automotives' breakthrough into the car-care field against giants such as Johnson's, Simoniz and Howard's; Damart's capture of 50 per cent of the rapidly expanding UK thermal underwear market; and more recently the successes of female retailing entrepreneurs in huge Body and Sock Shop advances – these are examples of outstanding success in the marketing of consumer goods where advertising is normally reckoned to be such a large factor in the marketing mix. It might be argued that new entrants in fields where products are more narrowly differentiated are more difficult to find (e.g. petrol, chocolate, cigarettes), but in the case of petrol there is also the important barrier of very high capital investment costs, while chocolate prices in the UK are lower than anywhere in Europe.

14. Public benefit from advertising

An argument in support of advertising and the public interest which is often ignored is that, by advertising, a supplier is identifying the company or the company's products. This attempt to create a distinction must be accompanied, if it is to be successful, by the setting of quality standards. Research has shown that, while it is sometimes possible to find that the price of certain strongly advertised products may be higher than those of a random selection of non-advertised goods, the variation in quality of the advertised products is much less than that of the non-advertised products. Advertising would therefore appear to reduce the risk to the consumer of buying low-quality products.

Control of advertising

Advertising is subject to regulations and restrictions imposed by voluntary bodies set up by the industry itself and by statutory controls. There follows brief review of voluntary bodies and codes of practice established and operated through advertising itself as well as some important statutes.

15. Advertising Standards Authority (ASA)

This body was established in 1962 and is independent of the adv
ing industry, although it is financed by the Advertising Assc
Members are appointed as individuals and not as represer
particular organisations or special group interests. Memb
sists of an independent chairman and twelve me'
connected with advertising and eight entirely indep'
tising interests. The committee, in addition to kee'
with the committee responsible for the British '
Practice, adjudicates on general advertising in'
putes among advertising bodies. It deals w
public and investigates action or inaction'
Code. The Advertising Standards Auth'
Health and Nutrition, Mail Order, Sa'

16. British Code of Advertising Practice
The Code covers such matters as:

(a) public decency;
(b) exploitation of superstition;
(c) appeals to fear;
(d) truthful presentation;
(e) protection of privacy and exploitation of the individual;
(f) advertisements directed to children;
(g) comparisons with other products, services and companies;
(h) testimonials, endorsements and related matters;
(i) pricing ambiguity;
(j) guarantees, warranties and related matters; and
(k) consumer and social responsibility.

Every month the Advertising Standards Authority issues a Case Report, free of charge. Many famous company names occur in connection with advertising complaints. Self-regulation is carried out very thoroughly. Recently, many 'green' claims in advertising have been most carefully investigated.

17. Other boards and codes

(a) *British Code of Sales Promotion Practice*. The fifth edition of this code was brought out in 1990 and covers a wide range of sales promotion issues, including consumer premium offers of various kinds, trade promotion activity, free offers, and charity linked promotions. This Code is administered by the ASA.

(b) *Direct Mail Services Standards Board*. This Board was set up in the early 1980s to monitor and bring about improvements in ethics and professionalism in direct mail advertising.

(c) *Public Relations and European Codes*. These include the Institute of Public Relations Code of Professional Conduct and the European Code of Conduct.

Students are advised to investigate in more detail regulating bodies and codes as appropriate to individual needs.

Statutory controls

e are many Acts of Parliament restricting or controlling particular ts of advertising. There is a growing amount of legislation aimed ecting the consumer. Students are advised to consult a spe- text for a detailed treatment.

lition, it should be remembered that much English law is in

the form not of statutes but of *common law*, which is base
decisions of various courts since the Middle Ages. Common
very pertinent to laws of contract and of tort – legal wrongs su
negligence and nuisance.

Legislation that students of advertising and marketing should in
vestigate further includes the following:

(a) Broadcasting Act 1990
Companies Acts 1985, 1989
Competition Act 1980
Consumer Credit Act 1974
Consumer Protection Act 1987
Control of Misleading Advertisement Regulations 1988
Copyright, Designs and Patents Act 1988
Data Protection Act 1986
Fair Trading Act 1973
Hire Purchase Act 1964
Lotteries and Amusements Act 1976
Race Relations Act 1976
Restrictive Trade Practices Act 1976, 1977 (The rules of EU competi-
tion policy are contained in Articles 85 and 86 of the Treaty of
Rome.)
Sale of Goods Act 1979
Sex Discrimination Act 1975
Trade Descriptions Acts 1968, 1972
Unsolicited Goods and Services Act 1971
Weights and Measures Act 1986
Wireless Telegraphy Act 1984.

(b) Bill of Sale, Broadcasting, Consumer Credit, Food and Drugs,
Games and Lotteries, Misrepresentation of Goods, Resale
Prices, and Unfair Contract Terms Acts.

(c) Food Labelling and Protection of Depositors Regulations.

19. Major new developments
The most recent developments concern further expansion of independent sound and television networks and stations, such as Radio
5, cable TV (e.g. Sky One, the Sports Channel) and satellite television,
now operating as B Sky B.

Readers concerned with legal aspects should refer to the Broadcasting Act 1990 and/or summaries or more detailed references.

20. Other codes and standards
Individual organisations within the advertising industry endeavour

standards by setting their own very specific
'ship or for accepting advertisements. Among

ing to the Standards of Practice', of the
Advertising.

vering the Acceptance of Advertisements for Dis-
by British Transport Advertising Ltd.

standards of Practice Regulating Contracts for Localised Advertising', drawn up by the Advertising Association.

(d) 'Form of Application by an Advertising Agency', for recognition by the Newspaper Publishers' Association Ltd, and the Newspaper Society.

(e) 'Standard Conditions of Insertion of Advertisements', in newspapers which are members of the Newspaper Publishers' Association.

(f) 'Standard Conditions of Trading', laid down by the British Poster Advertising Association and the London Poster Advertising Association Ltd.

(g) 'Advertising Film Standard Conditions', agreed by the Screen Advertising Association and the Institute of Practitioners in Advertising.

(h) 'Standard Conditions Observed by Producer House Members', of the British Direct Mail Advertising Association.

Advertising agencies

21. What are advertising agencies?
Advertising agencies are specialists in the planning, creating and placing of advertising. They function, therefore, between the advertiser and the media owners. An agency may assist in suggesting product features or sources of ideas. It may be asked to design trademarks and packaging, to advise on selling and promotional policy, and to plan advertising campaigns. It will have artists and copywriters for creative work or will arrange for this to be done. Agencies prepare advertising schedules of media to be used, and reserve and pay for the space or time (*see* 24 and 25 below).

22. Numbers and business transacted
There are over 700 advertising agencies in the UK with great variations in size of business transacted (billings), numbers employed and range of services offered. Almost all national advertisers (over 25,000)

use advertising agencies, even though they may have their own advertising departments. Many regional and local advertisers – and there are probably as many as 40,000 of these – use agencies to some extent. Some 70 per cent of all expenditure on advertising media passes through agency hands. More than half of the agencies are members of the Institute of Practitioners in Advertising, and these account for some 90 per cent of total agency business.

23. Institute of Practitioners in Advertising (IPA) conditions
Conditions of membership of the IPA by an agency are as follows:

(a) It is equipped to provide the kind and type of advertising service and marketing advice to which the advertiser is entitled.
(b) Its personnel includes Fellows and/or Members of the Institute.
(c) It promises to observe the Institute's standards of practice.
(d) It is free from any vested interest in advertising media or facilities.
(e) It will avoid advertisements of an undesirable, unethical or offensive nature.
(f) It will not canvass accounts of fellow members unless at the written invitation of the advertiser.
(g) It will not submit speculative advertisement designs or copy to any but its own clients except on payment of an adequate fee and only after an exhaustive study of a client's problems at first hand.

24. Agency recognition and the commission payment system: recent developments
Until 1979, 'recognised agencies' – that is, those 'recognised' by media owner groups: the Newspaper Publishers' Association, the Newspaper Society, the Periodical Publishers' Association, the Independent TV Association and the Association of Radio Contractors – were entitled to special standard commission rates on time and space purchases. This was, to most of the larger broad-service agencies, the system which enabled them to charge the media cost in full to clients, to offer them a wide range of other services and still to leave a satisfactory agency profit. The changing types and needs of clients, as well as media technological and creative developments, meant that clients' aspirations could often be met more effectively by independent narrow-line agency specialists operating directly with clients (if permitted to do so), or as part of a 'package' supplied by some larger agencies pleased to subcontract specialist campaign activities to specialist operators.

In 1979 the Office of Fair Trading's timely ruling under the terms of the Restrictive Trades Practices Act 1976 found the recognised agency/media commission scheme to be monopolistic. As a consequence, although the commission arrangement is still used by many large and medium-sized agencies, the door was opened to agencies to specialise in particular work for particular media, markets and communication developments (e.g. industrial and service markets, direct response/mail order operations, premium offers and incentives, sponsorship, etc.). Moreover, since 1981 media independents have become an important factor in the advertising world, can now be recognised by media owner bodies through their own Association of Media Independents, and have very considerably increased billing business annually.

25. Changes in client demand for agency services
It is significant that, while such regularly repeatable consumer goods suppliers as mentioned earlier (*see* p.101) remain at the top of lists of big advertising spenders, the following types of organisation have, in recent years, increased their advertising expenditure very considerably:

(a) Banks, building societies and insurance organisations (e.g. National Westminster Bank, Barclays Bank, Sun Alliance, Halifax Building Society, Prudential).
(b) Government departments (e.g. Health, Social Security, Defence).
(c) Direct selling/response organisations (e.g. Great Universal Catalogue, Book Club Associates, Franklin Mint).
(d) Privatised organisations (e.g. British Telecom, Electricity Association, British Gas).

There has also been, as previously indicated, a very considerable increase in such specialised areas as sponsorship.

26. Media and technological changes

(a) *The press*. The introduction of Web offset-litho and computerised systems has led to the introduction of one new national newspaper (the *Independent*), the relocation of printing plants, and intensive circulation competition. Other developments include the growing use of colour and an increase in 'free' newspapers.
(b) *Radio and television*. The Broadcasting Act 1990 set in train a whole host of changes in commercial radio and television. In addition to these changes, cable and satellite TV have also been introduced. Advertising students have been advised (p. 111) to consult specialist

journals and texts as well as the Broadcasting Act. One result will almost certainly be to reduce the opportunities to communicate with mass audiences, but to increase opportunities to pinpoint smaller potential audiences at a lower overall cost. The need for access to more specialised advertising agency staff (e.g. media buyers, planners, visualisers, layout specialists, typographers) becomes obvious. There will be an increasing tendency for creative personnel to be attracted by sheer novelty and technical advances, and the need for audience research and input–output measurement will be even greater. The trend towards more rigorous financial discipline in larger agencies is certain to continue as will the opportunity for smaller specialised organisations to meet more specialised cost-effective demands.

27. Full-service agency personnel
The agency link person is the *account executive* who works with the brand manager or appropriate company advertising executive. The account executive calls upon agency or outside experts to organise the campaign in line with the advertiser's objectives. The agency, therefore, employs or engages the temporary services of specialists in copywriting, creative art, typography, printing, and television and film production, as required. It has staff who specialise in, advise on and plan the use of various media, in addition to those who actually buy space or time. Larger agencies have ancillary services such as marketing research departments which may undertake tasks such as testing advertising impact or providing information necessary for campaign strategy. The large agency with high billings can afford to carry specialist staff whom even the largest advertiser would find difficult to justify economically, and the constant employment of that staff – often on related products in similar markets – can provide a wealth of experience on which to draw. Conversely, it could be argued that frequently repeated narrow experience can lead to creative sterility.

Agency organisations differ enormously and so do the needs of advertisers. An advertiser with a large marketing department of its own is unlikely to require the kind of strategic advice which is required by an advertiser with a small marketing staff.

28. Advertising organisations
The Advertising Association is sometimes described as the 'umbrella' organisation of the advertising industry and has been reconstructed as a federation of the following advertising bodies covering advertisers, media and agencies:

British Direct Mail Advertising Association (BDMAA)
British Printing Industries Federation (BPIF)
Direct Mail Producers Association (DMPA)
Graphic Reproduction Federation (GRF)
Incorporated Advertising Managers' Association (IAMA)
Institute of Practitioners in Advertising (IPA)
Incorporated Society of British Advertisers (ISBA)
Independent Television Companies Association (ITCA)
Newspaper Publishers' Association Ltd (NPA)
Newspaper Society (NS)
Outdoor Advertising Council (OAC)
Proprietary Association of Great Britain (PAGB)
Periodical Publishers Association (PPA)
Screen Advertising Association (SAA)

The establishment of the Communication Advertising and Marketing Education Foundation (CAM) was of considerable significance. The Foundation, sponsored by all sections of the advertising business, has, in association with adult colleges in the public sector and correspondence schools, established a diploma course and examination of a high standard which is making an important contribution to the advertising industry's recruitment and training programme.

29. Joint industry research and published data
In the UK a great deal of research is carried out by and for joint industry bodies on such key information areas as readership, circulation and viewing. Not only is this information important for the advertising industry in policy making, action planning, reviews, and marketing, but it is also important for their customers and potential customers, as well as for advertising industry public relations.

The following is a list of important joint industry research groups:

(a) *Joint Committee for National Readership Surveys.* Readership data are issued twice per year covering national newspapers and magazines as well as some specialist publications. The results are based on analysis of some 30,000 interviews based on A, B, C1, C2, D and E social grades – a demographic system set up initially for 'JICNARS Surveys'.

(b) *Joint Industry Committee for Poster Audience Research.* There is now a central data bank with information regularly updated and based on 175 target audience groups. Additional data are available on a geographical basis.

(c) *Joint Industry Committee for Radio Audience Research.* Samples of listeners complete diaries at thirty-minute intervals over seven days. The information gathered forms the basis of quarterly reports, and an annual report on audiences is also issued.

(d) *Joint Industry Committee for Cable Audience Research.* Since 1984, quarterly data and an annual research report have been issued.

Other research data sources

(a) *Audit Bureau of Circulations.* This is one of the oldest data sources of actual newspaper and magazine circulations. Together with British Rate and Data, and using information supplied by publishers' accountants, produces 'audited' net sales data. This audit covers 3,000 publications and is much used in the buying and selling of space.

(b) *Verified free distribution.* This is a comparatively recent source of circulation data. It covers the increasing number of newspapers, newsheets and magazines distributed free of charge. The information is collated and processed by an offshoot of the Audit Bureau of Circulations, Media Expenditure Analysis Ltd. This organisation covers media expenditure on TV and in the press and issues a *Quarterly Digest.* An enormous amount of comparative advertising data is available from this source, including regular lists of new advertisers, new brands, etc. which are published in *Marketing* each week.

Progress test 6

1. Give examples of advertising campaign objectives.

2. What is meant by the 'sales-task-approach' to advertising?

3. What is the difference between 'pull' and 'push' strategies?

4. Is advertising against the public interest?

5. What are the main provisions of the British Code of Advertising Practice?

6. What kinds of control over TV and broadcasting advertising standards are exercised in the UK?

7. What are advertising agencies and how are they paid?

Assignments

1. If possible, arrange to carry out interviews with the management of a variety of businesses in your area to find out the following:

(a) Are advertising agencies used and for what purposes?
(b) Is advertising ever tested in advance? (Give an example if possible.)
(c) Obtain examples of goals of particular advertising campaigns.
(d) How is success measured?
(e) How are target audiences described, if at all?
(f) How are advertising budgets fixed?

The above tasks may be allocated to small groups, each of which should prepare a written report. A group member should be ready to give a five-minute talk on the work carried out and be able to answer questions.

2. Using the questions (a) to (f) above as guidelines, arrange for students, individually or in pairs, to carry out interviews with the following:
(i)   the administrative manager of a local 'trust' hospital;
(ii) the administrative manager of a private hospital or nursing home;
(iii) the headmaster of a public school or a grant-maintained school.

Follow up the interviews with group discussions on the findings.

Advertising and promotion: campaign planning and evaluation

Basic steps in campaign planning

1. The six basic steps

There are six really basic steps in the campaign planning process:

(a) Objective – related to target market(s) (*see* 6:5).
(b) Message (copy and design).
(c) Media – selection and scheduling (including research and frequency).
(d) Marketing co-ordination.
(e) Budget.
(f) Evaluation – timing and methods.

These are outlined in 2–6 below.

2. The objective(s) of campaigns

The objective(s) of campaigns should be in line with the requirements of organisation management and, in turn, be part of the marketing plan. Those responsible for external communications – advertising, publicity, public relations, etc. – should contribute to the overall planning process and be responsible for organising and evaluating the necessary specialist activities.

3. The message (copy and design)

Advertisements consist of verbal symbols, illustrations, colour, movement, sound, etc. Both verbal and non-verbal symbols have denotative (dictionary or literal) and connotative (emotionally associated) communication potential. It is the task of the creative personnel in advertising to achieve the mix most likely to accomplish the purpose of the advertisement. One of the big challenges of the future is to establish an appropriate balance between science and art:

it is not a question of science versus art. Creativity and entrepreneurial flair will always be important in marketing. First, the advertiser has to decide who the target audience is and what message to communicate. Copy and design follow. The success rate which has often been achieved in the past almost entirely by flair and chance may be substantially increased in the future as a result of behavioural research into the communication process together with the realistic use of management science in media planning: for example, to determine 'reach' (i.e. of target groups) and 'frequency' of advertising at various cost levels.

Copy clearly depends on choice of media, and this and the next step will often be considered together. An early examination of copy is necessary, since the whole process of advertising is based on the ability to communicate a message to an audience, who should, as a result, react favourably to the product or service. In general, the most effective copy is that which concentrates on a limited selling appeal, and frequent repetition of a single appeal is a feature of many very successful campaigns. Certainly many campaigns are spoiled by the attempt to cover too many selling points in one advertisement. Campaigns may, of course, be planned to cover a number of single objectives over a given time, in line with a multiple communications strategy: to inform potential users of the company's technical achievements; to inform intermediaries in channels of distribution of a new product: and to inform users of technical or advisory services offered with a new product or service.

Advertising can be pre-tested to determine whether the intended message is being communicated, and comparisons of the effectiveness of a number of advertisements can also be made. Samples of prospective viewers or readers are exposed to advertisements and certain reactions are measured. Sometimes, tests are carried out on specially constituted panels. The tests may be conducted on the basis of aided or unaided recall of advertisements to which the panel or sample member has been exposed. It should be noted that these tests relate to the effectiveness of the communication as such and do not give a measure of sales results (*see* **9–11** below).

4. Selection and scheduling of appropriate media

Problems of media selection include the following:

(a) The extent of coverage required to reach potential buyers and the effective cost of reaching them (*see* **3** above).

(b) The comparative communication effectiveness of various media:

for example, the compatibility of the advertising or editorial material (*see* 11: **16**) with media audiences. An advertisement designed for the popular press might be totally unsuitable in a learned journal.

(c) The administrative, organisational and operating requirements of the media: for example, the operating frequency of publication and the length of lead time required for placing advertisements.

(d) Consideration of the ways in which competitors allocate expenditure to various media.

(e) The determination of advertising frequency – 'opportunities to view'.

(f) The size, positioning and/or timing of advertisements.

5. Co-ordination of advertising with the total promotional plan
Among co-ordination problems would be those of assigning tasks and expenditure to point-of-sale display, personal selling efforts, dealer-support programmes, handling and follow-up of enquiries, special promotional activity such as premium offers, contests, etc.

6. Determining and controlling the advertising budget
The size of the budget will, in practice, very largely determine the selection of media, but ideally budgets should be determined by companies after due consideration of the cost of achieving communication objectives.

Evaluation and research

7. Advertising contribution and research
Basically management need to know what contribution advertising makes to sales and profits. The complexity of the marketing mix makes precise evaluation extremely difficult. The sales-task method, which is based on a value judgement of the likely contribution of advertising (*see* 6: **6,7**), is gaining ground, but most attempts at evaluation are investigations into specific aspects of advertising in isolation.

8. Target audiences and media data
An advertisement has to reach a specified target audience if it is to have any chance of success at all, but no single media audience is likely to correspond exactly to the advertiser's target market.

Information on media and audience characteristics is readily available to advertisers, and the types of data may be classified as follows:

(a) Data on circulation or viewing (e.g. the circulation of newspapers and magazines, the number of people passing poster sites, the number of television sets switched on to commercial stations at given times of the day).

(b) Data on total audiences (e.g. information on the number of readers of a single copy of a newspaper or viewers of a television programme).

(c) Data gained from specific studies carried out by media owners, on, for example, incomes, spending patterns, buying habits and product usage of readers or viewers (*see* 3:**14**).

(d) Data on audience characteristics (e.g. analysis of readership by social, geographical or economic groupings).

1991 JICNARS social gradings were distributed as follows:

Group	All adults 15 +	Men	Women
A	2.7	2.9	2.5
B	15.1	16.0	14.2
C1	23.9	22.7	25.0
C2	27.8	30.6	25.3
D	21	21	17.3
E	12.7	9.4	15.7

Social grades used by JICNARS and agreed with Research Services Ltd are defined as follows:

	Social status	*Occupation*
A	Upper middle class	Higher managerial, administrative or professional.
B	Middle class	Intermediate managerial, administrative or professional.
C1	Lower middle class	Supervisory or clerical and junior managerial, administrative or professional.
C2	Skilled working class	Skilled manual workers.
D	Working class	Semi- and unskilled manual workers.
E	Those at lowest level of subsistence	State pensioners or widows (no other earner): casual or lowest-grade workers.

Even if the objective were simply to reach on one occasion a target audience defined in basic demographic terms (now accepted as a crude method of defining a target market), there would be the problem of selecting an effective economic media mix, but there are also other considerations, such as inevitable duplication and wastage factors (*see* **15**).

Attention must be drawn to the large amount of secondary data now available in addition to media ownership group statistics and reports. For example:

(a) *MEAL (Media Expenditure Analysis Ltd)*. Data on offer includes a *Quarterly Digest* based on 150,000 advertisements (press and TV) and weekly lists of and information on new advertisers, new and modified products, etc. published in *Marketing*.

(b) *TABS LTD Tracking*. This is an independent marketing research organisation offering weekly and quarterly data on the cost effectiveness of advertising by specially developed 'tracking' and scaling methods aimed at producing information on the strength of audience/customer reaction to advertising campaigns.

(c) *CACI 'Acorn Profile of Great Britain'*. The Acorn system involves a proprietary demographic model of Great Britain using 38 neighbourhood 'types' drawn from government census data refined to 11 'subgroups'.

(d) *Research Services Ltd and 'Sagacity Life Cycle Groupings'*. The basis of these groupings rests on the idea that individual aspirations and behaviour differ according to stages in personal life cycles (four stages), incomes and occupational groupings.

9. Media research
This is aimed mainly at:

(a) analysis of the actual size of viewing and listening audiences or readership of print media at particular times: and
(b) analysis of attitudes towards advertising messages.

Probability samples may be used and data may be collected by electronic devices, such as the television measurement system (*see* **3:12** (d) above). A number of private media surveys, such as the target Group Index for the British Market Research Bureau, provide, on a subscription basis, a mass of media information based on user purchasing, viewing habits, etc. related to specific markets (e.g. holiday and travel, financial services, toiletries and cosmetics). Most campaign research is, however, undertaken at periods of time after advertisements have been seen. Postal questionnaires and personal interviewing are employed, and selected respondents are sometimes asked to maintain diaries. Researchers may use 'aided recall' techniques which imply that memory is stimulated in some way: for example, by showing a list of programmes and inviting identification of those seen or heard. None of this research gives a measurement of the *sales effectiveness* of advertising.

10. Copy research

This is aimed at assessing the differences in impact of various sizes, themes, layouts, visuals, colours, etc. Research may be carried out both before and after the appearances of an advertisement. The tests used include the following:

(a) *Advertisement mock-ups*, shown to consumer juries who are asked to indicate preference, usually by ranking scales or by paired comparisons. The latter method involves a statistical calculation of the number of pairs possible from a given number of trial advertisements. (Paired comparisons are also frequently used for testing reaction to new products.)

(b) *Eye movement analysis*, using cameras to trace not only the direction of eye movement, but also the length of time spent on particular parts of an advertisement.

(c) *Readability studies*, aimed at assessing communication ease and effectiveness. These studies may include research into the understanding and emotional impact of words by people of different standards of education and from different cultural backgrounds, as well as studies of word and sentence length, etc.

(d) The *use of electronic equipment* to record favourable and unfavourable responses to advertisements.

(e) The *Schwerin test*, a method of assessing the effectiveness of advertisements in influencing consumers to buy the product. In a theatre situation an invited audience is exposed to TV or press advertisements. Before and after exposure, the audience is asked to place a number of brands in the order in which they would most like to win them as a prize in a lottery. Changes or shifts in preference are then assumed to measure the effect of the advertisement on the audience.

(f) *Recognition and recall tests*, widely carried out by personal interview (usually on the basis of a standard questionnaire). These vary mainly in the extent and method of memory stimulation.

(g) *Analysis of enquiries received* from advertisements specifically designed to elicit requests for further information. In mail-order selling and where salespersons can follow up enquiries, it is possible to establish an order conversion rate. The conversion rate may, however, depend very largely on marketing factors such as price or special product features.

11. Image research

An increasing number of studies are being made to discover what buyers – whether industrial, wholesale, retail or domestic – think about products, services and companies. Well-planned attitude studies may lead to changes in the total marketing strategy, and often to redirected emphasis towards company or product image building. There is a growing use of psychologists to undertake this type of research by individual or group discussion methods.

12. Test markets (*see* 4: **18, 19**)

The effectiveness of particular campaigns is frequently judged by setting up control and test areas so that, against other known criteria, differences in sales results may be observed. The problems of establishing controls and measuring a range of possibilities, within time constraints imposed by competitive reaction, are obviously very great. The decision to buy is, however, conditioned by price, product design and/or service benefits, personal selling efforts, advertising, promotions, user recommendations, availability, display and packaging – marketing forces within the control of the seller – as well as by forces outside the seller's control. A buyer must become aware of the existence of a product or service, understand its benefits, become convinced of the desirability of those benefits and take buying action. Ranged against the buying decision are such forces as competition, sales resistance, memory lapse and alternative uses of available resources. This complex of variables makes the establishment of research controls to measure the impact of advertising exceedingly difficult, and progress during the next decade will depend on four main developments:

(a) Clear definition of advertising goals as part of the total communications and marketing goals (*see* 6: **4**).
(b) More accurate definition of target audiences.
(c) Greater use of behavioural science concepts (*see* 3: **34**).
(d) The application of multivariate statistical techniques, such as factor analysis, with faster, more complex experimental analysis made possible by the use of computers. Multivariate techniques are necessary to examine relationships between sets of variables, such as attitudes on first purchase and second purchase, and advertising copy and frequency.

Media and costs

13. Circulation, viewing figures and media cost

The availability, cost and coverage of media differ tremendously in various parts of the world. In general, however, costs of space and time are linked to circulation or viewing figures.

Continuous monitoring of change is necessary. For example, during the past decade peak-time viewing ratings on television have declined steadily, and adult audience groups' peak viewing ratings have fallen even more sharply. This is in spite of the fact that considerably more commercial transmission time is available. In addition, loyalty to any one programme is progressively declining. This is in contrast to the steady high readership of Sunday newspapers, where there has been quite severe circulation competition.

During this period people tended to live longer, to leave home earlier, to live in smaller household units (one-quarter of households are single-person households; only just over one-third have dependent children). New leisure activities boomed, the working week became shorter and holidays longer, and more people had cars, travelled and ate out for pleasure. The government was announcing its privatisation plans and organising share issues. The introduction, extension and replacement of computer systems was advancing apace, while financial and other service organisations were diversifying and promoting and selling more aggressively. More leisure time led to more interest in tourism and leisure activities. Car markets were more competitive and promotion activities more aggressive.

During the period 1985 to 1990, taking 1985 as the base year at 100, by 1990 the index of retail prices stood at 133 and advertising costs at 137. Advertising at levels above these rates could be said to indicate increased advertising spending. The following table shows selected categories in which there was increased advertising spending in absolute terms:

Activity categories	1985	1990
Entertainment	100	339
Charity and educational	100	252
Publishing	100	228
Drink	100	193
Pharmaceutical	100	190
Institutional and industrial	100	179
Cars	100	175
Financial	100	170

Office equipment	100	168
Government	100	164
Wearing apparel	100	158
Retail and mail order	100	154
Toiletries and cosmetics	100	154
Leisure equipment	100	147
Holidays, leisure and transport	100	146

Data sources: *MEAL*; Advertising Association; Central Statistical Office; *Economic Trends*.

The table shows very considerable turbulence in marketing, and particularly in advertising expenditure. It should be noted that it does not show levels of advertising in absolute terms, but rather the most significant percentage increases. Neither does it show whether or to what extent advertising was at appropriate levels, in appropriate media or at appropriate times; nor, indeed, to what extent it was the cause of change or a reaction to change.

Advertising agencies have changed and a highly competitive field has become more so. Some programme contractors are providing in-house low-cost production, services or consultancy. More video tape is being used, and also more 165 mm film. Media-buying shops have been set up to concentrate on creativity and media contractors are now taking their work through specialised media-buying agencies. Computerised media scheduling is commonplace.

14. Some factors in assessing 'effective cost'
Many other factors enter into the calculation of the 'effective cost' of media.

(a) Circulation and viewing figures vary geographically, as do buying patterns. Television, for instance, is transmitted on a regional basis. It is therefore possible to direct advertising to specific geographical areas and this situation is frequently used to provide test market information. There is, however, an overlap situation: viewers can frequently receive more than one commercial programme.
(b) Television has a greater attention-pulling potential, especially if demonstration is needed, but social class coverage can be achieved on a more selective basis by use of press media.
(c) A single newspaper advertisement may be seen more than once by the same person. Sunday and weekly papers in particular are retained longer and provide additional opportunities to view. Some trade papers are circulated among several executives.

(d) It has been estimated that some 80 per cent of consumer purchases are influenced by women. Regional press has an average housewife readership of some 83 per cent. Sixteen million women over the age of sixteen read magazines. There is also some evidence that women's magazine readers are younger, more prosperous, more beauty and fashion conscious and more progressive than non-readers. The extensive use of colour in these magazines is another advantage, and is now also a feature of newspapers.

Two of the nineteen weekly women's magazines – *Woman's Own* and *Bella* – have readerships of over 3½ million; there are two fortnightly magazines, and over thirty monthly and ten bi-monthly publications. The monthlies have readerships ranging from just over one million to two million (*Prima*). It should be remembered that readership far exceeds circulation.

Many consumer magazines and journals are aimed at specific interest/sex/age groups, e.g. *Ideal Home, Homes and Gardens, Mother and Baby, Weight-Watchers, Clothes Show Magazine, Angling Times, Practical Boat Owner, Camping and Caravanning, The Economist, Practical Householder, Gramophone, Melody Maker, Computer and Video Games, Shoot, Fiesta* and *Care Bears*.

There are many business, professional and trade journals. Some of these are journals circulated to business and professional organisation membership. Others are on general sale. The following are merely examples of the wide range of occupational interest magazines: *Publican, Motor Transport, Professional Photographer, Autotrader, The Grocer, Furnishing, Investors Chronicle and Stock Exchange Gazette, Management Today, Marketing, Accountancy, Computing, Electronic Times, British Farmer, British Medical Journal* – well over 100 in all.

(e) Cinema audiences are divided roughly evenly between male and female. There is, however, a profound difference in terms of the age profile. Audience composition is approximately 20 per cent over 35 years old and 80 per cent under 35, of whom the majority are under 24 years of age.

Size and position of press advertisements, length, timing and programme proximity of television commercials, intensity of readership or viewership, editorial status and credibility, frequency of insertion or transmission and spread of expenditure among viewer media – these are all important variables to be considered in calculating advertising effectiveness in relation to cost.

Furthermore, it should be remembered that decisions to buy a product or service are almost always the result of formal and informal social interaction with a wide range of people. (This is particularly true of industrial and many service markets.) In addition, buying attitudes and spending patterns of individuals in similar socioeconomic groups vary.

The 'lag' or 'carry-over' effect of advertising is also of no little importance. Attitudes towards companies, products and organisations are often the result of a cumulative build-up of impressions over time.

Media selection and mathematical models

15. Difficulties in building advertising models
Major difficulties in model building are as follows:

(a) *Delayed sales impact.* Advertising may often be regarded as a form of capital budgeting.

(b) *Importance of quality as opposed to quantity.* Creativity in content and in presentation is a highly significant feature of many of the most successful campaigns. The cost, however, of many television advertisements campaigns in the 1990s often reveals extravagant use of technical media/camera developments, and it cannot be stressed too much that achievement of clear communication and marketing objectives within realistic budgets must come before creative 'production' novelty.

(c) *Isolating advertising from other components of the marketing mix.* A study of a list of winners of advertising awards to celebrate *Campaign* magazine's twenty-five years in 1993 reveals that the judgement of the advertising industry rests on very different criteria from that of many of the directors and senior management of the organisations promoted by several award winners.

16. Media selection models
During the past ten years or so there has been a great deal of activity – notably in the advertising industry and in academic institutions – to construct advertising models. An early model, Computer Assessment of Media (CAM) developed by London Press Exchange and constantly updated, is based on simulation. The model seeks to describe how a target audience is affected by a particular campaign and thus to determine how an advertising budget should be allocated among the various media available. The probability of a person receiving an impression (PRI) is calculated and modified by a selectivity weighting which takes into account the impact of times, days or editorial prestige.

Further modifications in accordance with, for example, the use of colour or special creative impact are made. The distribution of individual impressions can be used to arrive at a value-per-pound index.

Other models based on optimising methods, such as linear programming, are being used to arrive at media selection yielding maximum exposure subject to given constraints: for example, a set advertising budget, maximum use of certain media, and a minimum target audience exposure rate. Optimising is the process of allocating scarce resources in such a way that an objective is reached most effectively. Linear programming is a mathematical technique which can be used if the relationship between the variable resources can be expressed by linear equation. The computerised model is only an aid to judgement combined with the great advantages of speed.

Among the problems are the following:

(a) Omission of or judgement quantification of qualitative factors.

(b) Lack of precise knowledge of the effect of the timing and frequency pattern of advertisements.

(c) Lack of precise knowledge of the effect of the overlapping of readership among various media.

(d) Changes in the interest value of editorial or programme material – a very marked problem in television advertising. An advertisement appearing alongside a press report of an international soccer match or immediately after the presentation of a sporting event on television would have a different effect from one appearing beside an article or after a programme with an essentially feminine appeal.

(e) Models which seek to determine optimal solutions cannot handle as many variables as simulation. For example, various constraints which do not apply in practice have to be built into the model (e.g. an inside front cover of a magazine may have an utterly different effect from one of the inside pages; most magazines do not sell specific inside pages). A linear programming model, therefore, taking into account any inside page as a single variable, will lack sensitivity in relation to reality.

Descriptive conceptual and logical flow models, such as decision trees setting out the decision-making complex, flow, timings and responsibilities, may often have a worth exceeding that of sophisticated complex models which are often costly to develop, omit very important factors (e.g. behavioural) and require regular updating.

Advertising budgets

17. Methods of determining advertising budgets

Some of the most common methods of determining advertising budgets are as follows.

(a) *As a percentage of sales.* 'Sales' may relate to overall turnover, or to revenue received for individual products or groups of products. Some companies work on current sales figures; others on projected sales.

(b) *On the basis of competitive advertising expenditure.* While competitive advertising must be considered, no two companies are pursuing identical objectives from an identical base line of resources, market standing or other factors. Determination of budgets on the basis of, say, an identical percentage of gross sales revenue to that of competition is completely unrealistic.

(c) Both as a percentage of sales and in relation to competitive advertising expenditure.

(d) *As the amount remaining after deduction of other expense plus a predetermined return on capital.* This method appears to be based on the premise that it is impossible to determine the optimum level of advertising, but that it is right to advertise success to almost any level. Major objections lie in:

(*i*) the short-term emphasis which may lead to problems in longer-term advertising investment needs; and

(*ii*) the lack of consideration of alternative investment opportunities.

(e) *As a cost of achieving a given objective.* This is the most logical approach, but the difficulties of setting objectives and measuring their attainment have been previously discussed (*see* 6:5–7). This method may serve to determine the minimum and maximum limits, but there will usually be a considerable margin between these two. Objectives have also to be taken not only in relation to cost, but in relation to their contribution to profits.

Many companies apply information which has been developed through budgetary control systems, indicating profitability of markets, types of customer products, etc. Problems remain in that a great deal of marketing expense is arbitrarily allocated and there is great need for improvement of cost accounting practice applied to marketing.

If the 'objective' approach is used, however, the cost will be considered against other budgetary considerations, such as the total budget for promotion, for marketing and for the business as a whole.

If budgets have to be reduced, it is vital to reconsider the advertising objectives.

Market share objectives in relation to product-profit life cycles are certainly not new to companies involved in consumer goods markets. It is not uncommon to have relatively high advertising budgets in the introductory product-market phase in order to gain high distribution and/or market penetration. The subsequent level and role of advertising is then adjusted in line with market dynamics.

18. Market dynamics and advertising models

No model has yet been developed which is of practical value in predicting share changes attributable to advertising expenditure in complex dynamic situations. Of a number attempted, *Adbudg* and variations of it are among the most widely used. This model initially combines historical data and managerial judgement in seeking to establish four points of a potential demand curve associated with various advertising budget levels (e.g. the current level, a 50 per cent increase, a minimum, a maximum). Carry-over effects are also taken into the reckoning, and the model has been applied with some success – particularly in those mature market situations where there is essentially an oligarchic brand-share battle (e.g. razor blades).

Empirical evidence suggests that an advertising budget must be competitive not only to gain but to maintain brand leadership. Only some 5 per cent of brand leaders, in 30 product classes researched recently, had held their shares consistently on an advertising budget which, in relation to total product advertising, was proportionately lower than their sales revenue in relation to total product class sales.

Brand share *per se* is no justification for any level of advertising expenditure. Attempts to hold brand shares in a declining market can lead to declining profitability because of disproportionate advertising levels, price reductions, additional service packages, etc.

Advertising is one of many variables affecting attitudes and/or sales. Many attempts to measure effect have foundered, as we have seen, because the objectives of advertising are not sufficiently specific, and/or because target audiences have not been defined adequately for meaningful analysis. One factor which has until recently been ignored is variation due to environment. Empirical validation of expenditure has generally been based on two marketing areas at most. Ronald Fisher, an Englishman, expounded the principle of replication as far back as 1925, in a book on experimental design. In simple terms, when a variable is applied to a number of environments in orderly repetition, a normal variation stemming from the environment is measurable and can be removed by statistical routines described as the analysis of variance. This principle has, since the 1970s, been used by a limited number of advertising practitioners as well as academic researchers to assess the effects of given levels of advertising in several marketing areas, with very promising results.

One other development is worthy of mention – goal programming linked with sensitivity analysis. Linear programming methods, by definition, deal with unidimensional coverage. The goals of decision-makers are usually multiple and sometimes in conflict. Goal programming involves setting out objectives according to their priorities, together with decision variables such as level of direct mailings and level of sales force incentives, and assumptions such as the cost of borrowed capital and the level of fixed costs. The resultant simulation model is extremely flexible and allows for simulations with many variations of priorities and constraints in terms of objective outcomes.

Branding

19. Brand identity
A feature of advertising policy – particularly in the case of consumer goods – is to establish a brand identity. A brand identity may begin with a name (e.g. 'Kleenex', 'Tide'), but extends to other visual features such as typography, colour, package, design and slogans – features which should assist in creating, stimulating and maintaining demand. It is clear that branding could have a contrary effect if either the branded product were unacceptable to the consumer or the branding image were psychologically or sociologically ill-conceived.

20. Reasons for branding individual products
Among arguments in favour of branding are the following:

(a) Memory recall is facilitated. This could lead to more rapid initial buying action or greater frequency of buying and, hence, deeper loyalty.
(b) Advertising can be directed more effectively and linked with other communications programmes.
(c) Branding leads to the more ready acceptance of a product by wholesalers and retailers.
(d) Self-selection is facilitated – a very important consideration in self-service stores.

(e) Display space is more easily obtained and special promotions are more practicable.

(f) The importance of price differentials may be diminished.

(g) Brand loyalty may give a manufacturer greater control over marketing strategy and channels of distribution.

(h) Other products may be introduced more readily. (The failure of a brand may, of course, lead to undue resistance to other products.)

(i) The amount of personal persuasive selling effort may be reduced.

(j) Branding makes market segmentation easier. Different brands of similar products may be developed to meet specific categories of user.

The relevance of branding does not apply equally to all products. The cost of brand advertising and promotion may be prohibitive. Again, the success of branding may depend both on the nature of the product and on the behaviour characteristics of customers. Branding, for example, demands the ability to control quality; it is also likely to be more successful where product attributes are difficult to evaluate objectively. To take extremes, it is obviously easier to brand whisky than iron ore.

21. Branding, brand names and trademarks

'Branding' is actually a very general term covering brand names, designs, trademarks, symbols, etc., which may be used to distinguish one organisation's goods or services from another. 'Brand name' refers strictly to letters, words or groups of words which can be spoken. 'Trademark', however, is a legal term covering words and symbols which can be registered and protected. A legally protected mark can be a very valuable asset and prevent the spread of a market leader's brand name to generic application, covering a class of products or services – as has happened, for example, with 'aspirin' and 'cellophane'. International aspects of trademark registration require special study.

22. Corporate images: disadvantages

Instead of branding individual products, companies sometimes create product-family images or a corporate company image associated with all products. The potential cost saving of the approach is clear, but certain problems arise. These include the following:

(a) Difficulties of marketing different quality grades.

(b) Difficulties of marketing a range of products which it may be undesirable to relate closely.

(c) The risk of damage to existing lines by the introduction of unsuccessful products.

(d) The difficulties of devising sufficiently clear advertising and communications objectives and assigning expenditure. Companies which pursue an individual brand policy normally have brand managers who are concerned with the marketing and profitability of particular brands, and responsibility accounting methods can therefore be employed.

23. Corporate images: advantages

More and more organisations are beginning to realise the advantages of projecting appropriate corporate images. Organisations which have developed new visual corporate identities in recent years include ICI, Shell, British Rail, the National Westminster Bank, British Steel, Air India, Lufthansa and Unilever. The visible manifestations of a corporate image programme can be very widespread. The letters, symbols, logos and other design elements associated with it in the case of Shell, for example, appear on:

– media advertising
– promotional material
– road tankers
– sea-going tankers
– petrol pumps
– letter-headings
– sales aids
– buildings
– packaging
– uniforms.

There are, in fact, many reasons for developing appropriate visual corporate identities and projecting appropriate images. These include the following:

(a) The increasing importance of public relations – establishing the right relationships with governments, opinion-influencing pressure groups, and local communities in the vicinity of offices, factories and distribution centres.

(b) The need to attract and retain investment.

(c) The need to attract labour of the right kind in the right numbers.

(d) The growing realisation of the importance of good relationships with suppliers and institutions involved in forward distribution processes – wholesalers, agents and distributors.

(e) The need to foster a feeling of belonging within an organisation; this is particularly in evidence in large, widely spread groups and/or merged or restructured units.

(f) The realisation of the cumulative impact of multiple repetition.

(g) The need for broad-line companies set on growth strategies in financial services, construction, catering and entertainment to make increasing use of promotion and to take the corporate route.

(h) The growing internationalism of companies and customers.

> NOTE: In the marketing of many services and in organisational purchasing situations, selling and specialised technical information and discussion can be directed more effectively towards very specific client/customer problem areas peculiar to a particular person and/or organisation, especially if the marketing organisation is already well known and, in general, held in high regard. It is very important to recognise that advertising and sales should be complementary.

24. Branding, corporate images, communication and change

Communication involves senders, transmitters and receivers. It is perfectly obvious that the sender's ideas must be received, understood and accepted if the sender's objective is to be accomplished. Some of the important barriers to successful communication are as follows:

(a) The sender's message may not be received at all. Ask yourself what press advertisements you have seen today and what you can remember about them. Check on the number which actually appear in the papers you read.

(b) The sender's ideas have to be 'encoded' in copy and design elements which may not, in fact, reflect his or her true intention.

(c) The receiver may not understand the words or symbols used. Technical details of a computer, for example, may not be understood by an accountant who is involved in authorising purchase.

(d) The medium used may have low credibility. A newspaper may, for example, be read for amusement, but tend to have a disparaging effect on certain products or services advertised in it.

(e) The receiver is not just a blank screen waiting to reproduce accurately the message beamed on to it. The way in which he or she interprets a message will depend on many factors, such as the strength and nature of the receiver's needs and motivations, his or her past buying experience, education, ethnic and cultural background, and the influence of others to whom the receiver looks for value standards (reference-group influence).

A situation could arise in which one person is considering the personal purchase of a car and hand tools, and, at the same time, is involved in a work situation in the choice of a supplier of compressed air equipment. One large corporation could be the possible supplier in both cases. This situation illustrates the importance of thinking through, as fully as possible, the implications of the use of corporate identity and/or brand images. It is a question not simply of design and identification, but of knowing what ideas can be communicated to what audiences with what effect.

Corporate and brand images take time to build and it is foolhardy to discard a valuable image which has been carefully and expensively built up. On the other hand, organisations and markets change, and regular monitoring of communication effects is necessary to avoid the modern, efficient image of a company in 1985 becoming the image of an old-fashioned, slow-moving organisation in 1995.

25. Private branding and quality control
In recent years, wholesaling and retailing organisations which do not manufacture have been promoting their own brands – products supplied by manufacturing organisations with special labels and packaging. The most successful operation has been carried out by Marks & Spencer, who lay down precise specifications and exercise rigid quality control over manufacturers who supply 'St Michael' products. Multiple food stores are, however, increasingly involved in the branding battle – frequently without the resources to specify or control quality.

26. Reasons for the development of private brands
The major reasons for this wholesaler and retailer action are as follows:

(a) A desire to limit the control exercised by manufacturers of strongly branded products and to strengthen the retailers' negotiating position.
(b) A desire to create a company or store identity, and hence to create loyalty.
(c) A desire to introduce greater price variation. Private brands are frequently cheaper.
(d) A desire to protect margins. Intensive competition among powerful manufacturers sometimes leads to low retail and wholesale margins.

Small manufacturers are not unnaturally attracted by what appear to be easy markets, but larger manufacturers also frequently supply private brands, both to achieve given production levels and thus absorb fixed costs, and to take defensive action by accepting business which might otherwise go to a competitor and strengthen its costing structure or trade goodwill.

Packaging

27. Uses of packaging
Packaging may be considered from three basic standpoints:

(a) as a protective device;
(b) as a product utility factor; and
(c) as a form of promotion.

These were discussed in 4: **34–6**. Packaging is, however, a sufficiently important element in promotional communication to justify its discussion again at this point.

28. Communication and package design
The advent of self-service has created a packaging revolution. The package on the store shelf and in the consumer's kitchen is a form of advertising which is attracting increasing design attention – the design to be linked with other forms of advertising. A brand name of a package which cannot be reproduced effectively on television, for example, is useless to the detergent manufacturer. When buying depends to a great extent on impulse, package shape or colour may be the major means of creating product preference. Ideally, consideration of product design should include the following:

(a) Ease of identification in all selling situations (e.g. set against competitive products on store shelves).
(b) Appeal both in the shop and in the home. Contrast the likely household location of soap powders and paper tissues. Packaging should appear suitable for its likely location, as well as being attractive in itself.
(c) The ability of cartons or outers to be quickly converted into display units.
(d) The impact of product visibility (e.g. use of glass containers, visi-packs).
(e) The impact of colour and the problems of reproduction in other media.
(f) The pros and cons of returnable and non-returnable packaging.

Environmental considerations are important in this as in many other respects.

(g) Safety and customer convenience aspects (e.g. cap seals and pack seals).

(h) Directions for use. Legibility, appropriate language and simplicity are all very important.

(i) Legal requirements (e.g. ingredients lists, shelf-life dates).

(j) Differences in national and sometimes regional attitudes and behaviour.

(k) Linkage of packaging and media. The number of TV channels in Europe reached some 250 in 1990.

29. Packaging technology

Increased attention to packaging has led to a growing use of industrial designers as well as packaging technologists. Packaging costs are rising, and although the impact of the packaging revolution has been seen mainly in the field of consumer goods, its marketing potential cannot be ignored by industrial goods producers – particularly those who are tackling international markets. Packaging exhibitions in Tokyo, Copenhagen, Milan, Düsseldorf, Paris and Moscow have attracted much more than casual interest. In the past decade there has been a technological revolution in packaging and printing.

The growing cost, complexity and time required to develop package designs point to greater need for top management co-ordination and direction of packaging policy as a vital factor in achieving sales.

NOTE: What is good for the producer and the selling channel operator should be an advantage and certainly not a disadvantage to the end user.

Below-the-line media

The term 'below-the-line media' is regularly used to cover sales promotion and merchandising, sales literature, point-of-sale display material, direct mail and exhibitions. The commission system of payment does not apply to these media. Those to which it does apply – press, television, radio, posters and cinema – are classified in the advertising business as 'above the line'. A very considerable amount of the rapidly expanding below-the-line activity is handled by specialists with whom the advertiser may enter into a direct relationship.

A development worthy of special note is the marked increase in tailor-made special promotion activities designed for large retail and wholesale groups by consumer goods manufacturers. This development reflects the growing bargaining power of these buying groups.

30. Consumer promotions

Special sales promotions are part of indirect advertising programmes intended to stimulate awareness and quick action. They began as a feature of packaged consumer goods selling tactics directed at the consumer and/or the trade. They are also now an important part of the ever increasing number of direct-mail and mail-order operations. The following are examples of consumer promotion:

(a) Special price sales.
(b) Free sample distribution.
(c) Premium offers.
(d) Contests.
(e) Point-of-sale demonstrations.
(f) Coupon offers.
(g) Combination or banded-pack product offers.
(h) Competitions and free entry to prize draws.
(i) Reduced flight-price offers.
(j) Offers targeted at special age groups, such as the over-50s (Beefeater Emerald Club).
(k) Initial low-price offers (e.g. book, compact disc and cassette clubs).

Sales promotions in the 1990s have become a very important feature of service marketing: for example, in banking, private health schemes, investment, pension planning, travel and tourism, hotels and catering. They are increasingly used also in promoting sales of newspapers and magazines, by retailers and distributors of durable goods (e.g. furniture, kitchen equipment), by garden centre and DIY outlets, and in book, CD and video mail-order activities.

31. Trade and professional user promotions

The following are examples:

(a) Provision of display materials.
(b) Co-operative advertising schemes – assistance with blocks or space costs.
(c) Contests for sales staff.
(d) Special discounts.
(e) Special quantity rate terms.
(f) Invitations to free seminars and demonstrations – often with free travel and accommodation.

(g) Samples of products and miscellaneous 'gifts' (e.g. pocket calculators and other items for desk and/or study use).

32. Reasons for special sales promotions

Special promotions are almost invariably used at the time of launching a new consumer product to gain maximum dealer stocking, display space and customer attention. Costs vary from the high expense of free-sample distribution to 'self-redeeming' premium offers where goods bought at special quantity terms are supplied at bargain prices to customers who returned coupons or other evidence of purchase. There are so many special promotions in the more highly competitive areas of consumer marketing that it would be dangerous for a company not to be involved. Other reasons for the use of special sales promotions include the following:

(a) Stimulating a new use for a product.
(b) Encouraging more frequent use of a product.
(c) Appealing to a special segment of the market.
(d) Boosting sales in particular geographical areas.
(e) Encouraging the use of another product (combination offers).
(f) Attracting bargain-hunting non-brand-conscious buyers.
(g) Encouraging seasonal sales or stimulating off-peak period sales.
(h) Creating dealer interest and encouraging stocking.
(i) Securing shelf space.
(j) Encouraging movement of slow-selling lines.
(k) Attracting new users (e.g. catalogue selling, book and record club membership).
(l) Offsetting price competition.
(m) Assisting sales force presentations.
(n) Making contact with professional and technical personnel, bringing them together with other professional/technical people to attend special demonstrations, seminars and discussion groups.

33. Display

The importance of display in consumer selling cannot be over-emphasised. Manufacturers may have special display posters, stands, cards and other material designed for windows, counters, shelves and floors. Many manufacturers' salespersons are trained to set up displays, and in new food lines there is an increase of 'rack jobbing' – a jobber taking over responsibility for stock and display, with the retailer providing space at a somewhat lower profit margin.

34. Direct mail and direct response marketing

Direct mail may be broadly defined as a method of sending unsolicited advertising or promotional material through the post to customers or potential customers at specific named addresses. It is, therefore, distinguished from house-to-house personal distribution of literature, circulars, etc. It can be aimed at increasingly specific target groups in order, for example, to create awareness and interest in products and/or services, and to stimulate further enquiry or visits by salespersons or technical advisers. It should be distinguished from direct response selling, which is part of a new and growing field of direct response marketing. Direct response marketing may take the form of direct mailing and mail order, but other methods and systems of direct response marketing are now being widely practised or are in trial stages, for example British Telecom's trials on direct telephone ordering of films, videos, etc.

35. Response and cost effectiveness

Mailing may be used principally to provide information: for example, about new savings schemes, product modifications, price changes, etc. A great deal of mailing is, however, associated with direct action on the part of the recipient. Wincanton Contract obtained a 4.4 per cent response rate to a mailing shot aimed at managing directors and company secretaries in an early industrial marketing campaign to break into the contract hire market. This enabled highly paid sales representatives to concentrate on warm leads, rather than to be wastefully employed on cold canvass calling. It should be noted that this was an industrial marketing exercise involving high investment decisions – all too frequently direct mailing is associated with limited special ventures such as encyclopaedia campaigns. Costs per 1,000 shots can be calculated against a probable percentage reply to determine the cost per response. Response rates can then be translated into sales conversion figures.

Response rates will depend on many factors, among which the following are very important:

(a) The ability to maintain accurate, up-to-date lists of potential respondents by appropriate categories. The more personalised the approach, the better. Specialist mailing houses exist in many countries, but relevant data can often be obtained and updated from sales representatives and trade and professional associations.

(b) The mailing 'package' should be good enough to appeal to the respondent.

(c) Reply should be made easy: for example, business reply cards or envelopes should be included (in the UK, the Post Office covers licensing procedures in a special booklet). International regulations on mailing procedures should be checked.

(d) Personal and/or other forms of follow-up should be arranged speedily.

36. The Post Office – direct mail and mail order
The Post Office, not surprisingly, has been very active in promoting direct mail, and also mail order. The current pricing system, the Mail Sort Development, has been a major – but not the only – factor in bringing about a substantial increase in both mailing and mail-order activity. The Mail Sort system provides three price and delivery 'packages' covering speed of delivery (one working day, within three days, and within seven days), together with differential discounts based on the delivery timings, a minimum quantity condition of 4,000 letters or 1,000 packets and a minimum requirement of 85 per cent of individual mailings being properly postcoded.

37. Other factors affecting mailing and mail order
Apart from the Mail Sort pricing initiatives, the very considerable increase in mailing and mail order over recent years may be attributed to the following:

(a) A great expansion in the issue and use of credit cards.

(b) An extension of colour supplements in newspapers and magazines as well as inserts.

(c) More easily available mailing lists and sophisticated systems of their stratification, leading to more precise target markets in, for example, demographic, geographic and even behavioural terms (e.g. life styles). Mailing lists are also bought and sold by various national membership organisations.

(d) An increase in activity both by direct-mail houses and by organisations setting up their own mailing and mail-order systems.

(e) Press and other media involvement in joint promotion schemes.

(f) An increasing level of disposable income in certain consumer market target sectors, leading to increased interest in book clubs, CD and tape clubs, clothing and collecting (e.g. porcelain, prints).

NOTE: There is a great danger in indiscriminate mailing shots – often described as 'junk mail'. Specific targeting is extremely important. The Mailing Preference Service – recently introduced – allows consumers to have their names removed from mailing lists. Moreover, databases are becoming much more specific. EU data protection moves have a bearing on this area as well as many others.

38. Exhibitions, seminars and demonstrations

These are essentially specialist temporary marketplaces at which buyers and sellers meet. There are various types of exhibition: international trade fairs; national and local trade exhibitions and shows (e.g. for cars, agricultural and business equipment). In addition to these shows, at which competitor vies with competitor, there is a growing use of individual company exhibitions, seminars and demonstrations where there can be greater selectivity of audience – often at a lower cost. Sometimes the private exhibitions are mobile, and can be readily moved from one location to another by special vehicle or rail car.

Single company exhibitions, demonstrations, seminars and technical literature can be particularly effective with companies marketing high-cost machinery and systems. The German company, Windmoeller and Hoelscher Corporation, has used this technique in key world markets and is now a leader in the field of flexible packaging equipment.

> NOTE: An increasing use is being made of exhibiting at outdoor and indoor trade shows, and at large retail stores. Some organisations are able to combine special entertainment with publicity, such as the Whitbread Hop Farm in Kent.

39. Examining the reasons for involvement

Very careful consideration should be given to determining objectively the real reasons for entering any general exhibition. The following considerations may weigh heavily:

(a) A new product is being launched. It is the kind of product which cannot be physically demonstrated by sales personnel, but can be shown at an exhibition, seen by many potential customers and reported by the press, TV, etc.

(b) A new market is to be developed rapidly. Contacts can be made with potential customers, and an image created with considerable speed.

(c) It is important to maintain or gain the goodwill of sponsoring trade or professional organisations.

(d) It is the only way to make initial contact with professional personnel buying on behalf of a number of foreign governments, in international and multinational companies.

40. Cost effectiveness – some pointers

It is particularly difficult to assess the cost effectiveness of other than private exhibitions. Some sales may result, but these are rare, and in those cases where large orders are announced the deals have usually been virtually concluded in advance. Nevertheless, the following cautionary points should be noted:

(a) Steps should be taken well in advance to invite to an organisation's particular stand important customers and potential customers. Sales force reminders pay off.

(b) If the objective is to build prestige, the reverse effect may be obtained by having a stand which, because of size, position, lighting, exhibits, etc., compares unfavourably with key competitors. Missing the exhibition can be less damaging – and less costly.

(c) Staffing arrangments should be organised well in advance so that there are reasonable individual duty rosters, an avoidance of under- and overmanning, adequate briefing to competent personnel who will reflect the organisation's image effectively, suitable hotel reservations, a stand co-ordinator, etc.

(d) Less costly literature should be provided for the 'free loaders', who attend for entertainment, than for the serious prospects and customers. Literature aimed at clients or potential clients should be of the very highest standard.

(e) Attention should be paid to eye-catching stand design and exhibits in terms of the particular target groups. Working models and dynamic exhibits are invaluable. Interested parties should feel attracted to enter a stand, examine exhibits and ask questions.

(f) Staff should be trained to obtain sufficient information from interested potential buyers for speedy follow-up to be made.

(g) Close attention should be paid to press relations, with suitable news releases and visual material arranged before and during the exhibition.

41. Audio-visual aids for sales forces

In general, inadequate attention is paid to the communication process in person-to-person selling situations. It is known that over 70 per cent of our knowledge is acquired by reading and seeing; and that only some 20 per cent is acquired through hearing. It is also well known that a selling call should be a two-way communication process in which the potential buyer should play a positive role. In spite of this, many salespersons rely almost entirely on verbal communications dominated by themselves. The scope for visual material of all kinds in person-to-person communications is enormous. Many companies supply their sales forces with illustrated 'sales presenters', and more attention is now being given to attractive sample presentation kits, but there is comparatively little use of portable overhead projectors, sound tapes, video tape recordings, film strips, or desk-top 8 mm films with back-projection equipment. All these methods can also be used for small group presentations. This is a field which calls for intensive investigation. Recent video disc developments seem highly promising both for sales force use and point-of-sale activity.

42. Public relations (PR)
Publicity is a specialised marketing activity. Public relations is not. Public relations is defined by the Institute of Public Relations as 'the planned and sustained effort to maintain mutual understanding between an organisation and its publics'. It is a very important area of internal and external communications which is receiving growing attention and calling for increased expenditure and adequately trained and experienced personnel. The targets of public relations are very diverse and cover the following informal groupings:

(a) Employees – past, present and future.
(b) Customers and potential customers.
(c) Financial and investment consultants – present and future.
(d) Existing and potential shareholders.
(e) Existing, past and present suppliers.
(f) Financial and other relevant specialist media planners, writers and presenters.
(g) Communities and community leaders in the neighbourhood areas of offices, distribution depots, factories and/or other services.
(h) Local and central government elected members and opposition spokespersons.
(i) Business and professional organisation leaders.

> NOTE: There have been examples of PR being used by company directors simply and solely to influence key decision-makers in specific situations. Such activity is a denial of the true role of genuine planned and continuous programming as outlined above.
> The role of PR is, if anything, even more critical in international operations than in domestic operations.

43. Publicity
Publicity may be defined as news about products or services appearing in the form of editorial material, without cost to the sponsor, in

the press, on radio, TV, stage, etc. 'Without cost' refers to space or time costs, since good publicity programmes depend on the skill of publicity specialists.

Organisations often complain about how the media – press, television and radio – concentrate on the bad news. Very often the complainants have never properly investigated the ways in which they may have their 'good news' included. The requirements and workings of particular media must be fully understood if good publicity is to be gained.

The most common forms of publicity are as follows:

(a) The press release or news item.
(b) Photographs.
(c) Feature stories.
(d) News conferences.
(e) Works visits.
(f) Specific products or services used or shown free of charge in films, on TV or in the theatre, and editorial or reporter comment on exhibitions.

All of these require special handling and planning. Most press releases, for example, are thrown away because they do not fulfil the basic technical journalistic requirements of news agencies, regarding such matters as number of words, headline writing, opening paragraphs, development and final paragraphs, abbreviations, capital letters, etc. Many others are unsuccessful because of a failure on the part of writers to distinguish between press releases and advertising. The release has to be factual and newsworthy to the particular readership. Some companies, on the other hand, are able to handle press releases most adroitly, and it is interesting to note those companies concerned with industrial markets which not only secure favourable mentions, but have regular full-length articles by their production, research or engineering personnel featured in authoritative journals.

44. Some useful sources of advertising data

(a) *British Rate and Date* (*Brad*). This is a monthly publication giving detailed information on media facilities and charges.
(b) Evening Newspaper Advertising Bureau (ENAB). There is a considerable amount of regionally researched data available.
(c) Audit Bureau of Circulations (ABC). This is a body established by agencies, media owners and advertisers, issuing audited figures at six-monthly intervals. Audits show net sales, distribution, audience statistics, etc.

(d) *Nielsen Researcher*. This is a free publication by the worldwide independent market research organisation based at Headington, Oxford.
(e) Media Expenditure Analysis Ltd (MEAL).
(f) Legion Publishing Co. Ltd.

Sponsorship

45. Definitions
The Economic Development Unit in the 1980s defined sponsorship as follows:

(a) A sponsor makes a contribution in cash or in kind – which may or may not include services and expertise – to an activity which is in some measure a leisure pursuit, either sport or art within the broad definition of the Arts.
(b) The sponsorship activity does not form part of the main commercial activity – otherwise it becomes a straighforward promotion, rather than sponsorship. The sponsor does, however, expect some return in terms of publicity.

46. Development, expenditure and activities
There are nineteenth-century examples of sponsorship, such as *Wisden's Cricketers' Almanac* (over 120 years of age) and, later, Bovril's arrangement with Nottingham Forest following their winning the FA Cup in 1889, but sponsorship is really a twentieth-century phenomenon, starting in a really significant way in horse racing with the Whitbread Gold Cup of 1956. By the early 1980s sports expenditure had risen to some £100 million p.a. and in the 1990s was very considerably more. Horse racing has remained the major sponsored activity, but golf, soccer, athletics, cricket, snooker, tennis and motor racing are among the many sports beneficiaries. Arts sponsorship is to be found in connection with classical music, in the theatre, in visual art, opera, ballet, etc., and in local, regional and national arts festivals. Total sponsorship expenditure in the 1990s is estimated at around £250 million. The actual total, however, far exceeds the estimated figures, since the latter do not include the cost of entertaining, publicity and other support costs. Over 2,000 organisations are involved in the UK alone.

search and evaluation criteria
is an area of such importance that commercial organis-
tudents of business, economics, public relations and

marketing need to examine and research objectives, and input and output criteria – that is, apart from general altruism and goodwill. Companies are coming to accept the idea that wide-ranging exposure of company names, logos, cups, shields and awards must be beneficial commercially if others, and particularly competitors, are doing it.

Some universities, business school faculties and colleges, as well as business research organisations and professional bodies, are currently undertaking limited research and holding seminars and conferences to evaluate sponsorship. Among these are the Economist Intelligence Unit, the Association of British Market Research Organisations, the Market Research Society, the University College Dublin, the European Academy, Innsbruck, Cranfield Institute of Management and the London and Manchester Business Schools.

Some reasons for the rapid increase in sponsorship

(a) There is a widespread belief that TV is an effective communications medium in the case of sporting events, particularly where coverage is lengthy and there are action replays and highlights.
(b) Recent government decisions have already brought about and will lead to more commercial TV networks (e.g. satellite and cable).
(c) There is already and there will be more commercial radio air time – some national (e.g. Classic FM) and some local – and this medium is not restricted to the home. Car radios, for example, are installed in the majority of modern cars.
(d) Sports and arts organisations are unable to cope with the scale and costs of activities in the 1990s. Controlling and financially responsible bodies are looking more and more to outside business and commerce to maintain and improve their presence and standing in local, regional, national and international activities.
(e) There are more opportunities for businesses to display names, logos and associated promotional material in times of expanding and highly organised sports and artistic activities, particularly where restrictions once imposed on organisations and individuals have been removed.
(f) Service organisations which previously spent comparatively little on advertising and promotion have diversified, and professional regulations and restrictions have been lowered or removed. Sponsorship by banks and insurance companies is now on a very large scale. Cigarette and tobacco companies, now under a television advertising ban, are also among the most prominent sponsors.

Progress test 7

1. What are the five basic steps in campaign planning?

2. How are readership classes normally defined?

3. What methods are used in copy research?

4. What are the main problems in assessing 'effective costs'?

5. What are the most usual ways of determining advertising budgets?

6. What are the reasons for the development of private brands?

7. What are the main reasons for special sales promotions?

8. What are the advantages of direct mailing and what factors condition response rates?

Assignment

Obtain a copy of two different 'free newspapers'. Request information on the advertising rates of the two. Rate cards will normally be readily available and these may well contain readership data. Try to draw up a media plan for a local retail store covering two weeks, using one or both of the papers. Calculate the space cost and explain the reasons for decisions taken covering objective(s), timing and number of insertions, cost of space, and any methods of testing results.

Part three
Organisation for marketing

8

Organisation and control

1. Organisation structure and control systems

There is no model organisation structure which will meet the requirements of all types of business. Organisation structures depend on many factors, including the size of the business and its industrial classification, the markets it serves, its stage of growth, and the skills and experience of its people. Until comparatively recently, the application of the marketing concept could be seen most clearly in organisations marketing consumer products and in associated channel and distribution systems. In the last decade, however, the concept has been adopted wholly or partly by an ever increasing number of organisations marketing capital goods and industrial supplies. In both of these 'product-based systems' there appear to be three distinctive features of organisational structure, as follows:

(a) Certain specific marketing tasks – for example, marketing research and information, product-market planning, advertising and promotion, sales and distribution – are co-ordinated under a single executive.

(b) Clear formal communications are established between the chief marketing executive and the executives responsible for development, design, manufacturing and finance.

(c) Marketing performance is judged by profit and return on investment, not by volume of sales. There are, of course, other marketing performance measurement criteria arising from corporate strategic planning and goals, method of funding, etc.

The number of marketing executives employed will vary. Small companies may not be able to justify the employment of specialists for every marketing task. A marketing orientation depends not on the number of people employed in particular marketing specialisms, but on conformity with the principles listed above.

More recently, the marketing concept has become a feature of strategic and operating planning in other organisations:

(a) A vast range of commercial services, such as banking, insurance, tourism, sport, entertainment, hairdressing, domestic and commercial cleaning, and security services.
(b) Utilities, such as gas, water, electricity and telephone communications.
(c) Public and private hospitals, nursing homes for special needs and other organisations in health care.
(d) Institutions in entertainment and the arts, such as theatres, art galleries and museums, sports stadia.
(e) Educational institutions in the public and private sectors – schools, colleges and universities.

It will be noted that many of these organisations are not involved in the transfer of a product from seller to buyer. Products may be involved in the process, but the activity/process exchange is essentially a benefit: for example, improved health, a pleasurable experience, greater security against various risks, greater comfort, or better career prospects.

It should also be noted that some of the examples given cover a wide variety of organisational types, sizes, objectives and means of funding. Some have been recently privatised, some are owned by large public corporations, some are small and privately owned and operated, some are charities and non-profit-making organisations.

In all of these 'service' operations, customers and potential customers must have confidence. This confidence will depend, to some extent, on buildings, computers and machine systems of various kinds, but an enormous amount will depend on person-to-person contact and mutual trust.

Six important factors have to be taken into account when considering a marketing organisation to fit a particular situation:

(a) The number, diversity and specialist needs of products and/or services.
(b) The number, diversity and specialist needs of customers.

(c) The geographical spread of customers and products and/or services.

(d) The economies of scale which are feasible in terms of centralised specialist marketing services, such as marketing research, product-market planning, advertising and promotion.

(e) The extent and nature of specialist service support required by decentralised operating groups.

(f) The extent to which it is considered important to separate overall strategic planning and co-ordination tasks from ongoing operational tasks.

Some of the traditional concepts of organisation such as single lines of reporting are disappearing in new matrix-type organisational patterns. For example, a marketing manager may directly control some functional activities (e.g. selling, local intelligence and advertising) in a decentralised unit. He or she may report to a general divisional manager, while at the same time reporting to a marketing manager at headquarters who may be responsible for co-ordinating total marketing operations and services.

This chapter is concerned with the establishment of the information evaluation and control systems which guide a company towards the achievement of its marketing objectives and plans. This implies that appropriate information systems should be developed both for the planning of objectives (long and short term) and for the monitoring of performance achieved against objectives. The particular routing, form and frequency of the information will depend on the organisational position, responsibility and authority of line marketing decision-makers, and on the position and role of staff specialists. Contrast, for example, the information required for new product planning (*see* 4:**14**) and that required by a sales manager (*see* 10: **11** *et seq.*).

Evaluation and control

2. Evaluation and control mechanisms

A marketing system must have evaluation and control mechanisms built into it in order that actual performance may be measured against objectives and forecasted performance. Information indicating significant variances from plans must be fed back speedily to relevant decision points so that corrective action may be taken. Organisational structures with clear definitions of *authority*, *responsibility* and *lines of communication* are, therefore, an important element in any control system.

3. Reasons for variations from planned performance
Variations from planned performance will always arise because of the following factors:

(a) All plans are built on *imperfect information*.

(b) *Marketing decisions are complex* and there will usually be a large number of interacting objectives. Failure to reach any single objective may have a bearing on the attainment of other objectives: for example, in attempting to gain a given share of a market, profits may fall below target because additional sales expense has been incurred.

(c) *The marketing environment is constantly changing* and it is impossible to predict every eventuality.

(d) *Many organisations are becoming bigger.* This leads to the involvement of more and more people who are linked by information systems rather than by personal contact; the range of products and services extends; and the location of factories, service depots, customer service points, offices and warehouses becomes more diffuse.

(e) *Variations in performance in other systems*, such as supply, production, personel or finance, affect marketing performance.

(f) *Performance depends not only on the company employees*, but on the performance of wholesalers, retailers, agents, brokers, advertising agencies and others, who can never be subject to the same degree of control.

4. The importance of targets
An effective control system depends on the setting of realistic goals or targets. Targets should be quantified whenever possible. It is almost impossible to evaluate performance against general statements of objectives. However, it is also difficult to communicate intelligibly non-quantified objectives. Numerical targets make practical the fixing of tolerances – the extent of permissible variance. It is only by establishing control limits that management by exception can be applied; otherwise every minor deviation at every point of time at which information is received will throw up problems of decision.

5. Marketing plans – reasons for their development
During recent years there has been a very big move towards the construction of formal, written, annual marketing plans. These plans should ideally evolve from the medium- and long-range plans of the

organisation and thus avoid entirely short-term considerations which are inappropriate in dealing with product-market dynamics. Nevertheless, they will inevitably be matched to the annual corporate objectives and co-ordinated with the plans and budgets of other resource facilities – personnel, purchasing, finance, manufacturing, etc. The basic logic of marketing planning applies to services and products. Deregulation, as in financial services, has opened the door to increased segmentation, distinctive pricing strategies and the use of mass media promotions. In the remainder of this chapter, the word 'product' covers benefit packages marketed to various markets and segments by a vast range of product and service organisations. The advantages of a formal planning process are as follows:

(a) Diverse marketing activities can be co-ordinated into effective total action with known authority, responsibility, timing and communication networks.
(b) Non-specialist marketing activities can be more effectively examined and co-ordinated to meet marketing objectives.
(c) Crisis management can be reduced to a minimum.
(d) Measurements of performance can be more readily set against known standards.
(e) Corrective measures can be applied at appropriate decision points.
(f) Participation in planning can be encouraged and delegation can be more effectively practised, with resultant improved motivation.

6. Marketing plans – structure
In practice, marketing plans vary in detail and sophistication, but there are detectable common elements in the structural pattern which tend to have the following sequence:

(a) *The information base.* This is an analysis of the present position of the organisation: its profits, revenues, product-market shares, strategy and tactics, weaknesses and recent trends – economic, social, technical and competitive.
(b) *Environmental assumptions.* On the basis of the best evidence available, the effect is assessed of significant economic factors likely to affect the forthcoming year's programmes: for example, government measures; economic factors affecting such items as labour or material costs; spending capability or propensity; social and technical shifts influencing demand; and known or probable competitive activity.
(c) *Basic overall objectives, policies and strategies.* In a business organisation, these include profit and investment goals and product-market

priorities or emphasis, as well as strategies relating to product quality, leadership, pricing, distribution and promotion.

(d) *Specific goals and programmes of action.* These cover product-market segments, but are detailed in terms of specific sub-programmes for product planning, selling, promotion, distribution, after-sales service, etc. Responsibilities and task achievement timings are set out and agreed.

(e) *Planned expenditures.* The overall marketing budget is broken down into subgroup budgets and set against (f).

(f) *Quantitative and qualitative measures of performance.* Revenues, costs, market shares, etc. are readily quantifiable, but some important tasks, such as the development of personnel and the change of a company image, are not so readily susceptible to direct quantitative measurements. (*See* **12–13**.)

The profit-centre concept

7. Responsibility or profit centres
The increasing complexity of organisations and multiplicity of products are leading to devolution of responsibility. Closely controlled centralised operations are giving way to decentralised systems with greater emphasis on delegation. *Responsibility centres* are often set up, the responsibility for making a profit on particular operations being delegated to particular executives.

8. Types of profit centre
The whole marketing department may be treated as a profit centre. This implies that goods are really being purchased from manufacturing departments, and profits result from the difference between the cost of purchase plus sales expense and the revenue obtained from the marketplace. In this way, the chief marketing executive becomes responsible for achieving a given return on investment and will think in terms of *cost* and *revenue* rather than in terms of volume.

Profit centres may similarly be established for individual product lines or groups of products. Sometimes, the profit-centre concept is applied to types of customer or market segment, to branch offices or geographical sales, or to channels of distribution.

9. Information and distribution costs
In physical product-market situations there is certainly a great need to pay more attention to the costs of distribution, which in many cases

are not only higher than the cost of manufacturing, but represent more than half of the final selling price. Many existing accounting systems could be extended to provide more significant information on cost: sales representatives, for example, are frequently unaware of the cost of their calls, or the cost of providing special deliveries and services. Marketing management certainly needs to consider the various combinations of channels, products, promotional and sales effort, which will yield satisfactory return at the least cost. Information collection and distribution can itself be an unnecessary cost, however, and it is important to establish what information is needed, for whom, when, where and in what form. The speed of information output from computers makes it all the more necessary to determine information flow and needs precisely. This is, perhaps, all the more necessary in many service sectors, where the form and frequency of individual customer information requires very careful consideration. The financial sector is an obvious case.

The major bases of performance evaluation

10. Performance targets and budgets
These are both fundamental to overall performance evaluation.

(a) *Performance targets.* Based on market evaluation and resources available, overall targets should be set which lay down what is to be achieved in both the short and the long term.
(b) *Budgets.* A marketing budget agreed by top management should be drawn up to show the permissible cost in relation to achieved target. The budget is the major means of evaluating profit performance.

11. Long- and short-range budgets
A distinction should be made between *long-range budgets* covering three, five or ten years ahead, which aim to determine long-range capital, facility and manpower needs, based on an assessment of long-range plans for business growth, and *annual budgets*, which are a control device for the year ahead.

Long-range budgets are important if companies are to plan for growth and change. These budgets require an evaluation of the likely effect of external and internal events over the forward period, against the background of which new products will be launched. The budget will indicate the likely profitability of new and existing products, as well as market shares. Products which are likely to fall below given company profit objectives have to be analysed so that decisions may be taken on appropriate action – to modify, to increase sales effort, or to drop.

12. Quantifiable overall objectives
The company must establish clear long- and short-term objectives so that these may be incorporated in overall budgets as well as in departmental budgets.

Important quantifiable objectives may be:

(a) gross and net sales figures;
(b) market shares;
(c) profit expressed in monetary terms and as a percentage of sales;
(d) turnover of capital, inventory and accounts receivable;
(e) return on capital employed.

Profit on sales reflects performance in maintaining cost control; turnover reflects the speed at which capital in the business is being worked. Return on investment – a most important yardstick – can be improved by reducing costs or using capital more effectively.

13. Other overall objectives
Other important objectives may not be so easily quantified. These include:

(a) providing for staff training and development;
(b) providing for effective plant, buildings, offices, transport and staff utilisation;
(c) avoiding excessive variations in the level of business transacted;
(d) maintaining and/or improving market standing against competition;
(e) providing for a satisfactory level of shareholder dividends in both the short and the long term;
(f) providing for employee job satisfaction.

14. Responsibility budgeting
If profit, expense and revenue centres are established, and managers at various levels of an organisation are accountable for their performance in relation to budgets, it is important that the following conditions are observed:

(a) The executive concerned should understand and agree the particular budget. Pursuing the notion of management by objectives, the executive would not only agree, but also participate in the decision and perhaps even contruct his or her own objectives in line with major company objectives.

(b) An executive who carries a responsibility for profits must have the authority to make necessary adjustments to programmes in order to reach the profit target.

(c) Adequate information on performance should be available in the right form at the right time.

Information for marketing evaluation and control

15. Reasons for information

The provision of relevant information at the right time to the right people is the basis of an evaluation and control system. Information is required to:

(a) provide for evaluation and control of overall marketing performance;

(b) provide for evaluation and control of subfunctions and individuals within marketing departments or divisions;

(c) provide specific data for any action necessary in relation to products, marketing programmes or prices;

(d) provide information for sales and key customer contact personnel and management.

16. Main types of marketing control analysis

The most commonly analysed information supplied for overall marketing analysis falls under six headings described in subsequent paragraphs:

(a) Sales analysis (**17**).

(b) Product-market share analysis (**19**).

(c) Distribution and/or market segment performance analysis (**20**).

(d) Sales force and/or customer contact managers' activity analysis (**21**).

(e) Cost and profit analysis (**22**).

(f) Advertising analysis (**25**).

17. Sales analysis: information

Sales managers in many product-market situations tend to judge current performance by the volume of business and the size of individual orders. Difficulties arise if the only information available regularly is aggregate orders. Information needs to be broken down much further for evaluation and control. Possible breakdown categories in terms of unit volume and sales revenue are:

(a) products or other units of sale, which can be further divided into particular styles, sizes and/or other appropriate categories;
(b) customer type or size;
(c) sales territories;
(d) channels of distribution – geographical groupings or service sectors;
(e) terms of sale or transactions;
(f) key outlets.

18. Sales analysis: standards

Information received must then be set against standards, such as annual forecasts, previous month's performance and last year's performance. It is also important to measure performance against opportunity and not just against the company's own past record. This requires supplementary information from the field and marketing research reports. Regular reports on marketing expenses by various categories will also be required if profit targets are to be met.

One of the problems frequently encountered in actual operations is that sales analysis data arrive too late for effective action. In volatile consumer markets, for example, detailed analysis six weeks after the event may be much too late to enable effective corrective action to be taken.

19. Product share (brand position) analysis

Regular information on a company's own as well as competitive brand shares of the market is extremely valuable. Growth in volume of business – or, indeed, in profits – is no guarantee of complete realisation of opportunities. A 3 per cent improvement in volume is unsatisfactory set against an overall market growth of 15 per cent. Apart from immediate lost profit opportunities, loss of market share may reflect on future business prospects. A change in brand leadership may mean considerable modification of plans.

In certain fast-moving consumer markets such as pharmaceuticals and groceries, regular audits of brand share positions are undertaken by A.C. Nielsen and other specialist agencies (*see* 3:**12**). In industrial markets and consumer areas where the information is not readily available, a company may have to devise its own arrangements for taking stock checks. High sales stocks in the warehouse of an agent or intermediary may indicate a high level of anticipated demand *or* a decline in demand at the next point along the chain. Stock-level information must, therefore, be supplemented by data on the estimated usage level and flow of products: a stockpiling of all brands, for example, may indicate a general recession, either cyclical or permanent. In the case of financial markets – banking of various kinds, investment agencies, building societies, pension advisory services, etc. – money markets have been turbulent for some time, and international stock market movements are so fast that sophisticated special data delivery systems may be needed for key field managers.

20. Distribution analysis

In tangible product markets, it may be comparatively simple to codify outlets to reveal statistics on actual company transactions, but where products are transferred, say from wholesaler to retailer, it is more difficult to evaluate the performance of particular links in the distribution chain. Information on stock levels, stock condition, order sizes, and selling effort may be necessary at outlets where sales calls are not regularly made. Again syndicated information is sometimes available from outside sources, but the sales force may be required to check on display activities or to ensure that inefficient systems of withdrawal from stock do not mean that the newest stock is used first. Old or damaged stock reflects more on the manufacturer than on the final supplier.

One of the great problems in distribution evaluation is to establish standards of performance. As in other forms of evaluation, reliable standards are needed for really effective control. The problem of measuring the performance of distribution points with which the company is not in direct contact is obvious, but comparison of the performance of wholesalers and agents on the basis of one year's figures against another's is also inadequate. Does a 20 per cent increase by one wholesaler represent a greater effort than a 10 per cent increase by another? More attention should sometimes be paid to establishing standards in relation to potential and constraints. It may, for instance, be possible to measure the performance of various overseas agents by establishing relative potential indices based on such information as total population, rural and urban population, degree of industrialisation, educational standards, and extent of communications and transport systems in each region. Similar indices could, of course, be developed for home markets.

21. Field sales force activity analysis

Some of the previous analyses give an indication of a salesperson's performance: for example, sales by product in a particular territory. There are other measurements which may be necessary. A salesperson may have tasks other than actually effecting a sale, such as display and service. Again, if action is to be taken to raise the level of sales performance, it may be useful to have information on the following:

(a) Number of calls per day.
(b) Number of different calls per month.
(c) Ratio of orders to calls.
(d) Value of sales per call.
(e) Time spent on non-selling activities.
(f) Mileage covered in given periods, or mileage per call.
(g) New accounts opened.
(h) Expenditure and cost of obtaining sales.

22. Cost and profit analysis: difficulties of allocation

Some company costs might be said to cover basically manufacturing costs and marketing costs. Allocating manufacturing costs raises problems, but they are nothing like so great as those of allocating marketing costs. Marketing, like manufacturing, has the problem of overhead allocation (e.g. for managerial salaries), but manufacturing costs are allocated to processes and things manufactured, however arbitrary the allocation may sometimes be in practice. The ultimate output of marketing is a sale, but it is difficult to determine the allocation of marketing processes. Products, salespersons, advertising, distributors – all contribute to sales, but in ways which are difficult to quantify. Similarly, additional cost in manufacturing is likely to yield a given output, but it is much more difficult to estimate the effect on sales revenue of hiring extra salespersons or increasing an advertising appropriation. Marketing costs can only be viewed in terms of absolute accuracy in total; individual activity costs provide a basis for revision of the balance of these costs. This is a particularly difficult problem in service sectors, but it can be overcome. Most management consultants – not surprisingly perhaps – have set up systems appropriate to their own business activities.

23. Cost and profit analysis: methods

Nevertheless, measurement depends on being able to examine both cost and revenue. Margins, for example, might be increased either by increasing sales more than expenses, or by reducing expenses more than sales. It is difficult to adjust margins or to use budgets to regulate specific marketing activities, therefore, unless there is an attempt to break down marketing expenses. Cost and profit analyses are consequently carried out in three main ways:

(a) *By calculating gross margins for specific managerial units.* Gross margins are what remain after the cost of goods sold is deducted from sales revenue. Lower gross margins on certain products or in certain markets point to a need to investigate. Falling margins may, for example, indicate that there is something wrong with the marketing plan and marketing efforts may be badly directed.

(b) *By breaking down expenses into normal categories,* such as salaries, rent and supplies, and comparing the expense against the gross profit of a profit centre.

(c) *By allocating all direct and indirect costs* to specific managerial units and setting these against profits. The units may be territories, customer groups or product groups. There are very considerable problems of allocation: for example, when one salesperson handles products from two or three different product groups or calls on two or three different customer groups. Similar problems arise in the case of corporate product advertising, billing or mixed product–customer-type deliveries. Where product groups, outlet types, sales delivery arrangements and so on are reasonably well separated, it is possible and often very worthwhile to carry out this kind of analysis. The major consideration is to ensure that the benefits of undertaking the exercise exceed the costs.

24. Cost and profit analysis: interpretation

Interpretation needs care, since most cost allocations are arbitrary. Direct costs are simple – for example, costs of salespersons or advertising directly associated with a product – but costs of space, management salaries, taxes and corporate advertising present considerable difficulties. Distribution cost analysis in its purest state can rarely be the basis for an immediate decision. It is a yardstick – to some extent arbitrary – of measuring relative performance and should be regarded as a guide to areas requiring further investigation.

It may be found, for example, that by measuring total sales achieved against quotas there seems to be one star salesperson in a team. A gross margin analysis by product may reveal that the salesperson's effort and expense have been devoted mainly to an easy selling line which yields a lower gross margin than other products. If sales targets and expense budgets have been set on the basis of anticipated market demand and an expectation of balanced sales across the range of products, and if direct costs have been allocated on the basis of actual expense incurred by having the salesperson in this territory, the unbalanced selling could result in both a low gross profit and a small contribution to profit. This kind of analysis would indicate, in this case, the need for more balanced selling effort; in other cases there might be pointers to the need for purely increased sales volume or a reduction in selling expense.

25. Advertising analysis and mark-up

Advertising evaluation has been covered previously (*see* 7:**13–14**), but attention should be drawn to the fact that the costs of advertising are frequently given unfavourable publicity, while little mention is made of the costs of effecting distribution and sales through conventional channels by offering suitable margins of profit. While there are very considerable variations, and generalisations in terms of all goods marketed are impossible, the advertising of strongly promoted foodstuffs may account for 5 per cent of the final retail price against 20 per cent for retail margins. Wholesale margins are far lower and this explains why it is sometimes not only more effective in terms of sales revenue, but also cheaper in cost to arrange terms direct on a single margin with large retailers. Sums spent on research and development, too, are frequently insignificant compared with mark-up allowances.

Marketing costs are mainly fixed regardless of the level of the flow of goods – unlike the variable cost of manufacturing. Margins to intermediaries may be regarded as an economic cost, but they are not an accounting burden. If their role were taken over by company-owned wholesale warehouses and retail outlets, then rents, salaries and running expenses generally would become a fixed cost or overhead.

26. Determining marketing expenses

Companies find it difficult to assess whether they should increase or decrease marketing expenses – or indeed at what level they should be fixed at all. It might be simple to consider the costs of each marketing activity – selling, advertising, market research, channel costs, order processing and product planning. The problem here is that each reacts on the other. A method of isolating functions has been described under advertising as the sales-task approach (*see* 6:**6–7**). Other possible ways of investigating expense and effectiveness are as follows:

(a) Analysis of resources, results, marketing methods and expenditure of competitors.

(b) Analysis of customer attitudes and behaviour.

(c) Analysis of non-accounting statistical data: for example, difference in results of advertising carried out under controlled experimental conditions.

(d) Analysis of the relative importance of marketing activities in relation to sales. Similarly, analysis of expense within an activity should be measured: for instance, who is the least productive salesperson (in terms of contribution to profit), or which is the least productive form of advertising. This kind of approach would be used if profits were falling; it is a useful guide – but only a guide – when profits *and also expenses* are rising. Some attempts to reduce cost are unlikely to have any really significant effect, such as general requests to cut down on telephone calls or stationery.

27. Budgets and flexibility

From what has already been said (**10–14** above), it will be clear that, although sales budgets are essential and central to the company operation, variations in the constituents of the total marketing expenses have no inevitable consequence in terms of sales revenue. There is, therefore, room for flexibility in the light of unexpected happenings. It is important that a measure of flexibility in the constituents be maintained, since there will always be some unexpected developments in market situations. Often these developments will require adjustments in the way marketing expense is used in order to reach the planned marketing objectives; sometimes unexpected opportunities to exceed planned objectives will arise. Production expense may be affected by changes in wage levels or materials cost, for example, but the budgetary changes necessary are less complex and more predictable than in marketing. Indeed, production budgets are most likely to be affected by changes in sales.

Flexibility in marketing budgets should not lead to thinking in terms of an immediate reduction of constituents such as advertising, as demand falls. A fall in demand would affect the production budget in a manufacturing organisation and it might indeed be necessary to *increase* sales effort beyond the point of marginal return on sales cost in order to absorb uneconomic production capacity. One budget must be seen in relation to another, and none is more critical in its interrelated effect than the sales budget. An apparently high selling cost might be justified if the volume of sales generated were sufficient to enable high-productivity machines to be installed in the factory or offices, leading to reduced manufacturing/output cost and thus greatly improving the contribution to overall profit. Service sector organisations have special problems in regulating supply: for example, electricity supply, hotel accommodation, theatre reservations, stadia for sporting events, catering, public transport, car service and repair, and health care.

Very careful consideration has to be given to the need for and possibility of regulating supply and demand. Inventory regulation is not normally a possibility, as is so often the case in manufacturing industry, wholesaling and retailing. Among the supply demand regulator possibilities are the following:

(a) Taking no action and trying to explain.

(b) Generally pricing up or down (e.g. at various times of day, seasons of the year).

(c) Pricing down to special groups (e.g. older customers, children at special times with special offers).

(d) Offering special price rates to users at particular times (e.g. electricity Economy 7 schedules).

(e) Keeping customers and potential customers informed of time factors (e.g. postal announcements on Christmas collections and deliveries).

(f) Giving different types of service for different prices (e.g. first and second class mail, economy rail travel schemes).

(g) Hiring part-time and casual staff for peak-time demand periods.

(h) Providing special accommodation for waiting clients (e.g. restaurants, shops, video entertainment at airports).

(i) Pricing up for customer priorities (e.g. types of service/accommodation, etc.).

The effect of any systems to regulate demand should be tested, if possible, in limited 'control' situations before extending widely; and even then, they should be regularly revised.

28. Fixed costs and revenue

Most marketing costs are fixed, but variable costs are involved in activities such as short-term promotions, sales commissions and temporary salespersons. If a high fixed cost in selling is combined with a high fixed cost in manufacturing, the dangers of a fall in profit (resulting from increased wages and rents, reduced demand and falling prices) are clear; diversification, rigorous product development policies and a drive to differentiate products might be expected in circumstances of this kind.

29. Market development and investment

Although emphasis has been laid on the importance of comparing performances of products, of sales personnel, and of channels on the basis of profit contribution, it should be stressed that low contributions may arise initially and/or periodically because of the need to invest in sales training, or in cultivating certain intermediaries (e.g. voluntary group wholesalers), just as much as from the need to invest in product development and market introduction.

30. Financial reports and relevance

The rapid speed of punched card and computerised systems means that sophisticated information can be made available quickly. Consider the range of data which could be obtained from drawing up a product and a customer code for computer processing on the following lines:

(a) *Product*
  (*i*) Product line (e.g. filter paper).
  (*ii*) Product size (e.g. 3 cm).
  (*iii*) Product type (e.g. circles).
  (*iv*) Product grade (e.g. 4).
  (*v*) Product price (e.g. £0.55).
  (*vi*) Product quantity (e.g. 12 × 100).

(b) *Customer*
  (*i*) Name and address (e.g. Bryce and Co. Ltd, 29 Warren St, Tonbridge TN3 4BC).
  (*ii*) Industrial or business classification (e.g. chemical and allied industries).
  (*iii*) Size by potential sales revenue (e.g. £25,000 p.a.).
  (*iv*) Sales department (e.g. 4).
  (*v*) Salesperson (e.g. 6).

The possible combinations of information would be too much for an individual to digest, and it is therefore important to provide the right data for the right level at the right time.

The product manager concerned with product profit contribution may require summary reports by size, design, quality, revenue and margin. From this he or she might see slow-moving lines, uneven spread of sales and unexpected margins. More detailed reports may be necessary to follow through on significant variations from anticipated results.

The field sales manager is concerned not so much with profit contribution on single products as with volume or revenue targets and controllable expense. He or she may, therefore, need information on sales progress by territory and a considerable range of individual expense items such as office and equipment depreciation, salespersons' cars, stationery supplies, hotel bills and clerical salaries. The salesperson, on the other hand, would be unable to control variable expenses apart from personal travelling, hotel and entertainment bills. The area manager may need a regular record of these expenses, but the salesperson is primarily concerned with a record of sales and deliveries on his or her territory – in total by product and by individual account – plus, perhaps, records of outstanding customer debts.

31. Reports from field sales forces

Two problems arising from the various information systems described are, first, that there is a *time lag* between the event and the reporting of the event; and second, that the information is in *quantitative* terms. Supplementary verbal information may be necessary.

To remedy these defects, salespersons are usually asked to make periodic reports on their field activities to area managers, who similarly may provide reports for more senior executives. The frequency and detail of such reports must be carefully considered in the light of their value as evaluation and decision-making aids. Not infrequently, very detailed daily sales reports from representatives contain information which is not really required or is available from other sources – and the compilation of these reports reduces the time available for selling and/or planning selling calls.

Well-planned field reports may, however, provide faster or more extensive information in the following matters:

(a) Number of calls made on particular days.
(b) Sales made or not made, with some explanation.
(c) Economy of routing.
(d) Localised competitive activities.
(e) Significant customer or potential customer developments.
(f) Details of complaints about, for example, product performance or delivery.

32. Possible effects of sales reports

Field sales reports may lead to more effective operation in the following ways:

(a) By indicating the need for urgent training, motivation, or other remedial action.
(b) By acting as a constant reminder to the salesperson or field sales

executive that, each day or week or month, targets must be met if the annual target is to be reached.

(c) By providing fast information on the progress of special presentations or campaigns, or on sales tactics which are proving particularly successful.

(d) By giving information on such matters as the progress of product tests, special display activities and technical servicing.

33. Communication, evaluation and control

It will be seen that much of the information required for evaluation and control is passing along formal organisational channels. An inherent danger here is that information can be misunderstood or distorted, giving rise to suspicions, conflict and low morale. Marketing is an activity involving a particularly large number of informal groupings and personnel with wide individual differences. A purely bureaucratic, mechanistic approach to objectives, control and evaluation is, therefore, likely to lead to low morale and failure to meet imposed objectives. In a bureaucratic control system, sales reports, for example, can become mainly alibis – means of protecting the individual or the group. The purpose of control and evaluation must, therefore, be understood and accepted by the participants in the system, so that they constructively participate in achieving and setting objectives which satisfy not only the company and its executives' hierarchy, but the needs and aspirations of informal groups and individuals.

One of the key factors in the management of service organisations is that the personal element is experienced by actual or potential customers in much greater organisational depth than in the vast majority of product-marketing organisations. It is important that the personnel involved understand very clearly what their role is *vis-à-vis* the customer, and that the appropriate manner and action necessary to build and/or maintain confidence is represented over the telephone, in letters and/or in person. This confidence must be maintained in actual customer experience of the service, and this customer experience is more frequently communicated to or exchanged with other potential customers than is the case with products. Non-personal communications, such as letters, advertising, brochures, buildings and vehicles, must also be consistent with the kind of service satisfactions expected.

34. Marketing, information and microelectronics

The possibilities of microelectronics in terms of new product development are clear. In this chapter it is important to comment on the effect of the new technology on marketing information systems. Inside the company, the automation of order processing and production scheduling provides the opportunity for faster access to sales results, and these can be displayed and assessed at distant locations through terminals or telephone line links providing, for example, a sales representative with stock/delivery data, or a customer – or a negotiator – with cost data for the purpose of price calculations. External information, always expensive, will be easier and cheaper to capture: for example, by obtaining immediate access to distributor data, or by conducting consumer questionnaires by means of interactive terminals. A revolution will not just happen by acquiring hardware – or indeed software. Positive steps will have to be taken to create the climate for processing and decentralising the relevant decision marketing information. A programme of education, training and persuasion will be required if change is to be managed.

Progress test 8

1. What are the reasons for the development of formal marketing plans, and what elements do they consist of?

2. What are profit centres?

3. How might a company express its overall objectives?

4. What are the main types of marketing control analysis?

5. Why are there special problems in the allocation of costs to marketing activities?

6. What are the three ways in which cost and profit analyses are carried out?

7. In what way might information for product managers differ from information for field sales managers?

8. What is the purpose of field sales reports?

Assignment

Ask for an interview with the sales manager of a local company which employs several sales representatives. The companies could come from any sector, including manufacturing industry, distribution (e.g. retailers), insurance, publishing or wholesaling. Ask whether you can have a job description. What tasks does he or she consider to be most important in the job. What information is needed and where does it come from?

Write a report on what you discover.

9

Channels of distribution and delivery systems

Definition and types

1. Channels defined
The term 'channels of distribution' refers to the system of marketing institutions through which goods or services are transferred from the original producers to the ultimate users or consumers. Most frequently, a physical product transfer is involved, but sometimes an intermediate marketing institution may take title to goods without actually handling them.

2. Marketing institutions: types and functions
There is a very wide range of marketing institutions which carry out a variety of functions along the distribution channels. Among the most important are the following:

(a) *Retailers.* These are independent traders operating outlets selling 'at retail' to household consumers.

(b) *Wholesalers.* These are independent traders who sell 'at wholesale' to other business organisations either for the purpose of resale or for business use. The terms 'distributor' and 'jobber' are frequently used in American literature to describe the same type of trader. (Occasionally the terms have a different meaning: for example, American jobbers dealing in automobile components and packed-meat products frequently buy from distributors who own warehouses and then sell to retail outlets.)

(c) *Agents and brokers.* These are organisations which buy or sell on behalf of a firm in a manner defined by agreement. They normally earn their profit from commission payments made in return for their part in negotiating business transactions.

(d) *Distributors.* These are organisations which contract to buy a firm's goods and services, and sell to third parties.

(e) *Facilitating institutions.* These are organisations which neither take title to goods nor negotiate purchases or sales, but assist the marketing activities of manufacturers and the institutions mentioned in (a) and (d) above. Examples include:

(*i*) commodity trading exchanges;
(*ii*) trade associations;
(*iii*) advertising and marketing research agencies;
(*iv*) credit service organisations and finance companies;
(*v*) freight carriers.

Distribution is a highly dynamic field of activity. The following paragraphs cover, in the main, well-established systems. Some of the recent changes and innovating developments are as follows:

- vertical marketing systems
- warehouse clubs
- shopping centre developments
- telemarketing
- franchising
- networking
- delivery systems for services
- consumer co-operatives.

These will be covered later in the chapter.

Basic channel decisions

3. Direct selling

Some producers sell direct to end users. This type of operation is found more frequently in the marketing of industrial goods and services than in marketing to domestic consumers. Door-to-door selling and mail order, however, are examples of direct consumer marketing.

4. Reasons for the use of direct selling

Factors which stimulate direct marketing are as follows:

(a) The need to demonstrate a technical product, to supervise tests, to undertake complicated and perhaps lengthy negotiations, or to provide specialised after-sales service.

(b) The lack of active selling by intermediaries.

(c) Inability to persuade existing channels to carry merchandise stock.

(d) Unduly high intermediary profit margins, which might give rise to cost and price advantages under a direct marketing system.

(e) Inability of intermediaries to effect physical transportation.

(f) Industrial market structures with comparatively few potential buyers – often geographically concentrated.

5. Reasons against the use of direct selling
Factors which inhibit direct marketing are as follows:

(a) Lack of financial resources.

(b) The need to use capital to provide a better return on investment: for instance, a manufacturer of a range of games would under most circumstances utilise available capital more efficiently in ways other than by engaging large numbers of salespersons to call on thousands of potential occasional domestic purchasers buying in small quantities.

(c) Lack of 'know-how' in effecting final distribution. Retail store management calls for special skills: for example, in buying for resale, in shelf-space allocation, and in organising a predominantly female and often part-time labour force.

(d) Lack of a sufficiently wide assortment of own products to operate economically. Sales of individual items at retail are affected markedly by the assortment available.

(e) The existence of channels which are designed specifically to deal in assortments and to break bulk.

(f) A consumer market structure with large numbers of potential buyers geographically scattered.

6. Basic marketing processes
Marketing involves various basic processes:

(a) Bringing buyers and sellers into contact.

(b) Offering a choice of goods sufficient to gain the interest and meet the needs of buyers.

(c) Persuading potential buyers to develop favourable attitudes to particular products.

(d) Maintaining an acceptable price level.

(e) Physically distributing goods from manufacturing points to buying or use locations with the possible provision of additional storage points.

(f) Effecting an adequate flow of sales.

(g) Providing appropriate services, such as credit, technical advice and spare parts.

7. Channel decisions: effectiveness and cost
Channel decisions must, therefore, ultimately be based on the

realisation that failure to delegate the functions listed in **6** above to intermediaries will increase costs, and that increased costs must be justified by appropriate economic advantages in terms of profit, market penetration or other company objectives.

Over recent years, increasing attention has been paid to the very high percentage of costs often incurred in distribution – notably in transport, warehousing and stock. This has led to much development in vehicle contract hire, warehouse rental and the franchising arrangement so frequently encountered in department stores. There is, however, some movement towards more vertically integrated production–marketing systems. The integration does not necessarily take the form of complete ownership of channels. Producer co-operatives are appearing more commonly in some markets, such as agriculture.

8. Multi-channel decisions

A producer may decide to use more than one channel system in order to reach the market. A large-scale manufacturer of soaps and detergents may, for example, decide to market products to both domestic consumers and industrial users. To reach domestic markets most effectively and economically, the following decisions may be taken:

(a) Terms of sale for large chain groups will be negotiated directly by senior management. Delivery will be made to individual stores. Salespersons will have access to individual stores to arrange displays and to take orders under conditions negotiated centrally.

(b) Other large retail outlets will be sold to direct by salespersons allocated to particular territories.

(c) Salespersons will sell to wholesalers whose main resale activity will be concentrated on smaller retail outlets.

To reach a wide range of industrial users, it may be decided to effect distribution by various channels. Certain sectors of the market (e.g. restaurants, canteens) will be reached through well-established wholesalers. Other sectors (e.g. textile manufacturers) will be sold to on a direct basis, perhaps because of a need to demonstrate the technical superiority of specialised products or because a major share of the total market can be obtained by calling on a relatively small number of outlets in a limited number of geographical concentrations.

9. Physical distribution: logistics and the total systems approach

The increasing costs of physical distribution have attracted considerable attention, and operational research methods are being used in connection with the logistics of warehouse location and transportation utilisation. There is, however, a great need to explore in greater depth the complexities of existing and potential consumption systems. Vertically integrated ownership theoretically leads to greater control over – and more aggressive handling of – final markets, which in turn should stimulate derived demand. But control has to be bought, and the total investment has to be measured against the total resultant increased return and set against alternative opportunity investment. However, each point in the channel system has its own 'service package' offered to its own customer constellation at varying levels of effectiveness, cost and profit. There is growing interest in the total systems concept of physical distribution, whereby all aspects of the physical handling and distribution of goods and services are examined in close detail and linked to channel strategy. Specialised distribution contracting is also increasing.

Retailing

10. The functions of retailing
Retailing is the final link in the chain of distribution of consumer products. The functions that retailers perform are the consequence of the separation of distance, time and information between producers and consumers (*see* 1: **13**). Hence all retailers are involved in assisting in the physical movement of goods and in effecting a change of ownership. Retailers also hold stocks so that goods are available when required by the consumer, thus contributing to the reduction of the time separation. Retailers pass information on products to consumers and back to producers, so reducing the information separation.

11. Methods of retailing
The manner in which retailing functions are performed differs widely. For example, some retailers have van delivery services, while some rely on counter selling and others on self-service; some retailers hold wide stock assortments, while others hold very limited ranges; some retailers advertise in the press and run their own sales promotions, while others rely on personal service.

Retailing functions are performed by non-store (*see* **12–14**) and store establishments (*see* **15–36**).

Non-store establishments

12. Types of non-store establishment
Examples of non-store establishments are mail-order houses, vending machines, door-to-door sales organisations, mobile shops, market traders and credit traders, but these outlets only account for a very small proportion of retail business. The most significant developments in non-store retailing are considered in **13** and **14** below.

13. Mail order
Some 3.5 per cent of total trade is now conducted by mail order. The following may be included among the reasons for initial growth:

(a) Increased trading in branded goods that are known and accepted by potential customers.
(b) Congestion in major shopping centres, with parking and transport problems for shoppers.
(c) More married women in employment, who have less time to spend on shopping or are unable to visit shops during opening hours.
(d) Improved organisation by mail-order companies – central buying, better stock control, more effective use of advertising and, particularly, improved catalogues. This has led to higher operating margins.

Mail-order operations in the UK are most successful in certain sectors, such as soft furnishing (some 16 per cent of sales) and women's and children's clothing (some 12 per cent of sales). Great Universal Stores and Littlewoods are the largest operators. This is, however, a distribution system attracting many new entrants. The majority of operators use catalogues, and some agents use these mainly for their own buying. Until the 1990s mail order catalogues were aimed at middle and lower social group categories. Next have developed a catalogue (the Next Directory) which is clearly more expensive to produce and targeted at higher social income groups (40 per cent A and B groups). Orders may be telephoned; calls are at local rates and delivery is very speedy.

Increasingly, mail-order operators are improving their targeting, encouraging the use of credit cards and endeavouring to reduce the drain on profits caused by the very high percentage rate of returned goods. Another development is the introduction by Marks & Spencer of charge cards. Other bank credit cards are not accepted for payment, but may be used to back up a cheque payment. Data collected from charge card applications has been useful in targeting M & S mini catalogues.

Direct marketing
This term covers a wide range of activities notably in the marketing of technical products and in service operations (e.g. airlines, travel agencies, banking and insurance) as well as by non-profit organisations such as charities and political parties.

The operations may vary in detail, but in general direct marketing involves the delivery of messages by the marketing organisation through various media (including mail) and arranging for mail delivery.

There are now a substantial number of direct marketing agencies which organise campaigns (e.g. Wunderman Worldwide, Ogilvy and Mather Direct, Aspen Direct).

Direct marketing channels include the following:

(a) *'Off the page'*: for example, in newspapers or magazines, advertisements with coupons to be completed and mailed.
(b) *Club catalogues*. An outstanding example of this approach in the UK is the Automobile Association, which has developed this kind of business in products and services very extensively in recent years. AA services marketed now include not only car insurance but many other forms of insurance, including property. Mailing and telephoning are used extensively.
(c) *Telephone selling*. This has been used for some time by companies offering, for example, demonstrations of double glazing, conservatories and kitchen unit installations. This form of selling can be a considerable 'customer' irritant.

Electronic shopping development
The technology for transmission of screen images to be linked with telephoning is well developed and is likely to be a very major direct selling development in the UK as in the USA.

Viewdata (Prestel)
This should be distinguished from one-way transmissions such as Ceefax and Oracle. Specially equipped TV sets, selectively cheap microcopier links or appropriate software on hire enable many thousands of people to use systems of two-way visual exchange. Not only is this a reality in the case of mail order, but it opens up the possibility of actual transactions: for example, in the transfer of funds from one party to another in banking systems.

Other developments include teledata for information about goods, and for actually viewing and ordering them. Opinions among the public and the scale of development in the UK vary sharply, but major chains such as Sainsbury and Tesco cannot ignore this development, which is already creating some real transaction method changes in the USA.

In all these developments in 'electronic shopping', there are clearly real problems of information security. Voluntary and legal developments in data protection will certainly have to take place.

14. Door-to-door selling

The most interesting developments in this type of operation are associated with specific companies: for example, the Tupperware party selling system, or Avon Cosmetics, which use home selling by part-time women representatives paid on a commission basis. In both cases, major contributory factors to success have been the development of a leisurely social climate during the selling process, and the provision of ample opportunity for the demonstration and testing of products. Betterware have a very successful record of door-to-door selling, sales calls following hand delivery of catalogues.

Retail stores

Store establishments account for the major proportion of retail business; their organisation and operation is considered in some detail in **15–36** below.

15. Methods of classification of retail stores

Retail stores may be classified as follows:

(a) *By type or range of goods offered*. Some stores offer only goods in a highly specialised category (e.g. furniture, millinery, meat); others offer a wide range of different types of goods (e.g. a combination of food, drapery, hardware).

(b) *By the functions performed*. Some stores offer goods only by self-service; some offer delivery as well as self-service; others offer counter service and delivery.

(c) *By size*. Measurement of this may be based on the number of employees or the sales turnover.

(d) *By ownership* (e.g. independent, co-operative).

(e) *By location* (e.g. rural, urban).

These classifications are all important in specific marketing situations, but the present purpose is to examine general trends in retailing. The majority of shops in Britain are small in size and unincorporated: that is, owned by one individual or a partnership. The share of total retail trade transacted in shops which are part of an incorporated business (i.e. owned by private or public companies) is, however, constantly growing. The position of the independent (unincorporated) trader is first examined (16) and there follows a more detailed treatment of the developments in incorporated retail establishment (17–35).

16. The independent trader

The majority of shops in Britain are small and independently owned, but the percentage of total trade that these small establishments transact is constantly diminishing. Loss of market share is most outstanding in the case of grocery products.

(a) *Difficulties* encountered by the small trader include the following:
(*i*) Price competition from multiple organisations, who enjoy bulk-buying advantages as well as other organisational economies of scale. There is no longer the protection of resale price maintenance.
(*ii*) Lack of specialist expertise in the various functions of retailing, such as, buying, display, accounting and stock control.
(*iii*) Lack of capital to invest in modernisation: for example, provision of self-service facilities and accounting systems.
(*iv*) Location. Small traders usually lack the advantage of being in a major shopping centre where the customer is free to exercise choice over a wide range of purchases (but *see* (b) (*ii*)).
(*v*) Increased car ownership and the involvement of husbands in both buying and transportation tends to draw shoppers to the larger stores in the major shopping centres.

(b) *Advantages* that the small trader can offer customers include the following:
(*i*) Personal relationship with customers.
(*ii*) Convenience in being located near customers' houses or places of work.
(*iii*) Stock not necessarily limited to fast-moving items but catering for more individual needs.
(*iv*) Greater flexibility in arranging shopping hours.
(*v*) Overheads can be kept small because of siting, low labour costs, etc.
(*vi*) Greater flexibility in offering credit.
(*vii*) More flexibility in providing delivery service.

Incorporated retail businesses

Incorporated businesses are retailing establishments owned by public and private companies; their organisation and the main trends in their development are examined in **17–35** below.

17. Multiple organisations: chain stores

Chain stores are groups of retail stores of a similar type with a common ownership and some degree of centralised control. Multiples normally concentrate on a limited range of merchandise, such as groceries, furnishings, clothing and shoes. Variety chains, such as Woolworth and British Home Stores, are retail chains handling a diversity of goods.

The major multiples have, in fact, actively developed stores with sales areas of over 25,000 ft^2 (2,300 m^2) and it is these superstores which account for larger and larger shares of retail business. Some 75 per cent of all grocery turnover is now held by multiples and 55 per cent by the top five chains. Productivity in terms of sales per head soars. Nevertheless, it is interesting to note that one of the big retail successes in the 1970s and 1980s has been Kwik Save, which concentrates on smaller stores. Superstores are sited on the outskirts of town and have excellent parking facilities, but 30 per cent of households do not have a car and few customers anyway would drive 6 miles for, say, a piece of fish – especially at today's petrol costs. The organisational fragmentation of the co-operative movement has not been solved, and market share losses continue.

A further current problem relates to the range of items carried by multiples – how specialised should they be? Woolworth has in recent years disposed of many major outlets carrying highly diversified ranges, and has reinvested in more specialised areas of activity such as DIY. Tesco and Asda are officially classified as 'large mixed businesses with food', and Sainsbury has moved into some clothing and kitchen accessory lines.

Multiples have flourished particularly in central shopping areas, and their location, as well as their price advantages and stock arrangements, have probably contributed greatly to their success. More recently, the multiples have opened stores with greater sales areas, wider ranges, and vastly increased parking in out-of-town shopping centres, for example Merry Hill, Thurrock Lakesides, Dumplington. These superstores/hypermarkets have the following characteristics:

(a) Each has a selling area of at least 5,000 m^2 on one level, offering a wide range of foods and a more general range of non-foods.

(b) They apply self-service methods with payments at one point by means of 15 or more checkouts.

(c) They are usually located some distance from town and city centres.

(d) Each has an adjacent free parking area at least three times the selling area.

This move towards out-of-town shopping centres began mainly with the major grocery groups in the latter part of the 1980s. These groups extended their stock ranges very considerably to include such goods as stationery, magazines and newspapers, wines and spirits, cleaning materials, hardware, electrical goods, bakeries and delicatessen counters. There were regional differences in this movement depending to some extent on such considerations as individual company strategies, population densities and regional planning policies. Thus there was a comparatively high-level percentage development in Greater London, East Anglia and the South West as compared with Scotland, the North East, and the West Midlands. The next major movement was to the large 'mixed business' shopping centres, and this involved retail operations such as furniture, carpets and curtains, electrical hardware, and garden centres. Also of significance is the setting up of a Marks & Spencer outlet in the Metro Centre on the outskirts of Newcastle, and the activity connected with retail park developments as noted above.

The number of supermarkets/hypermarkets in the UK at present is some 500 and still increasing; there are some 900 in Germany, over 600 in France, and over 80 in Belgium.

18. The battle of shelf space

As multiples grow into regional and national organisations, they present new problems to the manufacturers whose products are handled by them. Their large share of business transactions means that major manufacturers may be able to restrict very considerably the number of actual selling calls made, but the need to acquire shelf space and display becomes more vital. So much are ultimate movements of goods (and profit) associated with shelf space that major retailing organisations – especially supermarket operators – are turning more and more to assessing stock assortments in such terms as sales per square (or linear) metre of space, or gross margin per unit of space per unit of time. Advertising and sales promotion schemes –

particularly the latter – are becoming more necessary to gain appropriate space allocation and to accelerate the movement of goods out of retail stores (*see* 2:**19**; 3:**27**; and Chapter 6).

In the final resort, however, the multiple organisation is concerned with long-run profit, and margins are as important as stock turnover. The more dominant multiples become in trade share, the more likely it is that they will be able to exert pressure on manufacturers' margins.

19. Private branding
Pressure on margins may be increased by the introduction of retailers' own private brands. Privately branded products are almost always sold on the basis of price. These private brands are rarely manufactured by the retailer organisation, but are supplied by both small and large manufacturers on the basis that spare capacity can be utilised or larger runs operated, margins being kept low by selling at prices sufficient to cover or slightly exceed marginal costs. Unless the retailer has a quality control organisation, there may be the temptation to lower quality standards; many private brands are certainly variable in quality. The argument of lower costs incurred by the manufacturer does not apply to all types of product, however, and is generally valid only in the case of products where a very large margin is normally allowed for advertising and promotion. A manufacturer may also be prepared to supply private brands on the basis that, if it does not, a competitor will. The potential dangers to the producer's own brands are, of course, obvious.

20. Marks & Spencer: the St Michael brand
In some cases, private brands were developed to overcome the problems of uniform pricing imposed by resale price maintenance (RPM), but the practice has grown since the abolition of RPM. The outstanding example of private brand marketing with rigid specifications and quality control is the Marks & Spencer operation. The 'St Michael' label has been used to create a distinctive quality/value for money image. No competing brands are sold, and marketing policy is based not on providing the cheapest product but on satisfying the needs of a large but well-defined market segment. Marks & Spencer has a constant updating policy and this is particularly necessary in clothing since the advent of more specialised competitive outlets (e.g. Top Shop, Dorothy Perkins, Principles (and Burtons), Miss Selfridge (Sears), Précis, Country Casuals and Benetton.

21. Principles of chain store operations

Significant general principles of chain store operations include the following:

(a) Large volume movement and a high break-even point. Success, therefore, depends largely on siting.

(b) Uniformity – store facias, layout and operational policies.

(c) Concentration on fast-moving lines – popular manufacturers' brands or private brands.

(d) Centralised buying.

> NOTE: Multiple domination clearly reduces the number of buying points: that is, the points into which the manufacturing organisation can actually sell. Overall there has been a very considerable reduction in the number of buying points. It is estimated that, in the UK, the 75 per cent of total retail grocery business transacted by multiples involved only 10.4 per cent of the total number of retail outlets. Over the last twenty years the number of independent retail outlets has fallen by 50 per cent and the number of co-operative outlets by over 60 per cent. It is interesting to note, however, that both independents and co-operative outlets have increased productivity per store by various means, such as special supply arrangements with symbol groups (e.g. Mace), a degree of self-service and an extension of opening hours (e.g. Co-op Late Shops).
>
> The number and types of salespersons required for 'selling in' has therefore been reduced drastically, but there is an increased need for promotional activity at retail outlets.

(e) Minimum customer service (cf. departmental stores, **22**).

(f) Group advertising and promotional activities.

(g) Close attention to pricing tactics, mark-ups and customer traffic flow in purchasing areas and/or exit payment points. The amount of customer service required remains a very serious problem.

Departmental stores

22. Characteristics of departmental stores

The departmental store is really a collection of 'shops' under one roof and ownership, each shop or department specialising in selling a special range of goods (e.g. clothing, furniture, footwear, cosmetics, electrical goods). Each department normally buys separately, exercises its own stock control and sets its own merchandising policy. There are, therefore, few economies of scale in terms of supply. The advantages must lie in providing service and convenience to customers under a general 'house image'.

23. Customer service
Customer service advantages may include the following:

(a) Provision of a wide range of specialised goods in one location.
(b) Freedom to move around the store to view.
(c) Provision of special services such as restaurants and telephones.

24. General principles of departmental store operations
Significant general principles of departmental store operations also include the following:

(a) Siting in major shopping centres in urban locations.
(b) Fairly extensive local advertising and specialised promotions, frequently in the form of special 'sales'.
(c) Delivery services.
(d) Staff trained in handling specialised merchandise.
(e) Provision of house services (e.g. carpet laying, curtain fitting).
(f) Increased leasing of space for 'shops within shops', and space leased to manufacturers (e.g. Berkertex and Jaeger).
(g) Trading-up in price to compensate for services provided and high overhead structure, but the movement of whole or parts of stores to new developing sites on the outskirts of towns and cities, together with subcontracting of services and increased leasing, is now very much more evident.

25. Characteristics of variety stores
A variety store is one which handles a wide assortment of goods not necessarily related to each other (e.g. toys, cosmetics, sugar confectionery, hardware). It may be independently owned, but is usually owned by a private or public company. A group of variety stores may, therefore, constitute a chain or multiple. Characteristics of variety stores include the following:

(a) Handling of a wide range of unrelated goods with customer opportunity to walk around store freely.
(b) Preponderance of 'convenience' or 'impulse' goods of low unit price.
(c) Absence of credit and delivery service.

(d) Siting in major shopping centres.
(e) Counter service and counter display.
(f) Very limited direct advertising.

26. Recent trends

Originally variety stores such as Woolworth operated mainly on the principle of low prices – the 'bargain' store. More recently, there has been some evidence of extension of the lines stocked to include higher-priced items such as cameras, radios, clothing and kitchen furniture. In some cases there are indications of trading-up.

Growing specialisation can sometimes be seen. Woolworth has been pursuing a policy of diversification by the acquisition of such businesses as B & Q (DIY) and Comet (electrical equipment) each with a distinctive product portfolio, and has renamed the whole group in a move to restructure the operation and redirect the money market image. W.H. Smith is clearly no longer essentially a bookseller and has made diversification acquisitions such as 'Our Price' selling videos, records, tapes, etc. These systems moves are in accord with US diversification into divisional structures. The original company trading names are retained and the end consumer is probably not aware of the name of the merged organisation. The Stock Exchange, on the other hand, is kept well informed.

The Marks & Spencer variety chain, as has been previously indicated (20), is unique in its adherence to a single brand with rigid control of specification and quality. Moves by Marks & Spencer in the late 1980s were a major acquisition of a US stores group and, certainly no less significant, following the setting up of their own credit card system, the 1988 launch of the St Michael Unit Trust.

The late 1980s also brought in the UK a dramatic increase in the establishment of retail trading parks in addition to continuing growth in the construction of new shopping centres.

In order to reduce operating costs, many variety stores have introduced 'cash-and-wrap' operations. Individual counters are unattended and customers take their intended purchases to cash-and-wrap desks located at various points in the stores.

27. Buying practices

The variety chain invariably has a centralised purchasing organisation, but there are wide differences in the delegation of purchasing power to individual stores. The Woolworth central buying organisation, for example, may negotiate contract prices and keep store managers informed, but the individual store and district managers are free to make their own purchasing decisions and to negotiate with manufacturers. In contrast, Marks & Spencer store managers do not have this negotiating freedom and are concerned with the regulation of quantity and assortment of specified goods from specified sources, and other localised and important managerial tasks.

Co-operative societies

28. Early developments in the UK
The co-operative movement began in Rochdale in 1844 and was based on the notion that consumers should themselves control production and distribution in order to eliminate the waste of a competitive capitalist system. Dividends were to be paid out from trading surpluses in proportion to purchases made. Each retail society was to have its own area of trading free from competition from another retail society.

29. Later difficulties
The movement progressed fairly well up to the 1930s, but has more recently encountered great difficulties. As the members control the societies, there have been tremendous differences in the attitude to change. Consequently, many retail societies have stagnated while others have made notable progress. Attention is drawn to the *Co-operative Independent Commission Report* of 1958. It should be noted that co-operative societies were pioneers in the two most significant changes which have occurred in the pattern of retail trading: namely, the introduction of self-service and the rise of supermarkets.

Failure to keep pace with competition, however, may be attributed to the following factors:

(a) *Poor management*. This stems first from the inefficiency of many management committees consisting of members with no business expertise – committees which are difficult to change because there is usually insufficient organised voting power to replace ineffective members. There is also often a lack of managerial skill in executive store managers because of poor selection, lack of training facilities and inadequate financial incentives.

(b) *Poor service*, which stems from poor management.

(c) *Lack of integrated policy* between production and distribution. Individual societies have not always supported the co-operative factories distributing the product through the Co-operative Wholesale

Societies (CWS) in England and Scotland. In turn, there has been a lack of marketing policy and direction in manufacturing and whole-saling organisations. Steps are now being taken to recruit more highly paid experienced marketing experts, and as the CWS has increasingly become involved in the financing of many retail societies, a greater measure of control of goods handled at retail is becoming possible.

(d) *Lack of member loyalty.* The original notion that members would shop exclusively at co-operative stores was impracticable. The in-creasing attractions of competitive retail outlets have shattered any remaining illusions of large-scale exclusive store loyalty. The attrac-tion of a dividend paid annually has decreased, and only recently have quickly redeemable 'Divi Stamps' been introduced.

(e) *The high degree of decentralisation* has made the economies of scale and improved efficiency techniques of more closely knit large retail organisations difficult to effect.

(f) *Problems in relation to pricing policy and dividends*, provision of capital reserves and accounting procedures generally.

30. Recent departmental and variety store developments
In the early 1990s further problems have required top-level rethinking in departmental and variety store businesses:

(a) Leasing of space has become commonplace. Arrangements with concession holders vary considerably, but usually involve more than simply an annual rental. There is usually some agreement involving a percentage of sales. The very first concession was in the field of women's fashions – Jaeger at Selfridges – as far back as the mid-1930s. It is estimated that over 300 companies will be involved in more than 30,000 separate concessions in the mid-1990s. The leaseholders some-times retain some space for themselves, but often move out of town/city locations to suburban shopping centres, with a concentra-tion on more sharply focused businesses giving specialised service as required (e.g. furniture, carpets, soft furnishings).

(b) A number of departmental stores have been involved in merged activity (e.g. British Home Stores – Habitat – Mothercare; Burton – Debenhams; Dixons – Currys). The rationale behind these mergers might have been in part to benefit from the effects of synergy – a matching process in which the combination of units used together are expected to produce results much more favourable than the sum of the individual parts.

(c) The problem of departmental stores was not made easier by the emergence of such niche marketing operations as Tie Rack with a narrow product range aimed at narrowly segmented markets, or Virgin Records with a fairly narrow product range targeted at fairly broadly defined markets. In addition to such developments, there has been relatively fast and wide geographical spread of highly distinctive product ranges (e.g. Laura Ashley, The Body Shop). It is not without significance that these particular outlets were planned and launched by women. Until recently, at the top level retailing was, in the main, male dominated. As in other areas, women are beginning to take a more prominent part in marketing strategy decisions, marketing research and other important marketing operations.

Manufacturer-owned outlets

31. Arguments against vertical integration
Vertical integration – complete control from production through to ultimate distribution – is comparatively rare for the following reasons:

(a) Most companies prefer to utilise limited assets – of skill as well as finance – in specialised activities from which they have the greatest opportunity of profits.
(b) Rarely is it possible to provide a satisfactory assortment of goods in retail outlets from a single manufacturer's range.
(c) Selling to other (now competitive) retail outlets becomes difficult, and the rate of retail growth must therefore correspond closely to the rate of manufacturing growth.
(d) The number and range of retail distribution points is inevitably curtailed.
(e) It is very difficult to adapt the level range and style of manufacturing output to the fast-changing requirements of the consumer marketplace. The difficulties of integrated tailoring operations, such as Burtons in the late 1970s, demonstrate this problem.

32. Arguments for vertical integration
Arguments in favour of an integrated manufacturing/retailing organisation include the following:

(a) Possible cost savings. The elimination of middlemen margins may provide the opportunity for pricing advantages.
(b) Provision of more effective service. This argument might apply particularly in the case of certain technical products or 'do-it-yourself' items (e.g. Marley tiles).

(c) More effective merchandising and broad-line stocking. The problems of introducing new or slow-moving items to large retail outlets have been previously mentioned (*see* **18** above).

(d) The growth of large-scale integrated organisations dominating distribution of a product range (e.g. footwear, petrol, alcoholic drinks, pharmaceuticals). If a manufacturer has difficulty in gaining adequate retail distribution because many retail outlets are owned by its competitors, it may have to protect its interests by investing in retailing: for example, Rank's flour is used in shops owned by British Bakeries, Spillers' flour in United Bakeries; the British Shoe Corporation (Sears) merged with Freeman, Hardy and Willis, Saxone, Dolcis, Manfield and other outlets, all retaining their pre-merger names in the marketplace.

Horizontal integration: strategy and examples

Merging of businesses at the same level of production or distribution of goods and services – horizontal integration – has been a very marked feature of recent retailing merger activity. Many of these mergers involved diversification, the original merged companies retaining their names in the retail marketplace, but not in the stock market. Examples are as follows:

– Do It All (W.H. Smith and Boots – joint venture)
– Texas Homecare (Ladbroke Group)
– Superdrug (Kingfisher Group already controlling Woolworth, Comet and B & Q)
– Boots (controlling over 450 car accessory outlets).

Horizontal integration: current signs of turbulence

(a) Following the withdrawal of the Manoplax heart drug with substantial losses, Boots shared losses with partners W.H. Smith in the DIY business. The original retailing business continues to increase its market share and own-label products, many of which have been developed in Boots' Laboratories and are to be found in Boots' retail outlets alongside a very considerable number of other supplier-labelled products. There has been a reorganisation of the major pharmaceutical business and some withdrawal from the DIY venture.

(b) Costco, the first of the 'Warehouse Clubs' which in the USA have gained considerable business in retail grocery markets by establishing a low price, large quantity business with customers using hand-handled trucks rather than trolleys. Early operations in the UK have led to much keener pricing on a wide range of 'essential', items by Sainsbury. Other groups – even Marks & Spencer – are lowering prices over a considerable range of merchandise. Customers in Warehouse Clubs have to become members and the store furnishings are truly warehouse like. Merchandise may extend from groceries to furniture, car accessories, office equipment and clothing.

Discount stores and franchising

33. Characteristics of discount stores
Discount stores, which began to develop in the USA in the early 1950s, became a significant factor in European channel systems in the 1970s. Basic features are as follows:

(a) Low price – the major appeal.

(b) There is a low mark-up with minimum customer service (mainly self-service). Gross margins on durable items and clothing may, for example, be up to 10 per cent below those operated in departmental, variety or multiple stores.

(c) Purchases are mostly for cash.

(d) Stores are usually very large (in the USA normally over 5,000 m^2 and sometimes exceeding 10,000m^2).

(e) 'Hard' goods are the major lines stocked, but some discount houses have added foods and other 'soft' goods.

34. Recent trends
It is interesting to note that there is already evidence in the USA that many discount houses are departing from the original warehouse-like, self-service, cash-down operation, and moving towards the provision of credit-financing arrangements, sales attendance and more attractive furnishings. In the UK, Comet already offers servicing guarantees for electrical equipment as well as financing arrangements. Discounters also use very many local media promotions.

35. Difficulties in classifying retail stores
It will now be evident that classification in terms of size, service and range of products carried may be possible in general terms, but that there is a great deal of overlap. There are small and large co-operatives, there

are independent traders who provide counter service while others have self-service, and there has been a reduction in the number of stores carrying a limited range of highly specialised items. The dairy sells sausages, the off-licence sells confectionery, and the multiple food store, perhaps, sells paint and kitchenware.

36. Franchising

One of the most interesting distribution developments of recent years is franchising. The franchisor supplies a name, products, services and general know-how, and the franchisee contracts to use all or a major part of the franchisor's services in an agreed manner within an agreed territory. What might be called 'first-generation' franchising (e.g. tied petrol stations, public houses and car distributors) has been around for a very long time. The present significant factor is the rapid growth into new trading areas (e.g. the restaurant and food industries, home cleaning, printing and copying, car rustproofing).

Probably the most interesting development in franchising is in the services sector. The service sector, as a whole, has developed fantastically during the past half century in the major industrialised countries. In the UK over 70 per cent of the working population at the end of the 1980s was employed in service industries, and this percentage could be further increased if we added self-employed persons representing over 10 per cent of total employment, many of whom are in the service sector. The following organisations are among those operating franchises in the UK: Benetton (fashion), McDonald's, Kentucky Fried Chicken and Wimpy (fast food), Prontaprint (printing design) and Dyna Rod (drain clearance).

Franchising may be attractive to manufacturers in that it offers some of the advantages of forward vertical integration without the risk of capital investment; to the franchisee it offers a degree of independence in operating a business of a size which may otherwise not be feasible. Personal service is a key factor.

A recent development in the growing franchising field of operations is the easing of the cost of entry and training. McDonald's, for example, is offering a spread of initial start-up fees over a longer period and a lowering of the level of bank finance needed. The banks do warn enquiring 'entrepreneurs' against operations which are in an experimental stage of high-risk business, but are generally ready to offer advice on investigation guidelines to those considering taking up a franchise.

Over 17,000 people in the UK are now dependent on franchising for their living, and turnover is estimated at £4½ billion. This movement is in evidence in Europe generally. Kärcher Clean Park, for example, is a German-owned self-service car wash with some 700 franchisees. The organisation is now moving cautiously into the UK and offers guaranteed loans to help in the purchase of initial equipment in addition to operational training and advice.

A recent important franchising development is in the business of milk delivery. A pioneer in this development was the Yorkshire-based Northern Dairies. Unigate, which supplies some 1.6 million customers from 120 depots covering an area from South Wales to Kent, has recently adopted the franchise system in a market where supermarkets were cutting into the milk market with prices at least 10p per pint lower. Unigate is pleased with the initial stages of the franchising operation. Franchisees pay a setting-up fee of £1,000 to cover initial training and put down a returnable deposit (£3,000 to £4,000). Training is given not only in selling techniques, but also in marketing and financial management. Guidance is also provided on setting up pensions and insurance. A very detailed marketing plan gives the social and demographic breakdown of a round and its earning potential. Each month there are business reviews providing ongoing guidance and sales targets. The milk 'float' is rented and royalties are paid on products which are collected daily from depots. Franchisees pay on a weekly basis. Unigate's target is to have a complete franchising system by the mid-1990s. It is estimated that the initial batch of franchise operations have halted a sales decline and, in fact, show an increase of 2 per cent. It is also estimated that franchise holders will increase earnings from some £240 per week to £400. The structural change was supported by a £6 million TV advertising campaign stressing personal service and 'greenness'. While milk marketing is the prime operation, it is clear that other products can be included in marketing plans (e.g. biscuits, soft drinks).

Network marketing

This is a multilevel direct marketing/sales approach which was initiated in the USA around the 1950s. It has fairly recently taken off to a limited extent in the UK. As in the best marketing operations, the product must be extremely good in terms of potential market demand if a particular operation is to succeed. It is a great advantage if it can be demonstrated quickly and easily. A speedy back-up service is also very important. It is dependent on a product which in a conventional marketing operation has an on-cost from product to user of some 40

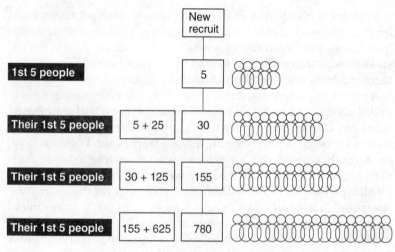

Figure 9.1 *Five stage example of pyramid growth*

per cent covering distribution mark-up, promotion and other kinds of marketing expenditure. When a person registers as a distributor of the product, the cost of doing so may be a mere £15 and investment rarely exceeds £75. The build-up of personnel takes the pattern shown in Figure 9.1.

Each network member receives a discount off the retail price (say 25 per cent). After the first level there is a wholesaler discount (say 15 per cent) and for very high sales performance a fourth 'bonus' (say 3 per cent).

For success it is clear that very good initial sales training is needed as well as a continuing communication programme, often in the evening. Network selling can be undertaken by otherwise employed personnel as well as unemployed persons.

Genuine network operations are subject to DTI regulations, the Direct Selling Association, the Multi Level Marketing Association and Trading Standards controls.

For more detailed 'case-specific' information readers should refer to the July 1992 issue of *Business Age*.

Wholesaling

37. The economic purposes
Wholesalers may be said to provide the economic utilities of time,

place and possession which may lead to economies in distribution – adequate stocks available at the right time in a convenient location.

38. Merchant wholesalers
Most wholesalers fall into this category – they buy and sell goods, taking title to the goods, then deriving profit from the marginal difference between the price at which they buy and the price at which they sell. Most merchant wholesalers undertake the following additional functions:

(a) They store goods.
(b) They undertake some advertising or promotional activity.
(c) They fix selling prices.
(d) They arrange credit terms.
(e) They make delivery.
(f) They offer advisory services.

39. Trade margins
Buying and selling margins vary widely, fluctuating in general with the risk carried and the range and effectiveness of the functions performed. If a wholesaler, for example, stocks expensive durable goods which require technical service, margins must be sufficiently high to compensate for these activities. It is, therefore, reasonable to expect that the manufacturer of refrigerators expecting a wholesaler to carry high stocks and provide servicing facilities would give much higher margins than a manufacturer of fast-moving canned food products. Sometimes, however, margins remain at a traditional level when original functions such as stocking and servicing are no longer carried out. This state of affairs may occur either because manufacturers are slow to recognise changed circumstances or because they are reluctant to take action in case they lose ground to competitors offering more favourable terms.

40. Size and specialisation
Some merchant wholesalers handle a wide range of general merchandise, but the majority specialise to a greater or lesser extent. Many are small and operate within a comparatively small geographical radius, but a number (particularly in certain trades such as grocery) are large and have regional and even national distribution. Examples of the various types of specialised wholesaler with a limited range of functions are described in **41–46** below.

41. Cash-and-carry wholesalers
These are at present mainly concerned with grocery products. They offer neither credit nor delivery services, and as a result operate on lower margins.

42. Rack jobbers
This is a recent development of truck wholesaling, previously limited mainly to perishable goods which may be collected from producers and delivered direct to retailers without the need for storage facilities. Rack jobbers are beginning to carry out a truck wholesaling function in supermarkets, where they may take over responsibility for maintaining stocks and the display of particular lines on particular shelves.

43. Brokers
Brokers negotiate sales between sellers and buyers. They take neither title to nor possession of goods. Profits are derived either on the basis of an average commission on value, or a commission on volume, or a predetermined fee based on sales. Brokers usually specialise in narrow ranges of products such as sugar, tea and cotton piece-goods. Specialisation is to be expected, since their value lies in their deep knowledge of particular markets and market conditions.

44. Factors or commission merchants
Factors do not buy goods, nor do they take title, but they do take possession and provide warehousing and handling facilities. Payment is normally by fixed commission. Whereas the broker represents the buyer and/or seller, factors represent the seller only. Factors are most commonly found where there are many small producers and a few large central markets through which products are resold, as in agricultural products.

> NOTE: The factors here described should be distinguished from factors who specialise in finance and who are really credit wholesalers. Credit factors may buy outstanding debtors' accounts and in doing so take over the function of a credit department. They also sometimes advise on customer selection and debt collection. Some finance factors have entered the business of stock financing: for example, in the case of car distributors, the dealer could take possession of cars in stock, but these would in fact be owned by the finance company to which sales revenue would go. Finance factoring is a growing business.

45. Selling agents

Selling agents are most commonly found where small manufacturers wish to be relieved of marketing responsibility so that very limited financial assets may be devoted exclusively to production. The selling agent usually works closely with the manufacturer over long periods, having complete responsibility for all sales. He or she accordingly sometimes supplies advice on style and design. Some sales agents work for one principal, but the majority carry a range of manufacturers' products, normally of a complementary kind. Selling agents sometimes carry the risks of credit loss and have considerable discretion over selling prices.

46. Manufacturers' agents

A manufacturer's agent differs from a selling agent in the following ways:

(a) He/she handles products in a limited geographical area only.

(b) He/she usually handles several manufacturers' lines, although these are normally, by terms of the agreement, non-competitive.

(c) He/she has little if any freedom to negotiate terms of sale and price.

(d) He/she usually has little control of product-styling design.

(e) He/she is rarely involved in credit collection and risk.

Manufacturers' agents commonly have warehousing facilities from which local deliveries are made, goods being held on consignment. Commissions are normally much smaller than in the case of selling agents, since the functions performed and the risks involved are smaller. Agency organisations vary in size, although most are comparatively small. They flourish particularly in circumstances where small manufacturers are endeavouring to tackle complex or widespread markets, such as industrial supplies and overseas markets. Automobile distribution is, however, conducted mainly through large-scale agencies which have exclusive area selling rights and usually, in return, act for one manufacturer only.

47. Wholesaler-sponsored voluntary groups or chains

The growth of large-scale retail operators is a threat to small independent traders and to wholesalers alike. To counter the threat, a number of wholesalers have combined to provide a central staff, while retaining control of the individual business. The central staff provides various services to all retailers which subscribe to the group. Members are expected to purchase a high percentage of their goods from a group wholesaler. Services provided by the central staff may include the following:

(a) Advertising and promotional support under a group name, (e.g. Mace, Centra, V.G.). Special promotions are arranged with manufacturers.
(b) Advice on merchandising, layout and equipment.
(c) Advice on retailing efficiency techniques, stock ranges, accounting and capital utilisation.
(d) Access to private label products.
(e) Financial assistance for shop improvements.
(f) Preferential insurance coverage terms.
(g) Special buying terms resulting from negotiation of bulk-buying contracts.

It should be noted that the voluntary group wholesaler movement lays great emphasis on assisting members to sell more effectively and enhance profits by greater all-round efficiency, and is not merely or primarily offering goods at cheaper prices. This movement has so far been most prominent in the grocery field, but may well spread to other retail outlets.

48. Retail-sponsored buying groups
Attempts have been made in various retail trades to establish group buying arrangements on a voluntary basis in order to obtain advantages of larger-scale purchases. Groups are usually formed on a very local basis, sometimes with a central warehouse and office being acquired. The progress of the movement in the UK has been much slower than in some European countries, and it seems unlikely that this form of group buying will become a major factor in the foreseeable future.

49. Producers' co-operatives
Producers' co-operatives are at present strongest in agriculture. They aim to provide a more planned and aggressive approach to marketing by:

(a) improving the quality of goods offered, through more rigid sorting procedures associated with the grading of produce according to set standards;
(b) undertaking co-ordinated promotional activities;
(c) regulating output levels in order to avoid the producer disadvantages of inelastic demand.

Producer co-operatives may be formed by the producers them-selves and the profit may be returned to the owners. On the other hand, the function of producer co-operatives may be absorbed by government-sponsored marketing organisations.

NOTE: There has been a growth in recent years of independent companies marketing for groups of producers: in horticulture, fruit farming, hotels and theatres.

Channel-choice problems for the manufacturer

Channel choice must be considered in the light of market coverage and control, product characteristics and market characteristics.

50. Market coverage and control
Distribution policy can be based on the following systems:

(a) *Intensive distribution.* This is a term used in different ways: limited geographical distribution as opposed to national distribution; maxi-mum distribution to all outlets of a specific type (e.g. chemists, grocers); or maximum distribution to every possible type of outlet.
(b) *Selective distribution.* This involves selection by the producer of the types of retail outlet through which the product may be bought. The decision may be made because of special services required (e.g. tele-vision sets), or because of the need to create an appropriate prestige image (e.g. certain cosmetics available from chemists only).
(c) *Exclusive distribution.* This is a further development of selective distribution. Particular outlets are granted exclusive handling rights usually within prescribed geographical areas. Wholesalers are given exclusive distribution rights more frequently than retailers. Some-times exclusive distribution or franchise rights are coupled with special financing arrangements for land, buildings or equipment (e.g. petrol station agreements).

51. Product characteristics
Those affecting channel decisions are as follows:

(a) *Frequency, value and quantity of purchases.* In general, low-value items bought in large quantity and frequently are widely distributed, using various channel combinations, whereas high-value items infre-quently purchased are sold by selective or exclusive distribution, or direct to the consumer.

(b) *Value in relation to weight and density.* The usefulness of intermediaries in the case of large, heavy items of low unit value may lie in their provision of local storage and bulk-breaking facilities.

(c) *Product life or seasonal demand.* Products which deteriorate rapidly or are affected by seasonal demand involve special problems of risk and inventory control which have a bearing on channel selection. Speed of movement is essential and channels tend to be shorter. Special storage (e.g. refrigeration) or transport (e.g. air cargo) may be necessary.

(d) *Product service requirements* (e.g. repair facilities, spares).

52. Market characteristics
Those affecting channel decisions include the following:

(a) *Market size.* If the market is large, the cost of performing all the marketing functions will probably be higher, and manufacturers may prefer or be forced to use intermediaries extensively. Cost could be reduced, of course, by limiting geographical distribution.

(b) *Market structure.* Consumer markets are inevitably dispersed. There are, however, differences in the concentrations of the potential users and distributors of products. Industrial customers require services of different types (e.g. technical advice, ready availability of spare parts), and although they are fewer in number, they may be widely scattered and have very different financial resources.

(c) *Market exposure.* Some products are bought almost on impulse, and sales are affected by exhibitions and special displays. Others require much more personal selling.

53. Decisions connected with channel selection
After consideration of basic channel problems **(50–2)** manufacturers are faced with more specific problems such as the following:

(a) *Organisation of selective selling.* In most types of business there are many outlets, but there is a disproportionate concentration of business in a small number of large units. This leads to 'selective selling' and the use of more than one channel, such as direct sales to large outlets, small outlets being supplied through wholesalers. Nevertheless, profitable operation may depend on securing wide distribution and/or promoting sales of slower-moving lines.

> NOTE: Selective selling should not be confused with selective distribution **(50 (b))**. By selective selling a manufacturer may succeed in obtaining intensive distribution.

(b) *Pricing structure* (*see* 5: **14, 15**).

(c) *Terms of sale.* As distinct from price, special credit arrangements, guarantees and arrangements for return of goods may be necessary.

(d) *Organisation of sales forces.* Sales forces may have to be organised partly by territory, partly by product type and partly by outlet size. Centralised buying has led to the creation of 'special outlet sales managers' in many companies.

(e) *Telephone selling.* The rapid growth of telephone selling must be mentioned. In-house operations in, for example, classified advertising, frozen foods and repeat subscriptions are not new, but there are now specialised telephone selling companies of which the leading six have been established within the past few years. Advantages are:

(*i*) quick advertising and assessable results;

(*ii*) rapid contact over a wide market;

(*iii*) cost advantages *vis-à-vis* personal selling calls.

Telephone selling companies have been linked with mailing in campaigns by large British and multinational plastics manufacturers.

In recent years, telephone selling has been used quite extensively by service companies such as those offering personal and household benefits (e.g. double glazing, security systems, building extensions, investment schemes). In these operations, the telephone call is only part of the selling process, intended to arouse interest and possibly fix an appointment for a visit by a sales representative.

(f) *Promotional support.* Channel choice will determine to what extent advertising should be used to *pull* products through the channels, and to what extent sales effort will be needed to *push* products through the channels (*see* 6:**10**). It may be necessary to supply private label brands (see 7:**21–4**).

(g) *Motivation and control of intermediaries.* Intermediaries are frequently order-takers, and problems of motivation and provision of sales training may arise. In selective or exclusive distribution systems, it will be necessary to evaluate the performance of intermediaries following careful selection. Replacements will have to be considered from time to time. Both intermediaries and channels which are the most suitable or feasible in the early stages of development of a business may cease to be so later on. In general, the further the manufacturer is removed from the ultimate consumer by links in the channel chain, the more difficult it is for it to control the flow of goods.

(h) Costs of stock holding.

(i) Costs of extending credit.

(j) Costs of invoicing, order processing, etc.

(k) Costs of transportation.

Delivery systems in service marketing

The need for making service facilities available in particular locations, in a particular form, to serve specified target markets with appropriate levels and types of service at acceptable cost requires a marketing approach. This is obviously now being recognised by those managing, for example, banking services, hospitals and other health care facilities, educational establishments and emergency services such as fire fighting. These and other particular service marketing aspects will be covered more fully in Chapter 11.

Progress test 9

1. What are the five main types of marketing institution?

2. What are the seven basic processes in marketing?

3. What are the main reasons for growth in mail-order business?

4. What are the advantages and disadvantages of the small independent retailer?

5. Define supermarkets.

6. What are the main general principles of chain store operations?

7. What have been the main difficulties of retail co-operative societies in recent years?

8. What are the main characteristics of discount stores?

9. What services do wholesaler-sponsored voluntary groups offer?

10. What is meant by 'intensive', 'selective' and 'exclusive' distribution?

Assignment

You are employed in an estate agency which has been taken over by an insurance company. What do you consider are the advantages you would be able to offer a prospective house vendor as a result of the change? Write notes which will be helpful to you in discussing the change with a prospective customer who has raised the question. You may wish to visit an estate agent who would be willing to discuss the matter with you.

Sales management

Sales forces: tasks and organisation

1. The role of sales forces

Sales forces are concerned with some or all of the six basic steps of the sales process (*see* 6:7). The closing of the sale may be the most important contribution to the process which most sales personnel make, but some may not be in a position to take orders, such as 'detailmen' who call on hospitals and general medical practitioners to convey information about the products of pharmaceutical companies. The five other steps involve a salesperson, however, in many activities. Among these are the following:

(a) He or she may provide merchandising services to speed up the stock turnaround (vital in retailing).
(b) The salesperson may act mainly as a specialist adviser: for example, on the installation of telecommunication systems.
(c) The salesperson may provide after-sales service and advice.
(d) He or she may actually deliver goods – van salesperson, bread roundsmen, etc.
(e) He or she may collect payment for goods delivered.
(f) He or she may be expected to advise on stock levels.
(g) The salesperson may train and motivate other salespersons, such as overseas agents and retail sales staff.
(h) He or she may report back on customer needs and reactions or on market conditions.
(i) The salesperson may progress orders and handle complaints.
(j) He or she may have a missionary or pioneering role, locating and opening up new business accounts.
(k) This salesperson may be part of a telephone sales team, as in advertising space selling and stock selling of frozen goods.

> NOTE: Many salespersons are concerned with the sale of intangible services, such as insurance. Many sales personnel are employed mainly to carry out sales activities at the premises of customers and potential customers; others spend

most of their time dealing with selling tasks at the premises of the vendor.

2. Selling and status

The range of products and services offered and the range of customer categories upon which salespersons might call are both enormous. Aircraft have to be sold to governments; milk has to be sold to housewives. Some products are bought repeatedly; others very infrequently.

The low status which attaches to the word 'salesman' in Britain derives partly from a popular ignorance of the diversity of personal selling tasks. Companies often attempt to overcome the status problem by using job designations such as representative and technical consultant. This is unfortunate, since all salespersons are concerned to a greater or lesser extent in actively persuading and educating prospective customers to reach the point of deciding to buy or to continue buying the company's products or services.

Company objectives and sales force decisions

3. Sales force decisions

A company must decide why it is employing a sales force: what role the sales force is to perform in the marketing mix. This basic decision will affect other decisions:

(a) What is to be the size of the sales force?
(b) How should the sales force be organised: for example, by products, by geographical territories, by customer categories?
(c) What is to be the comparative importance of the various activities of the sales force, such as actual selling, providing technical service, and display?
(d) What kind of men or women are required?
(e) What levels and systems of payment should be adopted?
(f) What structure (e.g. levels of management) is required?

4. Sales force size

The size of the sales force will depend mainly on the following factors:

(a) *The resources available to the company* and consideration of returns in relation to alternative forms of investment at particular times under particular conditions. A company with small financial resources will clearly be restricted in employing sales personnel, who inevitably carry a high burden of expense. A company may decide that it can meet its objectives by other means, such as investment in advertising, and therefore may rely entirely on mail-order selling.

(b) *The value of potential orders.* The expense of operation must be measured against the returns. The key factor is profitability. In some cases a company may be selling a particular piece of capital equipment at a price which easily covers the cost of direct sales representation. However, where unit margins are low and varied, a key consideration becomes the potentially profitable assortment of products which the salesperson has to offer. It is, therefore, logical to consider the minimum potential order value which will warrant the expense of personal representation.

(c) *The location and number of potential customers.* All other things being equal, consumer sales forces are larger than industrial sales forces since there are far more potential customers for consumer goods, scattered more evenly across wider areas. Industrial salespersons may, however, waste travelling time in visiting widely scattered accounts if too small a force is employed.

(d) *The buying habits and characteristics of potential customers.* Existing efficient channels of distribution (e.g. good wholesalers and retailers) may mean that fewer salespersons are required. Lack of efficient channels and the need for demonstrations and technical information – as in some industrial markets – may mean that the ratio of sales personnel to potential end users should be high. The *frequency of call* rate must also be taken into account here.

(e) *The product and customer range.* Different products may sometimes be handled effectively by one salesperson calling on similar types of outlet – or sometimes even on different types of outlet. The depth and breadth of product range may, however, lead to a position when salespersons become ineffective because they have too many products to handle, or products which require different technical knowledge, or sales journeys which are uneconomical.

(f) *Marketing policy.* The company may decide to concentrate on selective distribution or to attempt the widest possible distribution.

5. Sales force organisational patterns
Sales forces are normally organised on the basis of:

(a) geographical areas;

(b) product/service characteristics;

(c) customer types;

(d) customer sizes; or

(e) a combination of geography, product and customer types.

These five patterns are described in **6–10** below (*see also* **13**).

6. Allocation by geographical area

The possible advantages of a single salesperson assigned to cover all company products in a particular territory are:

(a) savings in travel expenses;

(b) better local and customer knowledge; and

(c) avoidance of multiple calling on the same customer.

The products offered, however, must be fairly homogeneous and within the technical competence of the salesperson to handle. In addition, the need for frequency of call must be judged against the number of calls which have to be made, when determining the extent of each salesperson's area.

7. Allocation by products or services

Sales force structures built around product specialisations have the advantage that highly qualified salespersons can be employed to deal with technical explanations and problems (e.g. pharmaceuticals, lifting equipment). This type of structure is favoured by larger companies which have highly diversified and specialised products/services, each making substantial profit contributions.

8. Allocation by customer types

Product specialisation selling may lead to the duplication of calling more than once on the same customers, whereas a specialised knowledge of different kinds of customer, their organisation, attitudes and product applications may be just as important as a specialised knowledge of the product. Sales forces may, therefore, be organised to call on particular market segments, such as laundries or retail outlets. The development of systems selling (e.g. of a range of items to furnish an office – carpets, curtains, filing cabinets, tables and chairs) often leads to customer-type organisations.

9. Handling large outlets

The significance of large outlets in relation to total market size has given rise to the practice in some companies of creating a sales force to handle key accounts. In some cases, key accounts, often termed 'house accounts', may be handled by the sales manager personally or by other sales executives.

Few generalisations are of any value, but where actual selling is a frequently performed and major role of the salesperson, a combination of fixed and variable compensation elements seems to be ideal. The fixed element has to be sufficiently high to provide for basic security and living standards; the variable element has to be sufficiently meaningful to both salesperson and company. A combination of fixed and variable remuneration has advantages in adjusting potential earnings according to changes in costs of living, changes the company's profit record and various combinations of seniority and selling achievement. The problems are to devise equitable systems and to set equitable targets.

17. Direction and control
Important factors are the following:

(a) *Economy in the use of time and effort.* The maximum amount of time should be spent on the outlets of major profit to the company. Waiting and travelling time should be kept to the minimum.

(b) *Arranging call frequency and rating.* Some outlets will require longer or more regular calls than others.

(c) *Development of business.* This includes increasing the business transacted with existing customers as well as locating and opening new accounts.

(d) *Reporting.* Reports will be required daily, weekly or monthly on calls made. Sales personnel should also learn to report back significant field intelligence (e.g. competitive activity, future developments by major customers). Reports on lost business or complaints will be required.

(e) *Evaluating the performance of sales personnel.* Salespersons' performance should be evaluated on quantitative factors, such as progress towards targets, comparison with past performance, and business development in relation to territory potential. Qualitative assessment will also be necessary, since the salesperson will have to undertake part of the selling process other than closing sales (*see* 6:7). It is increasingly common to find that sales personnel are appraised formally on their performance once or twice each year. Appraisal forms are frequently used and these often indiscriminately list quantitative and qualitative factors, such as attainment of target sales, condition of car, expenses against budget, and initiative. The primary assessment should be on the achievement of quantifiable objectives weighted according to their importance. Many of the qualitative factors on appraisal sheets refer to subjective assessments of personal characteristics or methods, and these should be considered only in so far as they may affect individual performance or company reputation and be susceptible to change by training or practice. A good appraisal scheme should be viewed by the salesperson as a mutually open exchange of views between him or her and the manager, a frank analytical performance check and, when necessary, a basis for agreeing on personal development action plans (*see* 19).

Motivation

18. Special problems of motivating sales personnel
Motivation of field sales forces provides special problems, for the following reasons:

(a) Salespersons meet frustration very regularly – every time they fail to make a sale or gain a favourable buying reaction. They can quickly lose confidence and future performance suffers.
(b) A salesperson works alone and lacks the immediate moral support of company colleagues. Sometimes a lack of company backing is felt if deliveries are late or invoices are incorrectly made out.
(c) A salesperson has irregular hours and is sometimes away from home. This may lead to special personal tensions.
(d) Few people are always self-motivating and of high morale, and a sense of reward or achievement is necessary for individuals to sustain effort if left entirely to their own devices.

19. Means of motivation
The need for a favourable working climate is therefore obvious. This can be stimulated in various ways:

(a) By providing helpful direction, such as assistance in field operations, by personal visits rather than perpetual written communications.
(b) By arranging sales and social meetings periodically.
(c) By arranging special sales contests.
(d) By making special efforts in writing and by telephone to keep personnel in the picture about company or area developments and progress.
(e) By encouraging positive suggestions for improved personal or company operation.
(f) By devising fair performance evaluation schemes, assisting people to develop their own capabilities, and providing a route to promotion or increased financial reward.

(g) By reducing unnecessary administrative procedures.
(h) By providing equipment and information to assist in the selling operation (e.g. sales manuals, sales literature, samples, demonstration models).

Market and sales forecasting

The remainder of this chapter should be read in conjunction with Chapter 8, 'Organisation and control'. All too frequently there is a lack of appropriate communication between sales, marketing management and other personnel. Ironically, this is a situation in which appropriate internal marketing is often required. The link between marketing plans and forecasting is reiterated in **28** below.

20. Basic forecasting considerations
Market and sales forecasting methods and procedures vary considerably from company to company, but there are really four basic considerations to be taken into account:

(a) The general economic environment and outlook.
(b) The particular industry environment and outlook.
(c) The outlook for the particular company and its products.
(d) Company and competitive marketing plans.

The above considerations should be related specifically to every product-market segment in which the organisation operates. For a company concerned with the marketing of tyres, for example, there would have to be a breakdown in terms of demand by tyre type, size and price bracket; by demand from original equipment manufacturers as opposed to replacement demand; by distributor size and type; and by geography. Products and services should also be considered in the light of the stage they have reached in the product-market life cycle. New products in markets where demand is mainly dependent on innovators should be distinguished from products on sale in mature, developed markets. Companies marketing similar products and services to a range of different industrial and commercial end users will find considerable variations in end-use demand trends and structure.

21. Forecasting time periods
Forecasts cover different time periods:

(a) *Short term.* The operating budget forecast covers the immediate financial year and is used to determine standard costs, prices, cash flow and similar matters.

(b) *Long term.* Forecasts are required for varying periods of time ahead, to provide for items such as major capital requirement, and new market or product developments.

22. Basic forecasting methods
Three basic methods are used for short-term forecasts, often in combination:

(a) Estimates (or guesses) by executives.

(b) Internal analysis of company data, such as using regression analysis (*see* 5:27).

(c) Analysis of company data related to other external performance criteria, such as economic conditions and industry trends. This form of analysis normally involves the use of statistical techniques such as correlation analysis (*see* 5: 27).

In any attempt to predict future demand from historical data, great attention should be paid not only to absolute levels of demand in specific product-market segments, but to monitoring rates of change. Key decision points occur where there are major directional changes in the typical S-curve of demand.

23. Sources of additional forecasting information
In order to supplement the information gained from various forms of statistical analysis, companies sometimes undertake the following exercises in addition to use of marketing research data:

(a) *Surveys of buyers' intentions.* It would obviously be impracticable to approach every potential buyer, or even to identify every one. Consequently, a sample is normally taken (*see*: **18–25**). Enquiries may be carried out by market research personnel, but sometimes sales forces are asked to co-operate. This method is more often practised when there is a comparatively small number of significant purchasers, as in some industrial markets. Difficulties arise if:

    (*i*) buyers are unwilling to give information (sales personnel may find this a major problem);

    (*ii*) buyers give deliberately false information; or

    (*iii*) buyers themselves do not really know.

(b) *Seeking the opinion of salespersons and sales executives.* The advantages should be:

(*i*) that the people in touch with actual buying conditions should know what is likely to happen;
(*ii*) that the forecasts will be readily available by products or areas; and
(*iii*) and that the sales force will support the forecast more readily because it has participated in the process.

This practice also has its greatest validity in highly technical selling fields. Adjustments have to be made to compensate for the over-optimism of some salespersons and the low estimates of others who fear that targets will be increased if sales estimates are high.

24. Problems in the analysis of internal data
Analysis of company data should take into consideration the following:

(a) Variations in demand – resulting from seasonal factors, cyclical changes in consumption and cyclical changes in inventory.
(b) Secular change – long-term trends of growth or decline in demand brought about by substitution or obsolescence.
(c) Random factors – chance or temporary changes in sales.
(d) Changes in the company's own market share position.

25. Statistical processess
Once seasonal factors are removed, random factors can be eliminated by the use of moving averages to produce a trend line (*see* NOTE 1 below). The problem now is to project the trend. Sometimes statistical means are used, such as the *least squares method* (*see* NOTE 2 below). There still remains the problem of allowing for changes in the business cycle which affect some types of industry (e.g. textiles) more than others (e.g. food). Sometimes it is possible to use *correlation analysis* to establish a relationship between specific materials or products, and demand for a company's own products. Thus a change in demand for retail products may be seen to have direct relationship to a change in demand for packaging, or a change in population to *per capita* demand for food.

NOTE:
1. A moving average is a moving total divided by the number of periods constituting that total. A moving total for twelve-monthly periods, for example, would be determined by dropping out the earliest monthly total and substituting the latest monthly total as it becomes available. For short-term forecasting, many

organisations are now using exponentially weighted moving averages, following a technique devised by Professor Holt of the Carnegie Institute of Technology. The weightings applied to a series of moving averages form a geometric progression. The latest data are thus given the greatest weighting and the diminishing weightings of previous data are systematically reduced by the use of a smoothing constant determined from examination of the nature of the demand curve.

2. It is most unlikely that the figures to be plotted on a graph will fall in a straight line which would immediately show the trend. The trend has, therefore, to be established by finding the line which would most nearly fit: that is, where the values shown on the line (the trend) would be nearer to actual values than any other line. The method of least squares is based on the mathematical concept that the best line is the one that minimises the total of the squared deviations.

26. Forecasting accuracy

The extent of forecasting error should be considered in the light of the cost of excessive stock-holding or out-of-stock situations and delivery hold-ups. It may not be economically justifiable to incur the cost of reducing errors by plus or minus 1 per cent, but it is certainly important to know the likely limits of error, and few companies are really satisfied with the reliability of their present forecasting procedures. If inaccuracy is seriously affecting profits, greater attention must be paid to preparing the basic economic assumptions, to securing relevant and reliable data and applying sound statistical techniques, and to analysing more closely the effect on demand of product policy, pricing and promotion.

27. Sales forecasting and sales targets

Sales targets are derived from a consideration of sales forecasts: that is, levels of sales anticipated at various levels of marketing expense. Sales targets do not necessarily coincide exactly with the finally accepted forecast, since targets are motivational tools (15) and may be set at a slightly higher level than the forecast in order to stimulate sales personnel to greater effort. Where salespersons are involved in the forecasting process, it should be noted that there is a real problem in practice in dissociating the idea of a forecast from that of a target. The experienced salesperson may well realise that his or her future earnings will be geared to this estimate of sales and make suitable downward modifications. Another source of possible distortion in a salesperson's estimates may arise in the form of upward modifications where there has been a history of delay or shortfall in deliveries on his or her particular territory (*see* **23**).

28. Marketing plans and forecasting – the link
Forecasting and marketing planning are complementary activities. Marketing plans are part of the corporate strategic and tactical decision-making process. The first stage is normally the identification and quantification of marketing opportunities, but consideration of resource availability, overall company objectives, risk, etc. enter into the picture. Before plans are put into action they will require top-level approval and the participation of those also concerned with forecasts (accountants, production managers, purchasing officers, personnel controllers, etc.). Marketing specialists take the lead in the forecasting process, involving sales personnel at various levels according to task and situation.

Progress test 10

1. What are the various functions which might be performed by sales forces?

2. What considerations might determine the size of a sales force?

3. On what bases might sales forces be organised?

4. What major problems occur in designing sales territories and routing? Is this a decision area where models might be useful?

5. What are the problems of providing financial incentives to sales forces?

6. Describe how and when fixed and variable salary elements might be used to create a purposeful sales salary.

7. How might salespersons be motivated?

8. What are the advantages and disadvantages of using buyers' intentions and sales executives' opinions in compiling sales forecasts?

9. What are the problems in interpreting company data for the purpose of forecasting? To what extent might exponentially moving averages help?

Assignment

Locate a firm which systematically evaluates the performance of its sales personnel. Explain how the system has been devised and comment particularly on:

(a) the frequency of the evaluation;
(b) who is involved in evaluating;
(c) whether the salesperson is involved and when; and
(d) the key objectives of the system.

Specific markets: the marketing of industrial goods and services

1. Definitions

The main principles of marketing as set out in earlier chapters apply to the marketing of all types of goods and services. The special characteristics of industrial markets and service industries, however, lead to special problems in the application of those principles.

Industrial goods and services are those bought by manufacturers, distributors and institutions (e.g. schools, government departments, extractive industries, agriculture and other commercial enterprises) for their own use rather than for resale.

Services may be bought not only by organisations such as those given as examples above, but by individuals or informal groups (e.g. club and society members). Kotler and Armstrong define 'service' as an activity, benefit or satisfaction that is offered for sale. It is essentially intangible and does not result in the ownership of anything. Its production may or may not be tied to a physical product.

2. A classification of industrial goods and services

There are four basic categories:

(a) *Capital goods*. These goods include such items as factory structures, machinery, office furniture and materials-handling equipment. Capital goods are treated by accountants as capital assets of a business, their value being depreciated over given periods of time.

(b) *Components and materials*. These include basic raw materials and partly or wholly processed materials and goods which ultimately form part of the products which are sold to customers (e.g. copper, tyres, sparking plugs, packaging).

(c) *Supplies*. Supplies are goods which assist production and distribution but are not included in finished products and, unlike capital goods, are not regarded as a capital investment. Examples include lubricating oils, stationery and cleaning materials.

(d) *Business services.* These cover a wide range of intangible services, such as business consultancy, office cleaning and advertising.

3. Special features of industrial products

There are certain features that distinguish industrial from consumer products:

(a) *Product similarity.* Industrial products have frequently to conform to national or international standards. This limits the extent to which a producer can differentiate his or her products from those of competitors. Again, buyers often lay down their own specifications. In general, the more a product is processed or fabricated, the greater is the possibility of differentiation.

(b) *Technical complexity.* Many industrial products call for a high level of technological skill and precision: for example, electric motors, paper-making machinery, hospital equipment, printing and packaging machinery. This factor means not only that there is often a need to maintain high investment in research and development activities and in manufacturing processes, but that it is frequently essential to supply technical assistance and advice. Provision for after-sales maintenance and for the supplying of spare parts is also frequently necessary.

(c) *High unit values.* Industrial goods, such as capital equipment, are frequently highly expensive items. The unit value of components and materials may be comparatively low, but the quantity required usually means that the value of total sales to individual customers is high.

(d) *Irregularity of purchase.* Materials which are used as part of finished products must be bought fairly regularly, but many other items, such as equipment, have a long working life and their purchase can be deferred. Components and materials are also frequently bought on a contract basis and the opportunity to obtain new business may arise infrequently.

4. Technological forecasting

Since traditional products and processes with high levels of committed investment are facing more rapidly the challenges of technological obsolescence, it is not surprising that considerable attention is being paid to a comparatively new type of forecasting – technological forecasting. Key questions which have to be answered include the following:

(a) What are the particular demand factors which promote the development of particular technologies?

(b) What are the total potentials for new technologies and at what speed will they be adopted in particular markets? The direction and speed of technology transfer are indeed a significant problem. The impact of nuclear and computer technology and satellite communications, for example, falls on government and private undertakings over a wide range of activities.

One of the techniques associated with technological forecasting is the *Delphi method*, whereby a panel of specialists is invited to express views on the probabilities of major technical changes taking place along a future timescale. The method involves a series of carefully planned sequential investigations. Further details of this and other methods at present being explored are outside the range of this Handbook.

The importance of these developments should be stressed, however, since it has been estimated that, by the year 2000, for every £1 spent on successful research in heavy industry, £25 will subsequently be spent on development work and £500 on commercialisation.

(c) Technological development is now a feature in some comparatively new fields, such as biotechnology. The biotech revolution came about in the USA some ten years before its emergence as a major development area in the UK. Some of these developments are in processes, such as blood filtration systems, the development of a compound to prevent rejection in kidney transplant, or new treatments for chronic kidney failure.

Research and development work in such areas as biotechnology are high risk over fairly long periods and call for very special marketing expertise – determining very real and pressing medical needs and the ability to move from research and testing so that distribution and marketing skills can be brought into play efficiently and quickly. Large multinationals such as Abbott have the capital and marketing skills needed, but there is evidence of the emergence of new companies linking in with distributors having the necessary marketing contacts and 'know-how'.

Company linkages are important: for example, the use by product/service-developing organisations of appropriately specialised agents in the marketing of specialised capital equipment and communication systems.

5. Special features of industrial demand
The following considerations are particularly important:

(a) *Derived demand.* The demand for industrial products is dependent on the demand for consumer products and/or services (e.g. the Channel Tunnel, construction, transport and rail links). A fall in consumer demand would quickly affect the demand for materials used in consumer goods, and a lack of buoyancy in consumer markets would lead to reluctance on the part of producers to buy new equipment or replace existing equipment. Government policies and economic measures are also very major factors. Because of derived demand, industrial markets are subject to greater irregularities in demand pattern than consumer markets, and the problems of forecasting are greater. Not only are there annual fluctuations; demand levels also often vary enormously from month to month.

(b) *Inelasticity of demand.* From the above it will be seen that lowering prices cannot be expected to have the same effect as in many consumer markets. If there is not ultimate consumer demand, the price of industrial goods and services is irrelevant. On the other hand, if there is a lowering in total demand, price reduction might provide an important advantage in the case of an individual company. Nevertheless, large price differences are unlikely, since producers will often be using similar materials from similar sources and competitors will probably react by reducing their prices. The greatest price fluctuations are to be found in markets for materials and components, where there are more suppliers competing for business than in capital goods markets.

6. Special features of industrial market structures

There are a number of marked structural characteristics of industrial markets. The most important are as follows:

(a) *Number of potential buyers.* It is clear that there are fewer potential industrial than consumer buyers. These buyers also have more specialised needs. Thus industrial markets consist of a number of special segments. The demand for certain products, such as agricultural machinery, will be limited to one specialised segment. The demand for other products, such as industrial oils, may be spread across a number of segments. The total number of potential buyers in different segments will vary tremendously: compare distributive services and aircraft manufacture. In all industrial market segments, however, a small number of buyers account for a very high percentage of the total market demand.

(b) *Geographical concentration.* Many industries are concentrated in particular geographical areas (e.g. paper making, car manufacture). On the other hand, the demand for certain products and services is geographically widespread (e.g. industrial cleaning materials).

7. Special features of industrial buying
Attention must be drawn to the following:

(a) Economic motives (*see* **8**).
(b) The group buying influence (*see* **9**).
(c) Professionalism (*see* **10**).
(d) Reciprocal buying (*see* **11**).
(e) Supplier loyalty (*see* **12**).

8. Economic motives
Industrial buyers are essentially concerned with the acquisition of goods and services which will provide measurable benefits in terms of ultimate profit. This, combined with the fact that the cost of purchase is often high, means that rational economic motives are much more significant than purely emotional considerations. Although industrial products are bought on a performance and benefit basis, however, it should be remembered that industrial buyers are subject to human emotions. Emotional aspects of buying may be seen, for example, in the following:

(a) Differences in attitudes of buyers towards features such as colour and design which may have no obvious economic value.
(b) Differences in attitudes of buyers towards particular sales personnel, sales literature and supplying companies.
(c) Differences in attitudes towards salespersons in general, which may have a sociological or psychological basis. The position and status of a professional buyer in the formal organisation structure, for example, will affect his or her attitude to sales approaches. One buyer with low company status may wish to bolster his or her ego by adopting a militant manner to sales personnel; another may be anxious to learn of new developments in order to gain a benefit for the company which might improve his or her own standing.

9. The group buying influence
The final purchasing order for industrial goods and services may be signed by one person, but the decision to buy is usually the result of the opinions of a number of people. These people may be motivated in different ways. The benefits seen by a manufacturing specialist may be minimised by an accounting specialist, for example. Again, persons who influence the buying decision may have different formal and informal status in their organisations. In general, research has shown that the larger the organisation, the greater is the number of people who influence buying decisions.

Robinson, Faris and Wind, in an important American research report *Industrial Buying and Creative Marketing*, have drawn attention to the differences in the 'decision-making unit' according to whether the purchasing decision is:

(a) a new buy;
(b) a modified rebuy;
(c) a straight rebuy.

Modified rebuy situations differ from routine straight rebuy situations in that some pressures exist to depart from routine: for example, a cost/profit squeeze or an existing supplier having to stagger deliveries. Modified rebuy and, particularly, new buy situations open up the real opportunities for a potential supplying company to contact a wide range of decision-makers and to offer creative ideas.

10. Professionalism

Industrial buyers are often not only familiar with technical and basic cost requirements, they may be specialists in such matters as evaluating sources of supply and deciding on the appropriate level of investment in stocks. Buying organisations are more and more concerned with setting basic standards of product and delivery performance, service requirements and so on, which must be met before a potential supplier can be seriously considered. The level of buying expertise varies tremendously. In general, the larger the buying company and the greater the expenditure involved, either in terms of capital equipment or in terms of cost of materials and components in relation to total costs, the greater is the professionalism of the actual buyer.

11. Reciprocal buying

This may be an informal arrangement whereby a buying organisation tends to favour suppliers who are customers. On the other hand, there may be strictly formal agreements. Formal agreements are not particularly widespread and have the great disadvantage of preventing buyers from obtaining the best value. It should here be pointed out that many large industrial organisations have highly diversified interests in different types of business. Sometimes there is complete control of capital; at other times there is a considerable percentage shareholding. Formal and informal reciprocal or transfer buying arrangements might be anticipated in such circumstances. Transfer arrangements apply to systems whereby one company or department buys components or processed materials from another, each ␣ operating as a profit centre. Sometimes when transfer arrangemen␣ are possible, buyers are still free to obtain supplies from outside sources if there are special advantages.

12. Supplier loyalty

Among industrial buyers there is frequently much greater loyalty to traditional suppliers than is the case in consumer markets. The reasons may be essentially emotional, such as the establishment of a personal relationship between buyers and sellers. Another important reason is that a new piece of equipment or new materials in industrial processes frequently affect total performance. Industrial buyers are therefore reluctant to change. Large organisations may have research and pilot plant facilities where prolonged testing can be carried out, and the period of negotiation for a major purchase may be quite lengthy.

Special features of the marketing mix

13. Industrial selling

Direct selling (i.e. from producer to user) is a feature of many industrial marketing operations. The main reasons for this shortening of the channels of distribution are as follows:

(a) There are fewer customers and these may be geographically concentrated. The potential size of orders is large. Thus fewer salespersons are necessary to establish direct contact, and the cost in relation to potential business is normally lower than in the case of direct personal selling to domestic customers.

(b) Considerable technical knowledge and demonstrations may be required in the selling process. The manufacturer's sales personnel can be expected to be more effective, therefore, than those of intermediaries who may handle a wide range of products. The use of sole agents with highly specialised product knowledge, territorial familiarity and customer contacts is often very successful.

(c) Many industrial items are bought to individual specifications and involve direct negotiation between buyer and seller on a technical level.

(d) Items of high unit value may require special credit arrangements which are more easily negotiated on a direct basis. Some items may be leased or rented.

ce of servicing and after-sales technical advice leads
efer direct dealings with manufacturers.

ers need a much more individual approach than
would be impossible in most cases to arrange for
monthly presentation of one particular brand with, per-
special price offers/advertising as in some retail market
situations. Individual benefits have to be sold to meet the needs of
particular organisations and people within those organisations.

NOTE: It is important that industrial salespersons should combine appropriate technical expertise and selling skill. There is a
danger that industrial sales staff may be appointed on the basis
of their technical qualifications alone, and there is frequently
insufficient training in selling skills provided.

14. Industrial advertising
Advertising is a much smaller constituent of marketing costs in
industrial than in consumer marketing. Apart from the fact that
advertising budgets are lower, there are many distinguishing features of industrial promotion, including those considered in **15–18**
below.

15. Use of mass media
As industrial markets are highly segmented, it is usually wasteful to
use mass media except in the promotion of corporate identity, where
mass media, public relations and sponsorship are playing an ever
greater role. Some companies do advertise in the national press for
the following reasons:

(a) To build up a corporate image of a large progressive organisation.
Large companies whose products may be used in many market
segments (e.g. ICI) are more likely to derive direct advantage from
mass communication media than smaller companies offering a
limited product range. Corporate images also serve to attract investment and personnel.
(b) To attract the attention of executives who may influence the
buying decision, but who rarely have the opportunity or inclination
to read specialised journals.
(c) To stimulate consumer demand for products which will reflect
on industrial demand. Consumer campaigns for artificial fibres and
plastics are good examples of this. The industrial manufacturer may
have much greater resources than the distributors along the distribution chain. In some cases, therefore, industrial manufacturers bear the

whole cost of such advertising; in others they may make a contribution towards the cost of advertising.

NOTE: Consumer campaigns organised by industrial manufacturers are often associated with branding (e.g. Terylene, Acrilan).

16. Specialised media
Industrial advertising is usually concentrated in the following media:

(a) *Trade press*. The range of journals is extremely wide; some are aimed at highly specialised readers (e.g. *Photographic Abstracts*), while others have a more general appeal (e.g. *Purchasing*). There are also considerable variations in costs of space, frequency of publication, circulation (often an estimate and not subjected to audit) and so on. This leads to specially acute problems in media scheduling and planning.

(b) *Business and professional journals*. These are ever-changing in number, format, circulation and influence. Professional journals often have a guaranteed circulation to members (e.g. *Work Study, Marketing*).

(c) *Direct mail*. There is evidence of the growing use of planned direct mail campaigns. In many industrial markets where prospective customers can be identified, are relatively few in number, and can be mailed at different times, use of this medium can bring valuable results: for example, in stimulating enquiries to be followed up by sales personnel or in keeping companies constantly informed of developments between sales visits.

(d) *Films and video*. Expenditure on documentary films for cinema showing could be justified by very few companies, but the specialised use of films and video is particularly appropriate in industrial markets. Industrial products are often large and difficult to demonstrate, especially if complex industrial processes are involved. Films can be used at trade shows, at national and international exhibitions, and at private company demonstrations. The use of special equipment for the showing of films by sales personnel on customer calls should lead to the stimulation of greater attention and interest.

(e) *Sales aids*. The provision of catalogues, price lists and sales literature is a vital part of any industrial advertising programme. Insufficient attention is often paid to the design and use of this material, and sales persons are inclined to rely too much on verbal descriptions and means of persuasion.

(f) *Exhibitions*. These are a feature of industrial marketing, but the large investment involved in participating in many national exhibitions is often unjustified except on the basis of keeping in line with competition. The case for arranging mobile exhibitions (e.g. in vans and special trains) is usually much stronger, as is that for participating in important international exhibitions (*see* 12: **55**).

17. Advertising agencies

Large agencies often concentrate on consumer goods campaigns because of the higher total expenditure and often better media discounts. There are sometimes, therefore, difficulties in finding agencies willing and able to undertake campaigns suitably geared to industrial users. Some smaller agencies specialise in this kind of work. Larger and more specialised agencies have become involved in the corporate image work previously mentioned. The increasing number of mergers has contributed to this, as have major government policies such as privatisation.

18. Establishing advertising objectives

Because of the range of specialised needs and buying motivations and the relative infrequency of buying, it is more difficult to establish clear objectives for a promotional programme in industrial than in consumer markets. The relatively low budgets and wide range of media available complicate the issue, and advertising expenditure is frequently wasted. It is particularly important that objectives should be clarified when resources are so scarce. Too many industrial advertisements attempt to communicate too much at one time, and too many campaigns are spoilt by attempting wide coverage at infrequent intervals.

NOTE: Publicity (*see* Chapter 7) is, of course, now a specially powerful industrial marketing tool.

19. Trends in organisation and negotiation

There is a real decline in purely geographically structured sales forces, and the following trends are clearly to be seen:

(a) More key account sales personnel specialising in large customers.
(b) More 'new account' salespersons requiring special qualities of enthusiasm, patience and ingenuity – pioneer selling as opposed to maintenance selling.
(c) More market- or product-centred sales forces geared to particular industries, specialised applications, buying policies and systems, etc.

A great deal more attention is also being given to developing negotiating skills and providing the appropriate background knowledge
skills to assist in, for example, financial services and product demonstration.

20. Conclusion
The total value of industrial goods and services bought in the United
Kingdom exceeds the total value of consumers' expenditure. This fact
together with the special complexities of industrial marketing
covered above should emphasise the importance of the adoption of
the marketing philosophy by all companies involved. Yet the process
of change from production orientation to marketing orientation is
slow. Vast sums are being spent on the research and development of
products, while the amount of money invested in analysis of the
markets to be supplied is still pitifully small.

The marketing of services

21. Definition
The increase in the service sector of industry is probably the most
outstanding factor of modern economically advancing societies. Of
course, all firms in business supply some aspects of service. It is
therefore difficult to define primarily service industries. W.J. Stanton,
in *The Fundamentals of Marketing*, has given an often quoted definition:

> Those separately identifiable, essentially intangible activities which
> provide want-satisfaction, and which are not necessarily tied to the
> sale of a product or another service. To produce a service may or may
> not require the use of tangible goods. However, when such use is
> acquired there is no transfer of the title (permanent ownership) to
> these tangible goods.

A useful quote from Gröngross from an article in the *European Journal
of Marketing* is quoted by Tom Cannon in *Basic Marketing*: 'The service
is the object of marketing, i.e. the company is selling the service as the
core of its market offering'. (See also the Kotler / Armstrong definition
in 11:1.)

22. Characteristics
The following are among those which have been quoted:

(a) *Heterogeneity.* This concerns the idea that services are very
frequently designed to meet the requirements of the individual

customer. Standard packages regularly appear, however, in tourism, banking, etc.

(b) *Intangibility.* The services offered by a tourist agency, an insurance company, a bank, a consultancy organisation, etc. are evaluated on the intangible working of a total service, which unlike a product is not judged or thought of primarily in terms of intangible elements, although intangible elements may be present. Contrast marketing a range of Ford cars and marketing a group of restaurants.

(c) *Inseparability.* It is said that, with a service, production and consumption take place at one time – hence the idea of inseparability. This concept may, perhaps, be most readily perceived in personal services such as financial services, insurance and travel agencies.

(d) *Perishableness.* Services cannot be stocked. A vacant hotel bedroom, and services such as electricity, gas, telecommunications and commercial advertising in TV time, have a regular fixed capacity which lacks the flexibility of being able to provide advance stocks to cope with fluctuating demand.

(e) *Lack of ownership.* The customer does not take title to a hotel room, to a hired car, or to a Barclaycard.

23. Service industries: vital aspects

(a) *Range and size.* Academic argument about definitions may well continue. The immediate vital aspects are the growth rate, the individual size of many operators, and the extremely wide range of service industries. Consider the following as examples: building societies, banks, distributive services of many kinds, leisure services, health and social care services, water, gas and electricity, tourism and travel services, consultancy of many kinds, security services, the Post Office, telecommunications, designers and architects, and non-profit-making organisations.

Corporate goals and strategies need to be decided and appropriate time allowed for effective analysis and implementation. Service packages should then be tailored to meet specific markets and/or market segment needs with an appropriate mix of material and human resources available at the right times and in the right places.

(b) *Personal aspects.* Services employ computerised methods more and more to cope with the speed, cost and flexibility necessary to meet a highly varied demand efficiently and promptly, and to cope with the development of the information systems required. Nevertheless, they are and will continue to be very large employers of labour. The need for economic operation in these vast markets is clear, but 'service' must retain the personal touch in its many varied markets, and be managed and staffed in such a way that the human element is always to the fore. It is difficult to achieve this objective when the time for individual customer contact in an increasingly competitive field is often very short and infrequent, yet memorable and vital to the customer. It would be dangerous to rely too heavily on particular aspects of the marketing mix, such as non-personal communications. The concept of the mix applies, but its complexity is even greater and must be used to overcome the danger of impersonal bureaucracy.

NOTE: Students are advised to attempt the assignment at the end of this chapter and, if possible, to discuss their findings and those of other students.

Progress test 11

1. Industrial markets are varied and complex. How might they be classified in order to examine broadly common characteristics of purchasing behaviour?

2. What is the special significance of demand elasticity in industrial marketing?

3. What are the special features affecting the industrial buying process which create selling problems quite different from those usually encountered in selling consumer products?

4. Why is 'direct selling' such an important factor in many industrial markets?

5. What are the special difficulties in devising advertising campaigns for industrial goods and services?

6. Comment on the characteristics offered by a number of writers in an attempt to describe service industry markets. Select a number of service markets and consider how well the quoted characteristics apply.

Assignment

Obtain statistical data showing employment in agriculture, manufacturing and services in a country, a major city and a small town in that country in 1970 and 1990. Comment on and suggest reasons for any major changes.

International marketing

The significance of international trade – the theoretical backcloth

1. The principles of comparative advantage

There is nothing new in the notion of international marketing. The *theory of comparative advantage* derives from the idea that nations will tend to capitalise on the possession of special natural resources or special skills, so that they can offer to other nations advantages in terms of price or special product/service qualities. They will import products which they themselves cannot produce as economically or as well. The theory is complicated in practice by shifting variables – wage levels, material costs, transportation costs, production methods and costs, scientific and technological development, educational standards and so on. In addition, financial (particularly foreign exchange) and legal problems complicate the issue, and various restrictions on free trade are imposed by governments. Again, there is a natural tendency to satisfy an unsaturated home demand before entering international markets.

2. The balance of trade

Nations lacking essential materials are compelled to import and must attempt to balance their trade by exporting.

The United Kingdom, lacking valuable raw materials and being highly industrialised, is particularly dependent on international trade. To maintain a balance of trade it is necessary to earn sufficient from visible and invisible exports to meet international obligations and finance imports and the outflow of capital.

3. Recent trends in international trade

The factors which have led to an accelerating rate of change in the pattern of international business are as follows:

(a) Social and economic (*see* **4**).
(b) Technological (*see* **5**).

(c) Legal and political (*see* **6**).
(d) International financing and investment.

These factors are, of course, interacting.

4. Social, political and economic factors (*see* 1:3**)**
Among major considerations are the following:

(a) Industrialisation.
(b) Education.
(c) Distribution of wealth.
(d) Demographic changes.
(e) Population size.
(f) Social and physical mobility (*see* 1:3(d)).
(g) Urbanisation.
(h) The development of political and economic trading blocs (see 6(d)).
(i) International and regional political and legal developments.
(j) Fundamental political changes (e.g. the demise of Communism in Russia).

5. Technological factors
Changes are taking place at an almost exponential rate. Examples are very evident: the use of nuclear power in generating electricity, the increased speed of air transport, international communication systems, automation and increasing mechanisation in industrial processes. International trade in manufactured products is increasing at a greater rate than trade in primary commodities. The need for primary commodities, however, does not increase in direct proportion to the growth of population or income. Countries which are industrialised tend to trade with one another more and more, so the gap between the economic development of industrially developed and non-developed countries tends to widen.

Transfers of technology between developed and developing countries amount to a mere 10 per cent of total technology transfers. This is a matter of worldwide concern which comes within the remit of UNCTAD (the United Nations Committee on Trade and Development).

The emergence of Japan as an economically developed country with the clearly formulated aim to obtain membership of several world economic organisations is highly significant in a world context. Currently, there appears to be a possibility that three major international groupings will develop:

(a) Greater Europe (EU and EFTA).
(b) North America and Mexico (NAFTA).
(c) Japan and East Asia.

The present situation in terms of population and GDP is as follows:

	Population	GDP
Greater Europe	380m	$6.5 trillion
North American Trade Agreement countries	360m	$6.2 trillion
Japan and East Asia	510m	$3.7 trillion

If economic development were to continue in line with that over the five-year period 1988 to 1993, a Japanese/East Asian economically tied group would outstrip both the European and the American groupings over the next twenty years.

More and more countries are becoming industrialised, and seek to develop their economies by international exchange. Those countries which are comparatively self-contained, such as the USA, are now very heavily involved in international marketing.

6. Legal and political factors

National and international bodies have been working towards the removal of economic and financial barriers. Examples can be seen in the following:

(a) *The General Agreement on Tariffs and Trade (GATT).* Since GATT was set up in 1948, there have been many long rounds of negotiations involving major industrial countries, a major result of which has been to reduce, on a reciprocal basis, hundreds of tariff barriers and customs duties. There are some 90 member countries which account for four-fifths of world trade. Recent negotiations have become even more difficult because of low growth and recessions in more economically developed countries. Greater evidence of protectionism has emerged: for example, extended negotiations on farm subsidies involving mainly France and the USA.

The *United Nations Conference on Trade and Development (UNCTAD)* has a wider brief than GATT, particularly in connection with finance and aid for development. It is open to all UN members. (*See* 5 for reference to UNCTAD in regard to technology transfer.)

(b) *The International Monetary Fund.* This organisation came into being in 1945 to devise and operate a system which would give stability to exchange rates and expand international liquidity – so necessary for the growth of international trade. Despite occasional difficulties, a system of fixed exchange rates geared to the American dollar held fairly well until the late 1960s, and world trade developed among the industrialised countries at an unprecedented rate. A slow-down in the development of international trade has been a feature of the 1970s and 1980s. This, together with the widespread use of mone-tarist policies to stem inflation, has also slowed down national growth rates in most industrialised countries, while unemployment levels have risen.

The *Organisation of Petroleum Exporting Countries (OPEC)* was set up in the 1970s. Agreement on prices and stabilisation among its mem-bers has not been entirely successful, but it has had marked effects on international trade – particularly the balance between developed economic areas and the less developed countries (the Third World).

(c) *The Organisation for Economic Co-operation and Development.* This organisation was set up in 1961 and has a membership of 25 western European states, plus the USA, Japan, Australasia, Turkey and the former Yugoslavia. Its aim is to foster the growth of the national income of its members through co-operation.

(d) *Economic trading groups.* One of the prime aims of these groups is to remove trade restrictions (e.g. tariffs, quotas) among members. The European Economic Community (EEC, or the EU as it has become since the 1993 European Union Agreement) was established under the Treaty of Rome signed in 1957. It came into existence in 1958 and Britain became a full member in 1973. Full membership in 1986 comprised Belgium, Denmark, France, West Germany, Greece, the Irish Republic, Italy, Luxembourg, the Netherlands, and the UK. Portugal and Spain are now also full members. Associate member-ship, with limited rights, is also possible. Full members of the European Free Trade Area (EFTA) were Austria, Iceland, Norway, Portugal, Sweden and Switzerland, with Finland as an associate member. All EFTA countries have signed agreements with the EC to Eliminate mutual industrial tariffs. Other groups are also emerging: for example, in South-East Asia, Latin America and Africa. At the same time a number of centrally planned economies survive in the remaining Communist countries, with external selling and buying conducted by state agencies.

(e) *Various forms of assistance* are provided to exporters by national governments.

7. Significance of recent trends

(a) *The emergence of multinational companies.* As a consequence of these changes, truly multinational companies are developing. Multinational companies may be defined as those which have manufacturing or other substantial investment overseas, and which make management decisions on the basis of global opportunities and global resources. A growing number of companies have reached this situation and have found the need to effect economies of scale by a variety of methods of international sourcing. The emergence of Japan in this context is highly significant.

(b) *The emergence of regionalism and nationalism.* The emergence of multinational companies has led many governments, urged on by organised labour, to reconsider forms of national protection of trade. In particular, the spread of American multinational operations is regarded as politically and economically dangerous in many quarters. At the same time, new independent national states have been formed, and countries which are considered less developed in an economic sense are pursuing policies which will transform them as quickly as possible from poor agricultural areas, with the majority of the population living at a mere subsistence level, to fully fledged industrialised societies, with total national and per capita wealth greatly enhanced. Among the schemes for some degree of economic integration, the formation of the following six regional markets is significant:

(*i*) East African Economic Community (Kenya, Uganda, Zimbabwe, Sudan and Tanzania).

(*ii*) Central African Customs and Economic Union (Congo, Gabon, Cameroon and Central African Empire).

(*iii*) Maghreb Common Market (Algeria, Tunisia, Morocco and Libya).

(*iv*) Central American Common Market (Guatemala, Nicaragua, Honduras, El Salvador and Costa Rica).

(*v*) Latin American Integration Association (formerly Latin American Free Trade Association) (all South American republics and Mexico).

(*vi*) Association of South East Asia (Thailand, Indonesia, The Philippines, Singapore and Malaysia).

(*vii*) NAFTA: North American Free Trade Association (USA, Canada and Mexico).

(c) *The Third World.* One of the great problems is the disparity in wealth and population between the so-called developed and industrialised countries (e.g. members of the OECD), and the diverse, essentially agricultural Third World countries, where over 1 billion people live in extreme poverty.

The conflicts between regionalism, nationalism and multinational private enterprise were well illustrated in the exercise of economic power in the mid-1970s by oil-producing and exporting countries, and the consequent policies and actions of multinational oil companies, oil-importing regional groups and national states.

The position of the UK

8. Productivity and international trade expansion
Britain's share of an increasing volume of world trade is falling. The decline is more marked in some industrial groups than others – notably in the more traditional industries, such as textiles.

Various reasons may be advanced, but all amount really to a failure to maintain a marketing advantage in increasingly competitive conditions. Sellers' markets have almost invariably become *buyers'* markets and, where attention has been paid to the specific needs of customers, companies and industries have been relatively successful (e.g. those that manufacture specialised paints, high-quality woollen goods, sports cars). Often exports have been increased in spite of pricing disadvantages. In general, however, the prices of German, Japanese and Italian goods have not risen as sharply as those of British goods. It could be argued that the Japanese have had the advantages of lower labour costs, but a similar argument is not completely true of Germany. Where price advantages have been gained by Germany, Italy, France and Japan, they have been achieved by marked improvements in productivity rather than by simple differences in wage rates. Improvements in productivity have been matched by, and to a large extent made possible by, aggressive overseas marketing and a philosophy of global growth. By the early 1990s, over 80 Japanese companies had businesses established in the UK, which had become the largest centre of a massive overseas Japanese investment.

9. Changes in demand patterns, markets and products
Apart from considerations of prices, productivity and increasing competition, it is clear that many of Britain's traditional markets have become self-sufficient and, indeed, are exporting some products in competition with Britain. It is also evident that world demand for the kind of products on which British international trade was mainly dependent before the Second World War has declined, or expanded at a much slower rate than the demand for other types of product. It may be argued that government policy in the early post-war years, often aimed at damping down home consumption to stimulate exports,

has had a dampening effect on industrial activity. It does not follow that a restriction of spending power in home markets will lead to increased attention on the part of manufacturers to export business. Home and overseas business are not mutually exclusive, and a healthy home market may well be a condition for competitive overseas operations – and in some cases, unless trade barriers are erected, a condition for survival at home.

One major factor leading to change in the UK position has been the relaxation of exchange controls. Foreign investment is being attracted into the UK (e.g. in car manufacturing and electronics) and British investment overseas has more than doubled in the last decade. This process of increased financial mobility in major developed countries has led to a high degree of industrial concentration in a limited number of world centres – particularly in the case of high-technology products. The Far East – and less developed countries such as Thailand, Singapore, Hong Kong and Malaysia – have profited from the offspin of the major developments.

The UK, the European Monetary System and Maastricht

For a considerable time the UK remained outside the European Monetary System (EMS), in which there are free capital flows, a single licensing system for banking, free competition in insurance, and a currency stabilisation system for full currency control, with participating currencies having a fixed rate against a European currency unit (the ECU). The ECU is based on a 'basket' of those currencies in the EMS. Apart from the UK, Greece and Portugal stay, by common agreement, outside the system at present because of the comparatively weak state of their economies.

The Spanish peseta went into the EMS in 1989 and, like the Italian lira, was and is allowed to fluctuate within an agreed percentage margin.

The UK went into the system very recently (8 October 1990) and came out again on 'Black Wednesday' (16 September 1992) when the British government pulled out to counter mammoth speculation in the currency markets. Other currencies, notably the French franc, have also come under great pressure. It was hoped by the British government that the lower international value of a floating pound would encourage exports and improve the balance of trade position. A year later there was little evidence of an improved overseas trading position in fairly widespread low-growth conditions.

10. Major opportunities for British trade

The opportunities for British exports of goods and services in the near future would appear to be in five main areas: western Europe, the USA, the Commonwealth countries, the Middle East and Latin America. It is the more highly industrialised countries which generate the highest level of world trade and these lie within the areas specified.

Future East–West trading within the former Communist bloc will call for a new type of economic relationship with special co-operative agreements. Examples are the export of 'know-how' and joint manufacturing arrangements such as those of the existing tractor manufacturing operations in Hungary and Romania with Steyr-Daimler-Puch of Austria and Fiat of Italy, respectively. There are and will continue to be considerable opportunities for 'exporting' management and operational skills, as well as for developing language and cultural exchanges.

Prior to the signing of the 1993 European Union Agreement at Maastricht there were many examples of mergers and other special exchange agreements as well as appropriately located capital investment in the 'new' Europe. Opportunities may well be taken to move into Europe by those internationally marketing concious Japanese companies already based in the UK (note Honda's reaction to the Rover-BMW agreement). An example of European activity was the Nestlé takeover of Rowntree, and its many successful brands could herald a wider-based European approach. In the late 1980s and early 1990s, takeover and merger activity in Europe was very marked: for example, in finance, cables, food processing equipment, packaging, brewing, electrical equipment and insurance. These activities were undertaken in order to slim down or concentrate activities to cope with and benefit from a unified European market. Harmonisation, however, will not provide simple answers to most of the questions raised in the following paragraphs. Opportunities need to be analysed very thoroughly if they are to be advantageous in a highly competitive world.

11. Analysing opportunities in world markets

It is likely that success or failure in world markets will depend as much on marketing expertise as on manufacturing or financial resources. The first consideration is to discover what the market wants and is likely to buy. It is therefore necessary to obtain the following basic information:

(a) *Population details:*
  (*i*) Total population.

(*ii*) Growth rate.
(*iii*) Geographical concentrations.
(*iv*) Income levels, distribution and trends.
(*v*) Consumption trends.
(*vi*) Family size and number of households – solidity of family groupings.
(*vii*) Language; religious, cultural and social groupings; and buying patterns and attitudes.
(*viii*) Educational standards.
(b) *Economic resources:*
(*i*) The existing structure of economic wealth – minerals, agriculture, manufacturing technology, financial services, research and development.
(*ii*) Likely changes in the economic structure and rate of change.
(c) *Communications* – the availability and cost of transport to and in the overseas territory (road systems, ports facilities, railways, airports, telephonic communications, etc.).
(d) *Location, climate and topography* – possible effects on resources and productivity.
(e) *Government policy and political philosophy*:
(*i*) Attitude to foreign trade and investment.
(*ii*) Taxation policy.
(*iii*) Economic planning and control; attitude towards particular products or industrial development.
(*iv*) Foreign exchange policy.
(*v*) Military demands on economic resources.

12. World demand: basic system

Analysis of world markets on the above lines will reveal certain basic similarities and differences arising from basic systems: namely, social, economic, technical, political and legal. Economic groupings and regulatory mechanisms are of increasing importance.

13. The social system

Nations develop social attitudes and customs which derive from their peculiar pattern of cultural development. Attitudes towards the family, social class structure, class mobility and material values, for example, have a basis in the oral and ethical standards of a community, standards often rooted in religious beliefs. Some of the effects on social systems caused by very different religions, such as Hinduism and Christianity, will be obvious; other attitudes, such as those towards colour, require close investigation. Significant differences in attitudes and customs are to be found in Christian countries. Attitudes towards certain products and advertising copy are different in France from those in Holland.

It should be noted that attitudes and beliefs tend to strengthen over time, and thus that countries are often associated or associate themselves with special abilities or characteristics. The German, for example, may consider himself technically superior but may be prepared to buy a Ford car combining German technical achievement and American styling. An image associated with particular countries persists long after the basis for the 'image' has disappeared. It is therefore more difficult to remove a reputation for poor delivery service than to create it. Changes can be effected, however. The Japanese reputation for lack of innovation has virtually disappeared, but major technological changes have been aggressively marketed. Attitudes towards personal mobility may have to change. Just over 40 per cent of managers in France's top ten companies now work outside France.

14. The economic system
Differences in market opportunities are frequently the result of differences in the following:

(a) Standards of living.
(b) Cost of labour, materials and equipment.
(c) Rate of population growth.
(d) Distribution methods.
(e) Spread of industrialisation.
(f) Availaibility of acceptable available currency, exchange values and credit.
(g) Communications.
(h) Privatisation.

Market similarities spring from economic similarities and the influence of mass consumption societies, international companies and international advertising. Patterns of consumption and income distribution follow similar trends according to broadly defined stages of economic development. The pyramid pattern of income distribution, with wealth concentrated in a few hands, moves through various stages until an ovoid pattern denotes a high level of industrialisation, with the incomes of the majority narrowly differentiated and well above subsistence level. Thus countries with a high per capita income level have an ever increasing demand for consumer luxury goods, while the demand for necessities remains fairly stable. The difference lies in the type of luxuries (e.g. telephones, refrigerators, washing machines, cars).

In the UK, the Conservative government's privatisation policy has led to very considerable changes in policies and strategies affecting capitalisation, profit and shareholder satisfaction, reinvestment, external and internal marketing, pricing, management structures, etc. The role of regulatory bodies at national and EU level is also of considerable importance.

15. The technical system
The development of technology depends on economic factors (e.g. the availability of capital and professional and skilled labour) and on political factors (e.g. high investment in defence projects, as in the USA). Changes in policy tend to arise frequently because of changing political and economic situations in the national and international scene: for example, the reduced threat of major wars, following political changes in Russia, the widespread slowing down of economic growth and the rise in unemployment levels. One of the major problems is that the 'technological gap', the difference in technical knowledge and its application, between the less developed economies and the developed economies of Europe, the USA and Japan is widening as a result of economic and political factors (*see* 4, 6 and 11 above).

16. The political and legal system
Political philosophies and government actions based on these philosophies affect the pattern of international trade. Moves towards liberalisation have been mentioned earlier (6), but among major differences are the following:

(a) The extent of state and regional political and economic regulations affecting control of particular economic situations.
(b) The attitude of governments towards, for example, the import and export of goods and currency, the investment of foreign capital and the use of foreign labour.
(c) Political stability. Frequent changes in government, as in Latin America, give rise to economic and financial instability.
(d) Business law and legislative procedures.
(e) Efficiency and integrity of civil servants.

17. Distribution patterns
The major differences between distribution patterns in various countries are due to the following factors:

(a) Economic factors (*see* 18).
(b) Social factors (*see* 19).

(c) Geographical and communication factors (*see* **20**).

18. Economic factors

(a) *Ownership.* In some Communist countries, for example, there is complete state control of the distribution process. In some other areas, state-owned enterprises or co-operatives co-exist with private institutions – but some major changes have already occurred and others might follow.

(b) *Number, physical size and turnover of retail outlets.* In general, the more economically developed a country is, the larger is the size and turnover of major retail and wholesale outlets. Average retail store sales in the USA are 35 times higher than in India, for example.

(c) *Functions performed and services offered.* Self-service is a feature of more highly developed Western economies. Other differences occur in the provision of credit, after-sales, stock-holding and risk-carrying, promotional and display facilities. These activities may require financial support from manufacturers or wholesalers where retailers are notably short of capital. Attitudes may differ surprisingly in important specific ways: for example, contrast attitudes towards and use of credit in the UK and Germany.

(d) *Assortment of products.* In general, the less developed the economy, the greater the degree of specialisation in channels.

(e) *Productivity and labour.* In more highly developed countries, great attention is being paid to economies of operation. This may lead to lower margins and a decline in personal service.

(f) *Industrial product distribution.* Where there is a lack of industrialisation, industrial goods are frequently handled by importers which carry a wide range of products. This presents difficulties in providing for technically competent after-sales service.

19. Social factors

(a) In many countries, manufacturing is considered to be more socially useful than distribution. The low status of wholesaling in many underdeveloped countries has, for example, led to the dominance of distribution by immigrant populations, who have also appeared in small-scale retailing in the UK.

(b) In all countries, various types of outlet have greater appeal for particular strata of society than for others.

(c) There are considerable differences in the extent to which buying is regarded as a social activity by both industrial and domestic customers.

20. Geographical and communication factors
In a large country with a comparatively underdeveloped economy and communication system, historical trading patterns and dispersion of customers may lead to a greater number of links in the distribution chain. One of the problems in this kind of situation is that there is often a marked difference in the attitudes and objectives of traders in the distribution chain. Lack of advertising media intensifies the problem.

Methods of exporting

Once a company has decided to enter overseas markets, decisions have to be made on the extent to which it should become financially involved and exercise control over various aspects of distribution.

21. Distribution: control considerations
Major factors to be considered are as follows:

(a) The physical distribution of products, including the maintenance of stock.
(b) Establishing contact with buyers.
(c) Providing information to buyers.
(d) Negotiating sales.
(e) Providing technical advice and after-sales service.

In the marketing of services, important factors to consider may include the following:

(a) The role and location of electronic devices for customer use.
(b) The roles, size, staffing and locating of specialist personal services.
(c) The extent to which specialist staff may be required to visit customers and potential customers, and where such staff should be located.
(d) The possibility of engaging, on a fee or contract basis, non-company personnel or agents of various kinds.

Every country has its established channels of distribution and the principles governing their selection are set out in Chapter 9. It is always wise to study the use of channels by competitive organisations. Various marketing institutions, however, provide specialist services in the field of international marketing in order to reduce the separation between producers and consumers (*see* below).

22. Specialist marketing institutions

The following marketing institutions may be used because they have expertise not possessed by the producer organisation or because they enable the producer to enjoy many of the opportunities afforded by overseas markets at a low level of financial investment and risk:

(a) *Export merchants.* Goods are purchased outright by the merchant in the country of origin. The merchant then takes over the task of reselling abroad. Use of merchants means that the manufacturing organisation has no control over marketing operations. Merchants usually handle many lines and may not attempt to sell a particular company's products aggressively. Non-differentiated commodities, such as raw copper, may be handled more successfully in this way than products which have distinctive benefits and company and brand identification. Export merchants do, however, offer advantages to small companies lacking resources or knowledge to export directly, or to large companies in areas with small market potential. Many export houses provide a wide range of valuable services, such as information on markets, agents, advertising and finance. Merchants are sometimes also able to carry out more effectively the barter arrangements which may be necessary in dealing with some countries.

(b) *Overseas company buying offices.* Many large companies establish buying offices abroad. Once an order is placed with an overseas supplier, it normally makes arrangements for transportation, invoicing, documentation and so on.

(c) *Export commission houses.* These organisations act as buyers on behalf of overseas companies. They try to locate suitable supply sources, putting buyers and sellers in contact. They are paid in the form of commission from the foreign firms they represent on the basis of sales ultimately negotiated.

(d) *Overseas agents or distributors.* The appointment of overseas agents or distributors has traditionally been a major method of exporting. Historically, British export success has been based very largely on the notion of finding distributors to stock, advertise and sell products, and to develop markets at a reasonable margin of profit. Personal contact on the basis of exchange visits was rare, and business was transacted almost entirely by correspondence. Unfortunately, this original tenuous arrangement often persists. Agents can still frequently perform a most valuable export-selling operation at the minimum risk, but great care must be taken in selection, and very considerable attention must be paid to training, motivation, direction and support (*see* 9: **2** (c)).

NOTE: Licensing (**29, 30**) also has the advantage of limited investment and low risk. Methods of international marketing involving much risk and investment are examined later (**32–41**).

23. Important factors in selecting agents

Because agents are so widely used, it is appropriate to examine in closer detail problems of agency selection, agency agreements (**27**) and methods of motivating agents (**28**). When the decision is taken to use agents, it should be realised that these agents will carry the major burden of effective selling, however much support (e.g. advertising and technical assistance) they may receive from the company engaging them. Careful selection is, therefore, absolutely essential. Factors to be considered in making the selection are examined in **24** and *25* below.

24. Business standing, reputation and policy

The following points must be taken into account:

(a) *Financial strength and reputation* with bankers and suppliers: credit policies.

(b) *Business success or prospects of success.* The record of sales growth over the past few years is a valuable selection pointer. Again, the significance of business with a new company would have to be considered. A fairly new agency with the right resources and development potential might sometimes sell more aggressively.

(c) *Integrity.* Agents must have a favourable reputation with the trade and be trustworthy in conforming to the spirit of agreements and plans made with the company they represent.

(d) *The number and type of products handled.* An agency will be more readily motivated if business with a particular company represents a significant part of its profits. Handling of competitive products or a very long portfolio of products would be most undesirable.

(e) *Business and technical competence.* It is important for agents to be able to take decisions quickly and efficiently without constant reference back to the manufacturer at home.

25. Marketing organisation and expertise

The agents' ability must be evaluated through careful consideration of the following:

(a) *Marketing strength.* This may be seen in the size and quality of the sales force, the quality and location of warehousing and office facilities, reputation with customers, customer coverage, pricing and advertising policies, and knowledge of the market and market requirements.

(b) *Ability to undertake market research* and to feed back reliable information on market development. The ability to communicate in appropriate languages is of great importance.

(c) *Provision of after sales service.* This also covers the stocking of spares. Ready availability of replacements, supply continuity and maintenance arrangements are often the key to success.

(d) *Marketing training.* An agency should be willing to co-operate with the home manufacturer in providing suitable training.

26. What agents want from the company

Some of the best agents may already have arrangements with competing companies. They will certainly look for readily marketable products and favourable conditions (e.g. commissions, credit, product guarantees, delivery reliability of product and spares, training, advertising support, technical support).

27. Agency agreements

Agreements should normally be kept as simple as possible, but very careful consideration must be given to defining certain essential rights which otherwise will possibly lead to dispute.

(a) Duration of the agreement. There may well be advantages in having the initial trial period reasonably short.

(b) Exclusiveness or otherwise of representation. Agents will naturally aim at exclusive representation; suppliers will have to consider the longer-term implications of exclusive rights over wide territories if business develops beyond the capacity of original agents.

(c) Payment, discount and tax conditions.

(d) Delivery conditions.

(e) Rights to additional or new products.

(f) Pricing policy.

(g) Use of trade names, trademarks, etc.

(h) Advertising, promotion and sales literature requirements.

(i) Inventory holding.

(j) Reports and information exchange.

It should be noted that often the law affords greater protection to the agent than to the overseas supplier.

28. Stimulating agents

Personal visits by home company executives to sole agents should be arranged on a fairly frequent basis. These should not be purely a matter of courtesy, but should be sufficiently long to measure progress and offer help and suggestions – generally to motivate and tactfully control. Some companies engage field forces (not always large, but highly mobile) who work with, train and motivate agents. Return visits by agency personnel not only create a sense of belonging, but provide opportunities for technical and sales training. Some companies have found that sales conferences of agents have generated tremendous enthusiasm and provided an invaluable means of exchanging ideas. Many companies find that sales targets provide a major incentive. Rewards can take various forms, such as a special pricing structure or additional promotional support. One problem is to establish and agree realistic targets. Potential must be taken into consideration – not simply past performance. If precise market data are lacking, potentials can often be established with adequate accuracy by using combinations of indicators, such as:

(a) per capita gross national product;
(b) percentage of gross national product accounted for by wholesaling and retailing;
(c) economic development status;
(d) literacy rate;
(e) percentage of population in towns and cities;
(f) industrial output;
(g) average household size;
(h) import volume and pattern; and
(i) population statistics.

A regular flow of well-planned bulletins, letters, publicity (*see* 7:**43**) and promotional ideas should be maintained to keep interest high.

29. Licensing (*see* **22**, NOTE)
Licensing takes various forms, including patent design or process licence contracts, trademark contracts, technical information contracts, and franchising contracts.

The exporting of expertise, which can be extremely rewarding, is a very underdeveloped area of British international trading. It is often the fastest way of entering overseas markets, and sometimes, as in centrally planned economies, the only possible way. It is clearly a method involving little expense, avoiding all distribution cost. On the other hand, it may not be the best way of maximising on overseas opportunities in the long run, and there is a risk of creating potentially serious competition. At this point it should be noted that successful international operations frequently depend on a combination of the exporting methods best suited to particular markets at particular points of time in relation to company policy and development plans.

30. Major reasons for entering into licensing agreements

A major reason for entering into licensing agreements is that no capital risk is involved. There are, however, other considerations:

(a) Licensing arrangements normally involve close collaboration, and, at a later stage, more direct involvement may be possible and desirable.

(b) Cross-licensing arrangements may be easier to negotiate. This is particularly important in view of the high cost of specialised research and development and the speed of scientific and technological change. Licensing arrangements can be used to obtain a higher return on the costs of research investment.

(c) Currency advantages exist as foreign currency is saved and there are few exchange difficulties.

(d) Some markets are too small or too risky for any serious consideration of capital investment.

(e) Licensees often have well-developed marketing organisations.

(f) Licensing may overcome the barriers of trading with nationally owned enterprises, or of trading in countries with strong nationalist tendencies. Newly established or developing countries, for example, may accept licensing agreements as a means of stimulating economic development without the risk of foreign domination of industries and markets.

(g) The customer reputation created through some licensing arrangements may assist in the marketing of other company products currently or later.

(h) There are advantages in diversifying the methods of receiving income from overseas.

31. Problems to be considered

(a) *Long-term risks*. Apart from the obvious problem of weighing risk against opportunity, licensing involves a number of potential dangers which must be seriously considered. It is important, for example, that there should be adequate safeguards for the maintenance of quality standards if a company's reputation is not to suffer. Companies with large financial resources must consider the long-term position most carefully. Patents and trademarks are valid for a limited period of time only and, if the real long-term aim is to enter more directly into overseas operation, the licensing period may have provided just the necessary time for the licensee to acquire the skills and marketing position with which it would be difficult – and certainly costly – to compete.

(b) *Legal factors*. Licensing agreements require specialist legal advice. They will often, in any case, require the approval of governments, but in the final analysis there has to be complete mutual confidence. It is now very rare for a company simply to agree to a set fee; almost invariably royalty payments based on the value of the business are built into the agreement, which may also contain provisions for the possibility of acquiring equity, termination arrangements, minimum volume conditions, renewal conditions, taxation and accounting procedures, degree of exclusiveness, and/or subcontracting rights.

32. Joint venture
Joint venture involves a capital partnership and may be arranged in connection with manufacturing activities, marketing activities or both. The cases for and against joint venture are considered in **33–6** below.

33. Advantages of joint venture

(a) *Political*. Like licensing, this is frequently a method which is acceptable to governments which strictly limit imports or the operations of wholly owned foreign companies. Local conditions may regulate the extent of such co-operation but, once established, joint ventures usually receive favourable treatment in matters of import licences, taxation and exchange control.

(b) *Financial*. Joint ventures are often regarded as the safest, easiest and least expensive method of engaging in international business. It may be possible to obtain local capital which is a safeguard against the risks of political and economic instability.

(c) *Commercial*. Such advantages may include acquiring new knowledge of manufacturing methods or research information. Access to new markets may be gained through a well-established distribution system.

34. Problems of joint venture
The most important ultimate consideration is probably the amount of control which can be exercised over the vital decision-making processes. Some companies will not enter into joint venture agreements unless they have a majority financial interest. Differences in manage-

ment philosophy, cultural attitudes, development plans or dividend policy, for example, may lead to considerable strife and possible deadlock. Legal agreements have to be supplemented by a tremendous amount of mutual confidence.

35. Major preliminary requirements

To minimise the risk of later difficulties there should be:

(a) a thorough investigation of the contributions that the parties can make to research, manufacturing or marketing expertise, plant facilities and equipment, and so on;

(b) a clear understanding of exactly what is required from the partners; and

(c) a clear understanding of profit pay-out policy – for instance, long-term investment at low returns or high immediate returns.

36. Decision making in joint ventures

Companies operating on a worldwide basis may find special problems in joint venture arrangements, particularly in relation to pricing and supply. Single ownership allows for the setting of corporate company objectives, profit standards and use of resources. Joint venture decisions cannot be based on the same premises.

> NOTE: *Management contracts* are very important in relation to developing countries. They may very well be important in the restructuring of business in former Communist countries in Europe and Asia. Basically an arrangement is made under which an experienced foreign company undertakes to carry out the usual management functions of a foreign enterprise, to operate it, and to train local personnel. The contract covers payment of the company and handing over of authority to locals once training is completed.

37. Wholly owned subsidiaries

Overseas companies may be involved in the whole commercial process from design through to manufacturing and marketing, or they may concentrate on a particular operation, such as purchasing, marketing or manufacturing, or the manufacture or assembly of parts. Whatever the extent of the operation, there is complete capital commitment and control.

The decision to invest in overseas establishments is normally the result of either failure to find a suitable alternative or belief that complete company control is essential for the most effective and profitable operation. It is large companies which usually move in this direction, but small and medium-sized companies might be wise to consider the possibilities since the investment need not necessarily be very high. The recovery of initial investment may be comparatively slow, however, and it is long-term advantages which should be taken into account. Statements that exporting is unprofitable often arise from short-term thinking. A substantial world business may be highly profitable, but time for build-up will certainly be needed.

38. Establishing overseas companies

There are two basic methods: acquisition, and starting from scratch. Special factors which may lead to foreign ownership include the following:

(a) *The volume of business expected.* This is very frequently the principal criterion in establishing overseas sales branches.

(b) *The need to provide specialised facilities.* It may be very important to establish adequate servicing, by way of spare parts, repair facilities and so on.

(c) *The strength of nationalistic feeling.* This may be reflected in official government policy by the provision of financial incentives, or tax or exchange benefits, but it may also be a matter of potential buyer sentiments. Customers may sometimes react more favourably to products which are produced in their own country. In consumer goods, in particular, customers are frequently unaware that the producing company is foreign.

(d) *Reduction of manufacturing overheads.* Domestic plant capacity may be of such a size that it is essential to have large world markets, and the establishment of overseas sales branches may lead to a more profitable total operation, even if these branches are not highly profitable in their own right.

(e) *Legal restrictions.* Prohibitive import duties or conditions, severe exchange restrictions or heavy tax burdens can sometimes be overcome. Sometimes it is necessary to establish an overseas operation in order to exercise a patent.

(f) *Rationalisation.* Ownership may lead to more profitable overall global operations by rationalisation of manufacturing, research, servicing and/or marketing activities.

(g) *Capital availability.* Overseas development may offer advantages in the reinvestment of profits or the raising of capital from local sources. In many cases long-term credit is easier to finance – and this is particularly important in the marketing of capital equipment.

(h) *Advantages in acquiring particular currencies.* These may be transferable to other overseas operations.

39. Risk factors
The extent of risk will obviously depend on the size of the investment, which may be small in the case of establishing sales, purchasing or warehousing facilities, or very large in the setting up of a large assembly or manufacturing plant. A major consideration will be the possibility of loss in the case of nationalisation. A marketing operation may incur a high running cost in terms of salaries, but large-scale investment in fixed assets (e.g. manufacturing installations and equipment) is a much greater reason to investigate the stability of government policy. Nationalisation is not the only problem. Currency and exchange rate stability are important considerations.

40. Problems of acquisition
Although acquisition may seem an attractive means of developing overseas trade on a large scale and quickly, it is important that any acquisition should be preceded by the formulation of a clear policy and a thorough investigation of the business to be acquired.

(a) *A clear acquisition policy.* In order to develop a truly international business most profitably, it will often be necessary to co-ordinate policy and rationalise resources. Heterogeneous acquisitions make these steps virtually impossible. The American General Foods organisation encountered enormous difficulties after acquiring businesses in many parts of the world on the very general basis of involvement in convenience foods markets. Convenience foods are difficult to define on a global basis. This raises problems of product policy which have direct repercussions on development and research. Many other problems arise from divergencies in accounting systems, personnel policy, business philosophy and so forth.
(b) *A careful investigation of the business to be acquired.* Investigations must be made to discover the following:
    (*i*) Financial standing and profitability record.
    (*ii*) Market standing and marketing organisation and methods.
    (*iii*) Personnel policies and, in particular, wage and salary structures.
    (*iv*) Research and development strengths or weaknesses.
    (*v*) Patents and licensing agreements.
    (*vi*) Plant and depot facilities and values.
    (*vii*) The strengths and weaknesses in the existing management

structure. This is a particularly important issue, since a great deal will depend on the ability and adaptability of the local management team.

(*viii*) Government regulations and controls.

Many companies use the services of brokers or consultants in locating suitable companies for acquisition. Really good prospects are difficult to find and an extensive search may well be needed. The use of legal and financial specialists will clearly be necessary in evaluating possible acquisitions, but other management personnel (e.g. research, manufacturing, marketing) will usually be required to carry out a complete investigation.

41. Organisation structure

It is usually impracticable – and unwise – to think in terms of setting up an organisational structure which is a replica of the home operation. There may be very real differences in market conditions, effective manufacturing methods, administrative procedures, growth rate and personnel capability. Very few companies have as yet succeeded in creating a fully integrated international operation – one which has no dominant domestic roots, but which is fully international in ownership, financing, management and operation. There is little doubt that such companies will increasingly emerge in the future.

The problems of corporate organisational structure are enormous. It is clear that there must be some degree of central control – but the problem is to determine the extent of that control, to establish the appropriate relationships between central staff and line management and decentralised managements.

The following are some of the questions that need to be posed:

(a) To what extent does central planning and direction conflict with the development of a decentralised profit-responsibility concept? What type of reporting system is needed?

(b) How is it possible to utilise the best managerial talent in the right place at the right time? To what extent is it possible to think in terms of truly multinational management structures? How can the problems of differences in standards and cost of living be overcome if management is to be moved from one operation to another?

(c) What should be the basis of evaluating the performance of different companies, considering the wide differences which exist in, for example, government taxation systems, currency stability, market structures and development problems, and cost factors?

(d) What special qualities are needed in the international manager, and how can he or she be trained and developed?

(e) To what extent should immediate or local considerations outweigh long-term and corporate considerations in determining the allocation of resources?

42. The international manager

Special qualities and/or qualifications are needed in the personnel selected to carry out operations. Far too little consideration has been given to providing the training and development programmes needed for British personnel working in overseas territories.

Overseas operations demand the following qualities:

(a) *The capacity and authority to make prompt decisions.* Overseas buyers are not likely to react favourably to people who have constantly to refer back to headquarters. Even an overseas representative will need to be much more capable of assuming responsibility of a managerial kind than his or her counterpart in home markets. He or she may well be responsible for guiding agency operations as well as for direct customer dealings.

(b) *Adaptability.* This characteristic is needed to cope with the wider range of unusual conditions surrounding the transaction of business.

(c) *Knowledge of languages.* The importance of language is too often underrated because of the ability of other nations to communicate reasonably well in English. Familiarity with non-verbal communication skills and negotiating customs is also of great importance.

(d) *Acceptance of the need for mobility.* The distances which may have to be covered and the possibility of international transfers makes it essential that individuals and families are prepared to adjust to a particular way of life. It may be necessary to provide special incentives to cover the possible additional cost of education, travel and home visits.

(e) *Health and energy.* Overseas operations are usually more demanding physically than domestic operations.

(f) *Knowledge of local customs*, culture and current events.

(g) *Tolerance* – a willingness to recognise that people with different cultural backgrounds have different points of view which are as valid as any other; and ability to work with and through people with diverse attitudes, beliefs and motivations.

(h) *Persistence.* It may frequently be necessary to pursue a line of action for a long time in the face of difficulties before success is finally achieved.

(i) *Reliability and attention to details.* Irritations and business loss may spring from slow, inaccurate or vague transmission of information. Weaknesses in administrative procedures leading to delivery delays, excessive correspondence or slow reaction to complaints intensify the doubts an organisation may have about doing business at all with overseas companies.

Whatever the form of overseas operation, it is clear that success depends to a very large extent on the calibre of the personnel involved, and there must be an acceptance that this usually means that top-level executives must themselves be more mobile and more directly in touch with the marketplace.

43. Organisational evolution
It is beyond the scope of this book to cover all the various organisational structures to be found in practice. A small export operation run entirely through agents may, at the outset, be organised by a small section of the home marketing department. This may develop into a separate export division with responsibility for market investigations, distribution systems, service, advertising and promotion. The establishment of overseas sales offices, assembly points and warehouses may follow. As the organisation develops, problems of communication and the relationship with the home operation will have to be resolved. The final step is the creation of a fully international corporation.

Marketing services and government support

44. The need for international marketing research
The differences in social, economic, technical, political and legal systems (**12–16** above) and in distribution patterns (**17–20** above) clearly indicate the need for particular attention to be paid to marketing research and promotion. The geographical separation of producers and consumers adds to the normal marketing problems of separation of time and knowledge or information (*see* **22** above).

45. International marketing research: the basic steps
There are four major steps in an investigation:

(a) Basic data concerning the market.
(b) General factors relating to the product and/or service.
(c) Specific factors relating to the market for the product and/or service.

(d) Specific factors which would influence the operation of the particular company.

46. Major problems to be resolved

The first two steps of this investigation are required for top-level policy decisions in connection with involvement in overseas areas. The third and fourth steps are required for decisions on distribution outlets, prices, terms and so on, but more important, on the specific products to suit specific markets. For product decisions, information on the following will be necessary:

(a) The effect of differing legal and exchange requirements.

(b) The advantages and disadvantages of standardisation of complete products or components.

(c) The need to adapt existing products to suit local conditions, functional or aesthetic design changes, packaging, branding and advertising, quality standards, specifications, and usage information.

47. Special problems in conducting overseas surveys

The techniques covered in Chapter 3 apply, but the following are some of the special problems which may arise:

(a) *The choice of the means of undertaking investigations.* These may include overseas agencies, British agencies, agencies with international associations, and company staff. The major problem is to weigh up the frequently conflicting considerations of efficiency, time and cost. A provisional estimate of a market may be prepared by experienced researchers in two or three days, whereas a more detailed investigation may require two or three months, including time for preparation of the survey, for execution, and for analysis and interpretation. Field interviewing can clearly involve high travelling expenses.

(b) *The value of published information.* Information from every possible source should be utilised, but it varies in reliability and statistics are often constructed on differing bases.

(c) *Language problems.* Large companies' executives may speak English, but surveys may need to cover respondents who are not bilingual. If the researchers cannot speak the particular language, interpreters have to be used, raising questions of additional cost and communication difficulties.

(d) *Terminology.* Definitions and technical specifications in connection with similar products may be widely divergent.

(e) *Differences in culture and traditions.* These may affect the willingness ndents to co-operate and the reliability of the answers they

as surveys are likely to be carried out in a series of stages. There
many markets to examine, and so few on which a company can
ntrate, that a screening process is essential. The first stage is
y to be primarily desk research aimed at eliminating countries
products offering inadequate profitable potential. Stage two
earch might require field investigations of the more promising
oduct-markets, and a third stage might be concentrated on depth
udy of a limited number of critical issues in the shortlisted product-
markets.

48. Selection of advertising agencies and media
Important matters to consider are the following:

(a) *Choice of agency.* As in marketing research, there are very large
international companies and local companies of various sizes; there
is also the possibility of using a British-based agency. The range and
efficiency of services offered require most careful consideration.
(b) *Differences in the quality and quantity of media available.* Contrast the
availability of commercial television, national daily press, magazines
and trade literature, for example, in France, the USA, Germany and
Britain. Accurate statistics on circulation and readership are often
difficult to obtain.
(c) *Direct mailing.* This is a form of presentation which is receiving
increasing attention. Obvious difficulties arise in obtaining full and
classified lists of potential overseas customers. Direct mailing can
often be most effectively organised in co-operation with local
agents.

49. Economic and social problems in promotion
Differences in economic and social systems (*see* **13, 14** above) create
individual promotion problems. Some of these problems are considered in **50–4** below.

50. Level of expenditure
The stage of economic development reached has a direct bearing on
the extent of advertising. Highly developed economies, as might be
expected, show a higher level of advertising expenditure than underdeveloped economies, but the level of expenditure is not directly
related to either national income or per capita income. In general,
however, companies should be prepared to spend comparatively

more on advertising in overseas than in domestic markets, since both they and their products will usually be less well known and have less intensive direct selling effort.

51. Distribution patterns
Differences in distribution patterns (*see* 17 above) may mean that there should be a totally different allocation of advertising expenditure: for example, if final distribution is mainly in the hands of small retailers, it may be difficult to obtain effective displays, but profitable to concentrate on promotions to large wholesalers.

52. Differences in customer motivations
Buying habits will be conditioned by income and assets available, but there will be differences in priorities and values. European countries with strong Protestant traditions tend to resist appeals based on labour saving, for example. Reports from many sources show that Swiss consumers reacted much more favourably to dishwashers promoted essentially on the basis of high water temperatures and sterilisation rather than on the basis of ease and convenience.

53. Differences in decision-makers
The influence of women and children differs tremendously in consumer goods markets. In industrial markets, management structure and styles have to be considered in determining the form and direction of communications.

54. International 'images'
There are obvious advantages in terms of both cost and effectiveness if a company can use the same kind of advertising copy and visual material all over the world. It is, however, rarely possible to reproduce identical promotional material for different markets. As well as problems in translation, illustrations must often be modified or completely changed: for example, a Smarties advertisement showing children physically handling the sweets and examining their different colours was completely unacceptable in Holland because of the Dutch attitude towards hygiene. Agents and distributors can often provide invaluable help in advising on idiomatic usage, appropriateness of copy and visual appeal. International advertising 'lead' agencies often work in liaison with local agencies.

NOTE: Legal regulations differ. Particular attention will need to be paid to restrictions in the advertising of food and drugs.

55. Exhibitions

The decision to participate in home exhibitions is not infrequently based on the notion of keeping in line with competitive practice rather than on calculated objectives in regard to communications and sales. Overseas exhibitions often attract much more serious buying attention and may be one of the most effective ways of communicating with potential customers.

It is important to plan for exhibitions well in advance. The most important should be carefully selected, and a timetable not only of the events themselves but of preparatory work must be drawn up. Apart from important matters of stand design, location and size, it will be necessary to prepare special literature and exhibits and to allocate responsible executives. The Department of Trade and Industry provides valuable advice and assistance to British companies wishing to take part in international exhibitions. In addition, through its overseas Fairs Directorate, the Department of Trade and Industry (DTI) organises British Pavilions and Information Stands and All-British Trade Fairs. British Weeks are also organised and financed by the DTI, and assistance is given in promoting British goods through special store promotions.

56. Co-operation in exporting

The cost of overseas marketing operations sometimes prevents companies from undertaking activities in which they could effectively participate if they were to look more closely at the possibilities of collaboration. Manufacturers' associations or voluntary groupings of firms could achieve great economies by co-operative effort in organising exhibitions, advertising, selling missions or visits by buyers. Co-operation in industrial markets may be necessary to supply a complete system, as in the building of oil refineries and power plants. Special consortia are sometimes set up for combined tenders. The DTI can assist and/or advise in all these matters and, for the smaller manufacturer, there is the 'pick-a-back' scheme which enables firms to contact successful exporting organisations which are willing to assist by offering certain selling facilities. The Chartered Institute of Marketing has established a company, Marketing Ltd, specifically to arrange for co-operative export marketing efforts.

The Board of Trade now offers valuable help to companies wishing to carry out research in overseas markets. This includes advice on research methods, costs, agencies, etc., as well as financial assistance.

57. Credit and insurance

Exporters face not only normal commercial risks of payment default, but the additional risks of shifting political circumstances, currency exchange and import restrictions. There is also, in increasingly competitive world markets, the problem of providing long-term credit. Most exporters have, therefore, to obtain finance from outside sources which themselves require reasonable guarantees against risk. Various national schemes have been developed in most industrialised countries to assist in the problems of credit and risk. Some schemes are private; others are state controlled (cf. Hermes Kreditversicherungs AG, Hamburg – a private company – and the Export Risks Insurance Corporation Ltd, Bombay – a government-owned corporation).

58. The Export Credit Guarantee Department

The Export Credit Guarantee Department (ECGD) is a government department set up to encourage the export of UK goods and services. It has two main functions: to provide insurance cover for exporters against the risks of non-payment by overseas customers; and to provide security so that banks will lend money to finance exports. It is possible to insure from the date of contract acceptance or from the date of the shipment. There are comprehensive policies covering the whole of a company's business or its export business, and specific policies for particular large individual export contracts.

(a) *Rates.* These vary according to the extent of risk involved and cover requested. Rates for special contracts, for example, are higher than those for comprehensive policies. However, even special policy rates are favourable. Basic cover ranges from 90 per cent of loss due to insolvency or default by a buyer, to 95 per cent of loss arising from political or economic conditions. It is possible to take out policies to cover special risks such as cost escalation, contracts involving construction work and capital goods export on credit terms of two years or more. An ECGD guarantee paves the way to bank lending at preferential rates of interest.

(b) *Cover.* ECGD cover provides the necessary collateral for normal bank financing, and various special guarantees to banks may also be negotiated. The main risks for which cover may be provided are:

(*i*) insolvency of the buyer;

(*ii*) failure of the buyer to pay within six months of acceptance of goods;

    (*iii*) wars, civil wars or revolutions;
    (*iv*) cancellation of UK export licences or the introduction of new export restrictions;
    (*v*) delay in the transfer of sterling to the UK.

59. The Diplomatic Service

It should be remembered that the Diplomatic Service, through its commercial services, is increasingly devoting attention to the promotion of exports by providing market information, advising on overseas opportunities and assisting in liaison between British and overseas companies and trade organisations.

60. Conclusion

It is evident that increasing home competition, the profit squeeze, increasing world industrialisation and the formation of economic trading communities will all combine to increase the need for consideration of marketing on an international basis. The distinction between home and export business will tend to disappear, and marketing strategies will be based on global rather than national patterns or segmentations.

The principles of marketing set out in Chapters 1–10 are as true of international as of home markets. Decisions have to be made on product policy, pricing, promotion, channels and organisation. Customers have to be understood, forecasts and targets have to be set, and performance has to be measured. Special knowledge and means of obtaining that knowledge are, however, required. Thus special training and experience must be linked with appropriate adaptability to the environment and linguistic ability. Not least important is the fact that company directors and top-level executives must become committed to the marketing philosophy and to more personal involvement in the actual fields of operation.

There is an urgent need to tackle what were described in a 1990 issue of the *Research Review* (Cranfield School of Management) as 'the major strategic management issues arising from acquisitions and mergers, globalisation and market restructuring'. This is at a time when research findings at Cranfield reported an absence of language training, of the development of real understanding of international cultural and business environments, and of career structures involving the possibility of international postings and/or secondments. It has also been reliably reported that in the UK only some 35 per cent of 16–18-year-olds are in full-time education or training, in contrast to 47 per cent in Germany and 66 per cent in France.

This is also a time when a very successful international marketing company – Gillette – with its razors and shaving products, its ownership of Braun, Parker, Waterman and other internationally known products, has called in consultants to examine a redirection of aspects of its corporate strategy. The reason is that 'it is not perceived as an international company,' according to a statement in November 1993 by its Chairman and Chief Executive, who sees internationalisation of business as 'an unstoppable trend'. He goes on to say that 'companies must respond to different national habits. The best way to do it is through personal advertising and PR approaches aimed at individual markets. The broad strategic attack should be an overall campaign.'

Progress test 12

1. What are the most significant recent trends in international trade?

2. What basic information is needed to analyse world market opportunities?

3. In what basic ways do international markets differ?

4. What specialist marketing institutions might be used by a company seeking entry to overseas markets at a low level of risk and investment?

5. List the important factors to be considered in selecting agents.

6. What are the major reasons for entering into licensing agreements?

7. Why and how do companies establish wholly owned subsidiaries?

8. What are the main problems involved in the acquisition of overseas companies?

9. What special qualities does the 'international' manager require?

10. What are the special problems of international marketing research?

11. What are the economic and social problems of international promotion?

12. What is the function of the Export Credit Guarantee Department?

Assignment

Choose three countries which are members of the EU. Your UK company is considering the marketing of a range of non-alcoholic drinks, which you have recently introduced successfully in the UK, to one or all of the three EU countries you have chosen. You have no continental European operation at present. What aspects of the following would you like to investigate now, and what methods would you use?

(a) the social and cultural environment;
(b) the economic and demographic environment.

You may make any reasonable assumption about the drinks concerned, the way they are marketed in the UK, the size of the UK operation etc. You may use press cuttings or seek interviews with manufacturers or agents.

Appendix 1

External sources of marketing information

There are many external sources of information; the more important can be categorised as follows.

Government publications

Census of Population. The Census (held every ten years) supplies details of population by age, marital status, occupation, social class, house ownership, sex and geographical area, and a considerable amount of social and economic data. This can be supplemented by the annual statistics produced by the General Register Office.

Statistics on Incomes, Prices, Employment and Production. This bulletin is published several times per year and is supplemented by the monthly *Gazette*. Details of employment and unemployment by industry and region, data on wage rates and retail prices, industrial disputes, etc., provide useful guides to purchasing potential by areas and income groups. More detailed analyses of incomes are available from Inland Revenue statistics.

Annual Family Expenditure Surveys. These give details of consumer spending on individual items by income groups and geographical areas. The survey is based on a limited sample of some 3,000 households.

Census of Distribution. This involves a partial analysis of distribution every five years and a complete survey every ten years.

Census of Production. This census, carried out every five years, gives information on manufacturing organisations, mining and quarrying, building and contracting and public utilities. The information includes details of materials and fuel purchased, stocks at the beginning and end of a year, annual output and sales analysis, expenditure on services, plant, machinery and vehicles, and value of buildings and land. Calculations of gross output, net output and net per person employed are made.

Monthly Digest of Statistics. This contains information collected by various government departments. The information is summarised in the *Annual Abstract of Statistics*.

The Business Monitor Series. This gives monthly or quarterly data on production over a wide range of industries as well as comparisons with past figures.

Overseas Trade Accounts. These are published monthly, showing, in detail, figures on imports and exports.

Statistical Classification for Imported Goods and Re-exported Goods.

Annual Statement of Trade of the UK with Commonwealth and Foreign Countries.

Trade and Navigation Accounts. A monthly publication.

The Export Service Bulletin.

UK Balance of Payments and the Economic Report.

Input–Output Tables for the UK. These are designed to show the flow of business from one industry to another, and cover industrial groupings.

Public Investment in Great Britain.

Company Assets, Income and Finance. This publication shows the net assets, profits, reserves and new capital of over 2,000 companies.

National Income and Expenditure Blue Book. Although all the raw statistics appear elsewhere, the data are processed in this annual publication to provide a particularly valuable source of social and economic information for both consumer and industrial marketing.

Special surveys published by the Social Survey Unit of the Central Office of Information.

The above publications are available from HMSO. Students should consult the *List of Principal Statistical Series Available*, published by HMSO.

Official international publications

United Nations Statistical Year Book
United Nations Monthly Bulletin of Statistics
United Nations Current Economic Indicators
United Nations World Economic Survey
United Nations Commodity Trade Statistics
Bulletin of the European Community
EFTA Bulletin
Statistics for Market Research in Europe and North America (Organisation for Economic Co-operation and Development)
Bulletin Générale de Statistiques (European Commission)
International Monetary Statistics (International Monetary Fund)
GATT Compendium of Sources (International Trade Statistics)
GATT World Directory of Industry and Trade Associations

GATT Analytical Bibliography of Market Surveys by Products and Countries
International Bibliography of Marketing and Distribution (Staples Press)

Other specialist publications

Quarterly Economic Reviews
Retail Business } The Economist Intelligence Unit
Marketing in Europe
A.C. Nielsen Indices – for food, drugs, pharmaceuticals, confectionery and
 tobacco
Statistical Review of Advertising Expenditure (Legion Publishing Co.)
Bradstreet Register
Dun and Bradstreets's Guide to Key British Enterprises
Kompass Register
Stock Exchange Year Book
Kelly's Directory of Merchants, Manufacturers and Shippers
British Rate and Data
Advertisers Annual
Consumer Marketing Manual of the UK
Industrial Marketing Manual

Newspapers, periodicals and journals (*=American)

London and Cambridge Economic Bulletin
The Times Review of Industry and Technology
The Economist
Financial Times
British Journal of Marketing
Marketing
Marketing Forum
Advertising Quarterly
European Business
Commentary
Scientific Business
*Journal of Marketing**
*Journal of Marketing Research**
*Journal of Advertising Research**
*Harvard Business Review**
Campaign
Retail Distribution Management
Industrial Marketing Digest
Which?
Anbar (Marketing and Distribution Abstracts)
Reviews published by the various banks

Institutions

Chartered Institute of Marketing, Moor Hall, Cookham, Berkshire SL6 9QH

Market Research Society, The Old Trading House, 15 Northburgh Street, London EC1V 0AH

Advertising Association, 15 Wilton Road, London SW1V 1LT

Incorporated Society of British Advertisers, 44 Hertford Street, London W1Y 8AE

Institute of Public Relations, The Old Trading House, 15 Northburgh Street, London EC1V 0AH

British Institute of Management, Management House, Cottingham Road, Corby, Northants NN17 1TT

Confederation of British Industry, Centre Point, 103 New Oxford Street, London WC1A 1DU

Institute of Export, Export House, 64 Clifton Street, London EC2A 4HB

Council of Industrial Design, 28 Haymarket, London SW1Y 4SP

British Export Houses Association, 16 Dartmouth Street, London SW1H 9BL

British Standards Institution, Linfold Wood, Milton Keynes MK14 6LE

Department of Trade and Industry, Ashdown House, 123 Victoria Street, London SW1E 6RB

Industrial Marketing Research Association, 2–11 Bird Street, Lichfield, Staffs WS13 6PW

European Society for Opinion and Marketing Research, Raadhuisstraat 15, Amsterdam

Central Office of Information, Hercules Road, Westminster Bridge Road, London SE1 7DU

HM Stationery Office, St Crispins, Duke Street, Norwich NR3 1PD

Communications, Advertising and Marketing Education Foundation Ltd, 15 Wilton Road, London SW1V 1LT

Trade associations

Chambers of Commerce

Banks

Embassies and Consulates

Appendix 2

Bibliography

Burnett, J.J., *Promotion Management*, West Publishing Co., 1988.

Cannon, T., *Basic Marketing*, Holt Business Texts 1980.

Channon, D.F., *Bank Strategic Management and Marketing*, Wiley, 1986.

Cowall, D., *The Marketing of Services*, Heinemann, 1985.

Elliot, K. and Christopher, N.G., *Methods in Marketing Research*, Holt, Rinehart and Winston, 1974.

Harris, D. and Walters, D., *Retail Operations Management: A Strategic Approach*, Prentice Hall, 1992.

Haywood, R. *All About Public Relations*, McGraw-Hill, 1990.

Keegan, W.J., *Marketing*, Prentice Hall, 1992.

Kotler, P., *Marketing Management: Analysis, Planning Implementation and Control*, Prentice Hall, 1993.

Kotler, P. and Armstrong, G., *Marketing: An Introduction*, Prentice Hall, 1987.

Lovelock, C.H., *Services Marketing: Text, Cases and Readings*, Prentice Hall, 1991.

Lovelock, C.H., *Management Services*, Prentice Hall International, 1992.

Maslow, A.H., *Motivation and Personality*, Harper and Row, 1954.

McGoldrick, R.J., *Retail Marketing*, McGraw-Hill, 1990.

Montinho, L., *Cases in Marketing Management*, Addison Wesley, 1989.

Paliwoda, S.J., *International Marketing*, Butterworth-Heinemann, 1992.

Appendix 3
Examination technique

1. Timing
Read most carefully the instructions relating to the questions to be attempted. Be sure that you understand how marks are to be allocated. In some papers there is a compulsory question: in others questions are divided into sections in order to ensure that students attempt questions covering as wide a range of the prescribed syllabus as possible. Having understood the directions, read the questions through once fairly quickly. At this stage it is normal for students to become unduly worried. Remember this and read the paper again more slowly, 'shortlisting' those questions which you believe you can answer most satisfactorily. Then make your final selection in accordance with the instructions given. Deduct a time allowance for reading through your answers at the end of the examination, and apportion the remaining time according to the mark contribution each question makes towards the maximum obtainable on the paper. Do not underestimate the cumulative danger of overrunning your time allocation for individual questions. Essay-type questions are very rarely awarded full marks, and there is almost invariably more to be gained by completing all questions as instructed than by adding small refinements to earlier questions attempted and having insufficient time for later questions.

If you are running out of time, make the best of the situation by listing salient points in note form or by covering the overall approach to a problem rather than by writing in full essay form or indulging in specialised calculations affecting a small part of the required answer.

2. Legibility
Examiners are usually marking large numbers of papers. They are not looking for copperplate handwriting, but they will naturally be inclined to ignore or be irritated by writing which is difficult to read.

3. Logical presentation
Written examination questions may occasionally be devised to test knowledge of facts, but more usually they are intended to examine the student's ability to use facts in investigating a problem or in analysing a line of argument. It is, therefore, of great importance to plan answers in such a way that they have a logical flow. Time spent on planning answers is time well spent.

4. Relevance of material

Read questions carefully and make certain you understand exactly what you are being asked. A lengthy answer is no guarantee of high marks. Students are apt to write down what they know rather than what they are asked. This leads to completely irrelevant answers or answers which are out of balance, with undue emphasis bring given to particular aspects.

5. Generalisations

Avoid sweeping and vague generalisations. Be as specific as possible by quoting actual examples, of company organisations, of marketing campaigns, of statements of writers and practising marketing specialists, etc.

6. Layout

Whenever possible emphasise your key points by suitable paragraph construction, underlining, use of diagrams and statistics. Clear and accurate diagrams and statistics often enhance an answer and make points more lucidly and rapidly than words, but avoid these devices at all costs if you are *unsure* of your facts.

7. Style

If you are a mature student who has not undertaken written examinations for several years, it is particularly important to practise written answers in advance of the examination as much as possible. Write in short, concise sentences, taking care to avoid ambiguous words and phrases. Define unfamiliar terms and make sure that your use of such terms is consistent.

Except in an emergency, do not write in note form. A definite mark allowance may be made for presentation, but if not, examiners will normally still expect students to show the ability to express themselves fluently.

8. Assumptions

In questions requiring analysis of problems, it is not unusual for the information supplied to be incomplete. It is expected that assumptions will be made, but that the assumptions will be stated and maintained consistently throughout.

Appendix 4

Test papers

Do not attempt these papers until you have thoroughly studied the text and can answer satisfactorily the questions in the progress tests.

Test 1

1. By what criteria would you decide whether a company were production or marketing oriented?

2. To what extent would you consider that the purchasing of industrial goods and services is a rational process?

3. Comment on the methods used by companies in determining advertising expenditure. What problems are involved in arriving at a decision and to what extent can these be overcome?

4. Under what conditions is it desirable to eliminate a product? What problems may have to be overcome despite the logic of any arguments put forward?

5. To what extent might channel decisions be conditioned by: **(a)** the characteristics of the product or products; **(b)** the practice of competitors? Illustrate your answer by reference to specific companies and products.

6. What would you consider to be the main responsibilities of a field sales manager controlling ten salespersons calling on grocery outlets? What considerations would you have in mind in selecting a person to take up such a position?

7. What do you understand by behavioural sciences? Of what importance is an understanding of behavioural sciences to a marketing research specialist?

8. What political and economic factors would you expect to be examined by a company before a decision is made to invest in setting up its own manufacturing or marketing organisation in an overseas territory?

Test 2

1. What do you understand by the term 'marketing mix'? Comment on the main 'mix' differences you might expect to find in marketing plans relating to **(a)** baby foods and **(b)** scientific instruments.

2. It is frequently stated that, the longer a person spends as a sales specialist, the less likely he or she is to develop ultimately into a good marketing manager. What do you consider is the validity of this argument?

3. What are the main problems in determining the size and type of samples for marketing research purposes in **(a)** specialised industrial markets and **(b)** mass consumer markets?

4. Discuss the various strategic considerations to be examined in determining a pricing policy. What are the special problems in pricing **(a)** completely new and differentiated products and **(b)** minor modifications of existing, narrowly differentiated products?

5. To what extent do you consider that existing voluntary controls in advertising provide adequate safeguards for the consumer?

6. What are the problems involved in evaluating the performance of a salesperson?

7. What do you understand by the 'product life cycle'? What are the advantages of understanding the concept in actual marketing situations?

8. Why do companies frequently appoint sales agents to represent them in international markets? Discuss the problems involved in the selection of agents.

Test 3

1. 'Marketing considerations must receive priority in company strategy and planning, but research and development, manufacturing and finance should have equal status with marketing.' Discuss this statement.

2. Discuss the major changes which have taken place in the pattern of retail distribution during the last ten years, and the effect these changes have had on the marketing policy of suppliers.

3. By what means is it possible to investigate purchasing behaviour and attitudes which are apparently irrational? What contribution might any findings make in devising a marketing campaign?

4. What procedures would you suggest for determining the priority which might be given to a number of new product possibilities?

5. Comment on the problems of evaluating the effectiveness of advertising. Discuss the significance and limitations of the most commonly used research techniques.

6. Discuss the advantages and disadvantages of licensing and joint venture in international marketing operations.

7. 'Relevant timely information is vital for effective marketing control.' Discuss this statement indicating the types, sources and frequency of data which might be required by **(a)** a marketing manager and **(b)** an area sales manager.

8. What are the special factors affecting marketing research investigations in connection with industrial goods and services?

Test 4

1. 'Marketing begins before production and ends after production.' Discuss this statement, particularly in the light of company organisational structures.

2. Explain what is meant by the following: **(a)** selective distribution; **(b)** intensive distribution; **(c)** exclusive distribution. Illustrate your answer by discussing distribution strategy in the marketing of **(a)** television receivers; **(b)** surgical appliances; **(c)** shirts; **(d)** motor cycles; **(e)** cigarettes; **(f)** agricultural machinery.

3. 'A matching of advertiser needs with media capacity is a prerequisite to the development of an effective advertising campaign.' Examine this requirement in connection with the marketing of **(a)** cars and **(b)** fork-lift trucks.

4. 'Costs, ultimately, set the floor to price.' Discuss this statement with particular reference to **(a)** the break-even concept and **(b)** discounted cash flow.

5. What are the objectives of branding products? To what extent is branding feasible and desirable in marketing industrial products?

6. What are the possible benefits of test marketing? What criteria might be used in **(a)** selecting areas and **(b)** determining the period of testing?

7. Why is it important for a company to know as accurately as possible the market share its product enjoys? How can the relevant data be obtained in the case of **(a)** cosmetics and **(b)** industrial detergents?

8. Distinguish between marketing research and marketing intelligence with special reference to the problems of overseas markets.

Test 5

1. 'Marketing calls for a combination of creative and analytical ability.' Discuss this statement in connection with the selection of staff in **(a)** a company marketing department and **(b)** an advertising agency.

2. Discuss the advantages and disadvantages of telephone interviews, mail questionnaires and personal interviews in marketing research investigations.

3. Comment on the most commonly practised procedures for forecasting sales. What factors would you consider in forecasting the sales of a new car model for a forward period of three years?

4. Discuss the problems of cost allocation in determining marketing budgets.

5. 'The pack protects what it sells and sells what it protects.' Comment on this double function of packaging with special reference to marketing cake mixes **(a)** to domestic consumers and **(b)** to catering organisations.

6. Why is personal direct selling a marked feature of the 'marketing mix' in the majority of industrial markets? How might advertising contribute to the accomplishment of the 'sales task'?

7. 'The more advanced a society, the more it counts the variety of its goods rather than the amount of those goods as an indication of the standard of living.' Examine the validity of this statement and the implications it might have for the international marketing plans of a company manufacturing domestic kitchenware.

Test 6

1. 'Where is our company going? Where should it be going? What is our business, anyway?' Consider the relevance of these three questions posed by T. Levitt of the Harvard Business School to company chief executives in connection with long-term planning and the marketing concept.

2. Discuss the reasons for the emergence of 'product' and 'brand' managers in larger multiproduct companies. Would you expect similar advantages and disadvantages in introducing brand-product management in connection with industrial and consumer markets?

3. Why have many retail organisations promoted 'private label' products? How is this development affecting the marketing policies of manufacturers offering products of a similar type?

4. 'The fact that the industrial buyer seeks the best value is not tantamount to saying that a seller can never get a high price.' Comment on price elasticity in industrial markets and ways in which industrial salespersons may overcome price objections.

5. To what extent do you consider that ability and competence in marketing are transferable? Discuss this question with particular reference to the following suggested transfers:

(a) from industrial products to consumer products selling;

(b) from industrial market research to consumer market research; and
(c) from marketing management of consumer goods to marketing management of industrial goods.

6. Examine the advantages and problems of discounts and credit as forms of buying motivation.

7. What free external sources of advice and information are available to the manufacturer who wishes to export from the UK?

8. 'Because an individual's values are conditioned by the social class structure he perceives, consumer buying behaviour reflects class differences.' Comment on the limitations of the conventional socioeconomic class definitions most frequently used in defining market profiles in the light of this statement.

Index

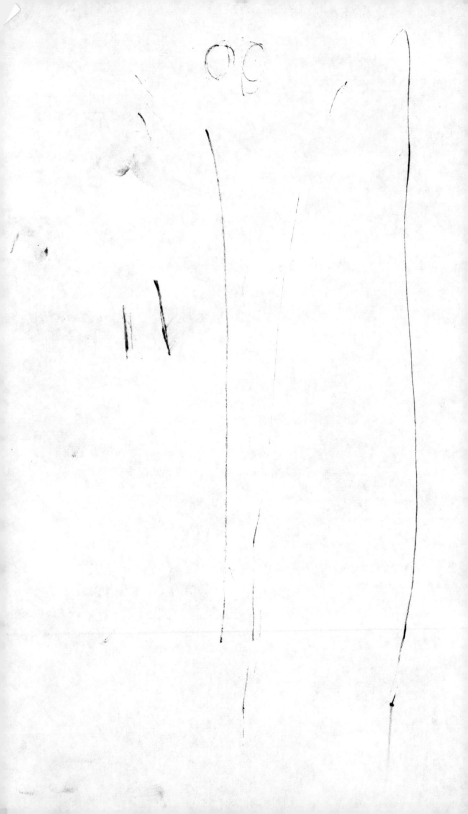